CURRENT ECONOMIC ISSUES

17TH EDITION

READINGS IN ECONOMICS, POLITICS,
AND SOCIAL POLICY FROM
DOLLARS&**SENSE**

EDITED BY JAMES M. CYPHER, ROB LARSON, ALEJANDRO REUSS, CHRIS STURR,

AND THE *DOLLARS & SENSE* COLLECTIVE

CURRENT ECONOMIC ISSUES, 17TH EDITION

Copyright © 2013 by Economic Affairs Bureau, Inc.

ISBN: 978-1-939402-09-7

Published by:
Economic Affairs Bureau, Inc. d/b/a *Dollars & Sense*
1 Milk Street, Boston, MA 02109
617-447-2177; dollars@dollarsandsense.org.
For order information, contact Economic Affairs Bureau or visit: www.dollarsandsense.org.

Current Economic Issues is edited by the *Dollars & Sense* collective, which also publishes *Dollars & Sense* magazine and the classroom books *Real World Macro, Real World Micro, America Beyond Capitalism, The Economic Crisis Reader, The Economics of the Environment, Grassroots Journalism, Introduction to Political Economy, Labor and the Global Economy, Real World Banking and Finance, Real World Globalization, Real World Latin America, Real World Labor, Striking a Balance: Work, Family, Life, Unlevel Playing Fields: Understanding Wage Inequality and Discrimination,* and *The Wealth Inequality Reader.*

The 2013 *Dollars & Sense* Collective:
Betsy Aron, Arpita Banerjee, Nancy Banks, Ellen Frank, John Miller, Kevin O'Connell, Larry Peterson, Linda Pinkow, Paul Piwko, Smriti Rao, Alejandro Reuss, Dan Schneider, Bryan Snyder, Chris Sturr, and Jeanne Winner.

Co-editors of this volume: James M. Cypher, Rob Larson, Alejandro Reuss, and Chris Sturr

Cover design: Chris Sturr
Cover photos:
Former PT Kizone workers protest in Jakarta, Indonesia, June 2012. Credit: United Students Against Sweatshops.
Supporters of union bus drivers in Vermont picket on April 4, 2011. Credit: © Mark Collier.
Members of the Chicago Teachers Union picket on Sept. 10, 2012, Credit: firedoglakedotcom, Creative Commons Attribution-Share Alike 2.0 Generic license.

Production: Chris Sturr, Dan Schneider

Printed in U.S.A.

CONTENTS

Chapter 1

THE ONGOING CRISIS

Article 1.1

INEQUALITY, POWER, AND IDEOLOGY
Getting It Right About the Causes of the Current Economic Crisis

BY ARTHUR MacEWAN
March/April 2009; updated November 2012

It is hard to solve a problem without an understanding of what caused it. For example, in medicine, until we gained an understanding of the way bacteria and viruses cause various infectious diseases, it was virtually impossible to develop effective cures. Of course, dealing with many diseases is complicated by the fact that germs, genes, diet, and the environment establish a nexus of causes.

The same is true in economics. Without an understanding of the causes of the current crisis, we are unlikely to develop a solution; certainly we are not going to get a solution that has a lasting impact. And determining the causes is complicated because several intertwined factors have been involved.

The current economic crisis was brought about by a nexus of factors that involved: a growing concentration of political and social power in the hands of the wealthy; the ascendance of a perverse leave-it-to-the-market ideology which was an instrument of that power; and rising income inequality, which both resulted from and enhanced that power. These various factors formed a vicious circle, reinforcing one another and together shaping the economic conditions that led us to the present situation. Several other factors were also involved—the growing role of credit, the puffing up of the housing bubble, and the increasing deregulation of financial markets have been very important. However, these are best understood as transmitters of our economic problems, arising from the nexus that formed the vicious circle.

What does this tell us about a solution? Economic stimulus, repair of the housing market, and new regulation are all well and good, but they do not deal with the underlying causes of the crisis. Instead, progressive groups need to work to shift each of the factors I have noted—power, ideology, and income distribution—in the other direction. In doing so, we can create a *virtuous* circle, with each change reinforcing the other changes. If successful, we not only establish a more stable economy, but we lay the foundation for a more democratic, equitable, and sustainable economic order.

A crisis by its very nature creates opportunities for change. One good place to begin change and intervene in this "circle"—and transform it from vicious to virtuous—is through pushing for the expansion and reform of social programs, programs that directly serve social needs of the great majority of the population (for example: single-payer health care, education programs, and environmental protection and repair). By establishing changes in social programs, we will have impacts on income distribution and ideology, and, perhaps most important, we set in motion *a power shift* that improves our position for preserving the changes. While I emphasize social programs as a means to initiate social and economic change, there are other ways to intervene in the circle. Efforts to re-strengthen unions would be especially important; and there are other options as well.

Causes of the Crisis: A Long Time Coming

Sometime around the early 1970s, there were some dramatic changes in the U.S. economy. The twenty-five years following World War II had been an era of relatively stable economic growth; the benefits of growth had been widely shared, with wages rising along with productivity gains, and income distribution became slightly less unequal (a good deal less unequal as compared to the pre-Great Depression era). There were severe economic problems in the United States, not the least of which were the continued exclusion of African Americans, large gender inequalities, and the woeful inadequacy of social welfare programs. Nonetheless, relatively stable growth, rising wages, and then the advent of the civil rights movement and the War on Poverty gave some important, positive social and economic character to the era—especially in hindsight!

In part, this comparatively favorable experience for the United States had depended on the very dominant position that U.S. firms held in the world economy, a position in which they were relatively unchallenged by international competition. The firms and their owners were not the only beneficiaries of this situation. With less competitive pressure on them from foreign companies, many U.S. firms accepted unionization and did not find it worthwhile to focus on keeping wages down and obstructing the implementation of social supports for the low-income population. Also, having had the recent experience of the Great Depression, many wealthy people and business executives were probably not so averse to a substantial role for government in regulating the economy.

A Power Grab

By about 1970, the situation was changing. Firms in Europe and Japan had long recovered from World War II, OPEC was taking shape, and weaknesses were emerging in the U.S. economy. The weaknesses were in part a consequence of heavy spending for the Vietnam War combined with the government's reluctance to tax for the war because of its unpopularity. The pressures on U.S. firms arising from these changes had two sets of consequences: slower growth and greater instability; and concerted efforts—a power grab, if you will—by firms and the wealthy to shift the costs of economic deterioration onto U.S. workers and the low-income population.

These "concerted efforts" took many forms: greater resistance to unions and unionization, battles to reduce taxes, stronger opposition to social welfare programs, and, above all, a push to reduce or eliminate government regulation of economic activity through a powerful political campaign to gain control of the various branches and levels of government. The 1980s, with Reagan and Bush One in the White House, were the years in which all these efforts were solidified. Unions were greatly weakened, a phenomenon both demonstrated and exacerbated by Reagan's firing of the air traffic controllers in response to their strike in 1981. The tax cuts of the period were also important markers of the change. But the change had begun earlier; the 1978 passage of the tax-cutting Proposition 13 in California was perhaps the first major success of the movement. And the changes continued well after the 1980s, with welfare reform and deregulation of finance during the Clinton era, to say nothing of the tax cuts and other actions during Bush Two.

Ideology Shift

The changes that began in the 1970s, however, were not simply these sorts of concrete alterations in the structure of power affecting the economy and, especially, government's role in the economy. There was a major shift in ideology, the dominant set of ideas that organize an understanding of our social relations and both guide and rationalize policy decisions.

Following the Great Depression and World War II, there was a wide acceptance of the idea that government had a major role to play in economic life. Less than in many other countries but nonetheless to a substantial degree, at all levels of society, it was generally believed that there should be a substantial government safety net and that government should both regulate the economy in various ways and, through fiscal as well as monetary policy, should maintain aggregate demand. This large economic role for government came to be called Keynesianism, after the British economist John Maynard Keynes, who had set out the arguments for an active fiscal policy in time of economic weakness. In the early 1970s, as economic troubles developed, even Richard Nixon declared: "We are all Keynesians now."

The election of Ronald Reagan, however, marked a sharp change in ideology, at least at the top. Actions of the government were blamed for all economic ills: government spending, Keynesianism, was alleged to be the cause of the inflation of the 1970s; government regulation was supposedly crippling industry; high taxes were, it was argued, undermining incentives for workers to work and for businesses to invest; social welfare spending was blamed for making people dependent on the government and was charged with fraud and corruption (the "welfare queens"); and so on and so on.

On economic matters, Reagan championed supply-side economics, the principal idea of which was that tax cuts yield an increase in government revenue because the cuts lead to more rapid economic growth through encouraging more work and more investment. Thus, so the argument went, tax cuts would reduce the government deficit. Reagan, with the cooperation of Democrats, got the tax cuts—and, as the loss of revenue combined with a large increase in military spending, the federal budget deficit grew by leaps and bounds, almost doubling as a share of GDP over the course of the 1980s. It was all summed up in the idea of keeping the government out of the economy; let the free market work its magic.

Growing Inequality

The shifts of power and ideology were very much bound up with a major redistribution upwards of income and wealth. The weakening of unions, the increasing access of firms to low-wage foreign (and immigrant) labor, the refusal of government to maintain the buying power of the minimum wage, favorable tax treatment of the wealthy and their corporations, deregulation in a wide range of industries, and lack of enforcement of existing regulation (e.g., the authorities turning a blind eye to off-shore tax shelters) all contributed to these shifts.

Many economists, however, explain the rising income inequality as a result of technological change that favored more highly skilled workers; and changing technology has probably been a factor. Yet the most dramatic aspect of the rising inequality has been the rapidly rising share of income obtained by those at the very top (see figures), who get their incomes from the ownership and control of business, not from their skilled labor. For these people the role of new technologies was most important through its impact on providing more options (e.g., international options) for the managers of firms, more thorough means to control labor, and more effective ways—in the absence of regulation—to manipulate finance. All of these gains that might be associated with new technology were also gains brought by the way the government handled, or didn't handle (failed to regulate), economic affairs.

Several sets of data demonstrate the sharp changes in the distribution of income that have taken place in the last several decades. Most striking is the changing position of the very highest income segment of the population. In the mid-1920s, the share of all pre-tax income going to the top 1% of households peaked at 23.9%. This elite group's share of income fell dramatically during the Great Depression and World War II to about 12% at the end of the war and then slowly fell further during the next thirty years, reaching a low of 8.9% in the mid-1970s. Since then, the top 1% has regained its exalted position of the earlier era, with 21.8% of income in 2005.   Since 1993, more than one-half of all income gains have accrued to this highest 1% of the population.

Figures 1 and 2 show the gains (or losses) of various groups in the 1947 to 1979 period and in the 1979 to 2005 period. The difference is dramatic. For example, in the earlier era, the bottom 20% saw its income in real (inflation-adjusted) terms rise by 116%, and real income of the top 5% grew by only 86%. But in the latter era, the bottom 20% saw a 1% decline in its income, while the top 5% obtained a 81% increase.

The Emergence of Crisis

These changes, especially the dramatic shifts in the distribution of income, set the stage for the increasingly large reliance on credit, especially consumer and mortgage

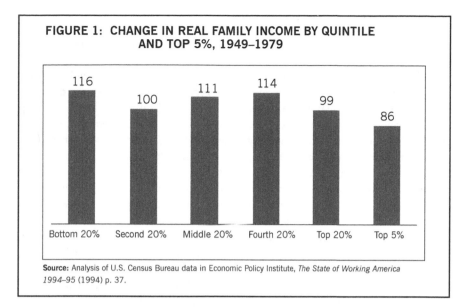

FIGURE 1: CHANGE IN REAL FAMILY INCOME BY QUINTILE AND TOP 5%, 1949–1979

Source: Analysis of U.S. Census Bureau data in Economic Policy Institute, *The State of Working America 1994–95* (1994) p. 37.

credit, that played a major role in the emergence of the current economic crisis. Other factors were involved, but rising inequality was especially important in effecting the increase in both the demand and supply of credit.

Credit Expansion

On the demand side, rising inequality translated into a growing gap between the incomes of most members of society and their needs. For the 2000 to 2007 period, average weekly earnings in the private sector were 12% below their average for the 1970s (in inflation-adjusted terms). From 1980 to 2005 the share of income going to the bottom 60% of families fell from 35% to 29%. Under these

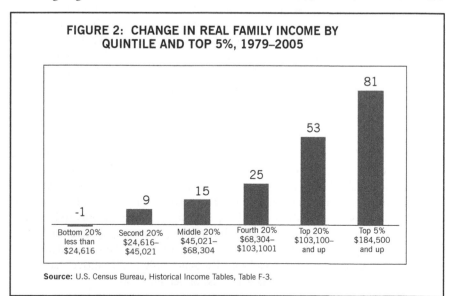

FIGURE 2: CHANGE IN REAL FAMILY INCOME BY QUINTILE AND TOP 5%, 1979–2005

Source: U.S. Census Bureau, Historical Income Tables, Table F-3.

circumstances, more and more people relied more and more heavily on credit to meet their needs—everything from food to fuel, from education to entertainment, and especially housing.

While the increasing reliance of consumers on credit has been going on for a long time, it has been especially marked in recent decades. Consumer debt as a share of after-tax personal income averaged 20% in the 1990s, and then jumped up to an average of 25% in the first seven years of the new millennium. But the debt expansion was most marked in housing, where mortgage debt as a percent of after-tax personal income rose from 89% to 94% over the 1990s, and then ballooned to 140% by 2006 as housing prices skyrocketed.

On the supply side, especially in the last few years, the government seems to have relied on making credit readily available as a means to bolster aggregate demand and maintain at least a modicum of economic growth. During the 1990s, the federal funds interest rate averaged 5.1%, but fell to an average of 3.4% in the 2000 to 2007 period—and averaged only 1.4% in 2002 to 2004 period. (The federal funds interest rate is the rate that banks charge one another for overnight loans and is a rate directly affected by the Federal Reserve.) Corresponding to the low interest rates, the money supply grew twice as fast in the new millennium as it had in the 1990s. (And see the box on the connection of the Fed's actions to the Iraq War.)

The increasing reliance of U.S. consumers on credit has often been presented as a moral weakness, as an infatuation with consumerism, and as a failure to look beyond the present. Whatever moral judgments one may make, however, the expansion of the credit economy has been a response to real economic forces—inequality and government policies, in particular.

The Failure to Regulate

The credit expansion by itself, however, did not precipitate the current crisis. Deregulation—or, more generally, the failure to regulate—is also an important part of the story. The government's role in regulation of financial markets has been a central feature in the development of this crisis, but the situation in financial markets has been part of a more general process—affecting airlines and trucking, telecommunications, food processing, broadcasting, and of course international trade and investment. The process has been driven by a combination of power (of large firms and wealthy individuals) and ideology (leave it to the market, get the government out).

The failure to regulate financial markets that transformed the credit expansion into a financial crisis shows up well in three examples:

The 1999 repeal of the Glass-Steagall Act. Glass-Steagall had been enacted in the midst of the Great Depression, as a response to the financial implosion following the stock market crash of 1929. Among other things, it required that different kinds of financial firms—commercial banks, investment banks, insurance companies—be separate. This separation both limited the spread of financial problems and reduced conflicts of interest that could arise were the different functions of these firms combined into a single firm. As perhaps the most important legislation regulating the financial sector, the repeal of Glass-Steagall was not only a substantive change but was an important symbol of the whole process of deregulation.

The failure to regulate mortgage lending. Existing laws and regulations require lending institutions to follow prudent practices in making loans, assuring that borrowers have the capacity to be able to pay back the loans. And of course fraud—lying about the provisions of loans—is prohibited. Yet in an atmosphere where regulation was "out," regulators were simply not doing their jobs. The consequences are illustrated in a December 28, 2008, *New York Times* story on the failed Washington Mutual Bank. The article describes a supervisor at a mortgage processing center as having been "accustomed to seeing babysitters claiming salaries worthy of college presidents, and schoolteachers with incomes rivaling stockbrokers'. He rarely questioned them. A real estate frenzy was under way and WaMu, as his bank was known, was all about saying yes."

One may wonder why banks—or other lending institutions, mortgage firms, in particular—would make loans to people who were unlikely to be able to pay them back. The reason is that the lending institutions quickly combined such loans into packages (i.e., a security made up of several borrowers' obligations to pay) and sold them to other investors in a practice called "securitization."

Credit-default swaps. Perhaps the most egregious failure to regulate in recent years has been the emergence of credit-default swaps, which are connected to securitization. Because they were made up of obligations by a diverse set of borrowers, the packages of loans were supposedly low-risk investments. Yet those who purchased them still sought insurance against default. Insurance sellers, however, are regulated—required, for example, to keep a certain amount of capital on hand to cover possible claims. So the sellers of these insurance policies on packages of loans called the policies "credit-default swaps" and thus were allowed to avoid regulation. Further, these credit-default swaps, these insurance policies, themselves were bought and sold again and again in unregulated markets in a continuing process of speculation.

The credit-default swaps are a form of derivative, a financial asset the value of which is derived from some other asset—in this case the value of packages of mortgages for which they were the insurance policies. When the housing bubble began to collapse and people started to default on their mortgages, the value of credit-default swaps plummeted and their future value was impossible to determine. No one would buy them, and several banks that had speculated in these derivatives were left holding huge amounts of these "toxic assets."

Bubble and Bust

The combination of easy credit and the failure to regulate together fueled the housing bubble. People could buy expensive houses but make relatively low monthly payments. Without effective regulation of mortgage lending, they could get the loans even when they were unlikely to be able to make payments over the long run. Moreover, as these pressures pushed up housing prices, many people bought houses simply to resell them quickly at a higher price, in a process called "flipping." And such speculation pushed the prices up further. Between 2000 and 2006, housing prices rose by 90% (as consumer prices generally rose by only 17%).

While the housing boom was in full swing, both successful housing speculators and lots of people involved in the shenanigans of credit markets made a lot of money. However, as the housing bubble burst—as all bubbles do—things fell apart. The packages of loans lost value, and the insurance policies on them, the credit-default swaps, lost value. These then became "toxic" assets for those who held them, assets not only with reduced value but with unknown value. Not only did large financial firms—for example, Lehman Brothers and AIG—have billions of dollars in losses, but no one knew the worth of their remaining assets. The assets were called "toxic" because they poisoned the operations of the financial system. Under these circumstances, financial institutions stopped lending to one another—that is, the credit markets "froze up." The financial crisis was here.

The financial crisis, not surprisingly, very quickly shifted to a general economic crisis. Firms in the "real" economy rely heavily on a well-functioning financial system to supply them with the funds they need for their regular operations—loans to car buyers, loans to finance inventory, loans for construction of new facilities, loans for new equipment, and, of course, mortgage loans. Without those loans (or with the loans much more difficult to obtain), there has been a general cut-back in economic activity, what is becoming a serious and probably prolonged recession.

What Is to Be Done?

So here we are. The shifts in power, ideology, and income distribution have placed us in a rather nasty situation. There are some steps that will be taken that have a reasonable probability of yielding short-run improvement. In particular, a large increase in government spending—deficit spending—will probably reduce the depth and shorten the length of the recession. And the actions of the Federal Reserve and Treasury to inject funds into the financial system are likely, along with the deficit spending, to "un-freeze" credit markets (the mismanagement and, it seems, outright corruption of the bailout notwithstanding). Also, there is likely to be some re-regulation of the financial industry. These steps, however, at best will restore things to where they were before the crisis. They do not treat the underlying causes of the crisis—the vicious circle of power, ideology, and inequality.

Opportunity for Change

Fortunately, the crisis itself has weakened some aspects of this circle. The cry of "leave it to the market" is still heard, but is now more a basis for derision than a guide to policy. The ideology and, to a degree, the power behind the ideology, have been severely weakened as the role of "keeping the government out" has shown to be a major cause of the financial mess and our current hardships. There is now widespread support among the general populace and some support in Washington for greater regulation of the financial industry.

Whether or not the coming period will see this support translated into effective policy is of course an open question. Also an open question is how much the turn away from "leaving it to the market" can be extended to other sectors of the economy. With regard to the environment, there is already general acceptance of the principle that the government (indeed, many governments) must take an active role in regulating economic activity. Similar principles need to be recognized with regard to health care, education, housing, child care, and other support programs for low-income families.

The discrediting of "keep the government out" ideology provides an opening to develop new programs in these areas and to expand old programs. Furthermore, as the federal government revs up its "stimulus" program in the coming months, opportunities will exist for expanding support for these sorts of programs. This support is important, first of all, because these programs serve real, pressing needs—needs that have long existed and are becoming acute and more extensive in the current crisis.

Breaking the Circle

Support for these social programs, however, may also serve to break into the vicious power-ideology-inequality circle and begin transforming it into a virtuous circle. Social programs are inherently equalizing in two ways: they provide their benefits to low-income people and they provide some options for those people in their efforts to demand better work and higher pay. Also, the further these programs develop, the more they establish the legitimacy of a larger role for public control of—government involvement in—the economy; they tend to bring about an ideological shift. By affecting a positive distributional shift and by shifting ideology, the emergence of stronger social programs can have a wider impact on power. In other words, efforts to promote social programs are one place to start, an entry point to shift the vicious circle to a virtuous circle.

There are other entry points. Perhaps the most obvious ones are actions to strengthen the role of unions. The Employee Free Choice Act may be a useful first step, and it will be helpful to establish a more union-friendly Department of Labor and National Labor Relations Board. Raising the minimum wage—ideally indexing it to inflation—would also be highly desirable. While conditions have changed since the heyday of unions in the middle of the 20th century, and we cannot expect to restore the conditions of that era, a greater role for unions would seem essential in righting the structural conditions at the foundation of the current crisis.

Shifting Class Power

None of this is assured, of course. Simply starting social programs will not necessarily mean that they have the wider impacts that I am suggesting are possible. No one should think that by setting up some new programs and strengthening some existing ones we will be on a smooth road to economic and social change. Likewise, rebuilding the strength of unions will involve extensive struggle and will not be accomplished by a few legislative or executive actions.

Also, all efforts to involve the government in economic activity—whether in finance or environmental affairs, in health care or education, in work support or job training programs—will be met with the worn-out claims that government involvement generates bureaucracy, stifles initiative, and places an excessive burden on private firms and individuals. We are already hearing warnings that in dealing with the financial crisis the government must avoid "over-regulation." Likewise, efforts to strengthen unions will suffer the traditional attacks, as unions are portrayed as corrupt and their members privileged. The unfolding situation with regard to the auto firms' troubles has demonstrated the attack, as conservatives have blamed the United Auto Workers for the industry's woes and have demanded extensive concessions by the union.

Certainly not all regulation is good regulation. Aside from excessive bureaucratic controls, there is the phenomenon by which regulating agencies are often captives of the industries that they are supposed to regulate. And there are corrupt unions. These are real issues, but they should not be allowed to derail change.

The current economic crisis emerged in large part as a shift in the balance of class power in the United States, a shift that began in the early 1970s and continued into the new millennium. Perhaps the present moment offers an opportunity to shift things back in the other direction. Recognition of the complex nexus of causes of the current economic crisis provides some guidance where people might start. Rebuilding and extending social programs, strengthening unions, and other actions that contribute to a more egalitarian power shift will not solve all the problems of U.S. capitalism. They can, however, begin to move us in the right direction. ❑

Inequality, Power, and Ideology: An Afterword
November 2012

When this article was written in early 2009, the U.S. economy was in a severe recession, which came to be called the Great Recession. The economic downturn—defined in terms of a drop-off in total output, or gross domestic product (GDP)—had begun at the end of 2007. Although the recession came to a formal end by June 2009, when GDP started to grow again, economic conditions continued to be very poor. With slow economic growth, unemployment remained high, falling below 8% only in late 2012, and many people simply gave up looking for work and were not even counted among the unemployed.

Several factors contribute to an explanation of the weak recovery from the Great Recession. When economic downturns are brought about by financial crises, they tend to be more lasting because the machinery of the credit system and the confidence of lenders have been so severely damaged. Also, while the Great Recession developed in the United States, it spread to much of the rest of the world. Conditions in Europe, especially, have hampered full recovery in the United States.

The continuing economic malaise, however, also has its bases in the political conditions of Washington, in the weakness of the federal government's response to the Great Recession. While it is possible to debate the extent to which the weak response has been the responsibility of the recalcitrant role of Republicans in Congress versus the limited actions of President Obama, there is no doubt regarding the several aspects of that weak response:

- ·The fiscal stimulus implemented at the beginning of 2009, the American Recovery and Reinvestment Act (ARRA), was too small. This action did stem the decline of the economy, probably preventing things from getting much worse. But given the severity of the downturn, the ARRA was insufficient to reestablish growth that would have moved the United States strongly back toward full employment.

- ·Programs to relieve the dreadful damage done to millions of homeowners have been minimal, leaving families in dire straits and leaving the housing market in the doldrums.

- ·The Wall Street Reform and Consumer Protection Act, the Dodd-Frank bill, was enacted in 2010. Yet it was a weak bill, failing to deal with the most serious problems in the financial sector—for example, leaving several banks "too big to fail." Also, many of its provisions were sufficiently vague to allow the Wall Street firms to use their influence to blunt its impact.

- ·The huge bailout of the financial sector, the Troubled Asset Relief Program (TARP) and other actions of the Federal Reserve, probably did make an important contribution to preventing an even worse financial crisis. But TARP was a tremendous boon to the bankers who had been instrumental actors in bringing about the crisis. There were other actions that could have been taken. Moreover, the continuing weak response of the economy to the Fed's continued efforts to stimulate economic growth demonstrated the insufficiency of monetary policy to deal with a severe economic downturn.

Even if the government's actions had been more forceful, the underlying causes of the crisis remain unaddressed—economic inequality, power, and ideology remain largely as they were as the crisis emerged. Figure 3 shows that from 2005 through 2011, all groups have seen their incomes decline. However, with those at the bottom suffering the most severe decline, income inequality has increased. Also, there is no indication that the power of the elite has been curtailed. Indeed, with the evisceration of campaign finance regulations (the Citizens United Supreme Court decision in particular), money and power are increasingly tied firmly together.

What of ideology? The outcome of the 2012 election suggests that a majority of the electorate rejects the leave-it-to-the-market ideology that has supported inequality and the concentration of political power and that led into the crisis. Whatever the limits of the Obama administration, it portrayed itself with rhetoric of social responsibility and promised some regulation of markets. Regardless of the limited extent to which reality in the subsequent years will match this rhetoric, the actions of a majority of the electorate suggest that there are some possibilities for positive change. Moreover, when the Occupy Wall Street (OWS) movement appeared in late 2011, it forced a discussion of basic issues of inequality, power, and ideology onto the public agenda. Whatever happens to OWS, it is likely that these issues will continue to be well recognized.

The sorts of changes advocated in this article, changes that would affect the underlying causes of the economic crisis, continue to be necessary. They also continue to be possible. —*Arthur MacEwan*

An elaboration of the points in this afterword is contained in the book that grew out of the original article: *Economic Collapse and Economic Change: Getting to the Roots of the Crisis*, by Arthur MacEwan and John A. Miller, M.E. Sharpe Publisher, 2011.

Article 1.2

UNEMPLOYMENT IS DOWN, SO WHAT'S THE PROBLEM?

BY ALEJANDRO REUSS
May/June 2013

The "headline" unemployment rate, or U-3 by its Bureau of Labor Statistics (BLS) designation, has declined from a peak of 10.0% in late 2009 to 7.5% now. The unemployment rate—the number of unemployed people as a percentage of the labor force (the employed plus unemployed)—is still abnormally high. Before the onset of the current crisis, it had been this high for only five months (May-September 1992) in the previous 24 years.

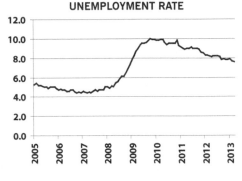

UNEMPLOYMENT RATE

The jobs situation now is certainly drastically different from 2008-2010, when unemployment was increasing dramatically—there's no argument about that. At the bleakest point of the recession, in each of two consecutive months (January-February 2009), over half a million more people went from being employed to unemployed than from unemployed to employed. In March 2013, in contrast, over 250,000 more people went from being unemployed to employed than the reverse. But the end of the employment freefall is hardly the same thing as a robust recovery.

The trend in the employment-to-population ratio—a much less familiar indicator than the headline unemployment rate—tells a different tale. This figure is the number of employed individuals as a percentage of the working-age civilian noninstitutional population. The civilian noninstitutional population excludes military personnel, people in prison, and so on. Working age, meanwhile, is defined as 16 years and over. So there are two big differences between this measure and the unemployment rate. First, the numerator is employment rather than unemployment (so it's looking at the other side of the employment coin). Second, the denominator is not the size of the labor force (the employed plus the unemployed), but the civilian noninstitutional population (which also includes people who are not in the labor force, or NLF). Here, we see not an employment situation that has turned decisively toward recovery, but one that has flatlined for more than three years.

EMPLOYMENT-TO-POPULATION RATIO

Employed, Unemployed, or Neither

How can the unemployment rate have gone steadily down for about three years with hardly a budge to the employment-population ratio? Shouldn't the two move in opposite directions? (They did during the freefall of 2008-2010.) To get a handle on this, we have to look at the way the "headline" unemployment rate is calculated, starting with the official government definition of unemployment. For the BLS to count someone as unemployed, three things must be true:

1. That person cannot be employed. In this context, being employed means working at all, whether full-time or part-time, "for pay or profit." People who work for wages, work at a business they own, or work even without direct pay at their family business are counted as employed.
2. That person must be actively looking for a job. That means doing things like filling out job applications, visiting an employment office, going to a job interview, etc.
3. That person must be available to start work. This means that someone who is looking for a job, but would not accept a job that required them to start immediately (for example, a student who would not be ready to start until after graduation, some months in the future) is not unemployed for the purposes of calculating U-3.

People who are not employed (meet criterion #1) but are not actively looking for work or are not available to work (do not meet criteria #2 or #3) are classified as not in the labor force. In effect, then, we have defined three distinct groups: employed, unemployed, and not in the labor force. The employed and unemployed, together, constitute the labor force. The working-age population, meanwhile, is divided between those in the labor force and those not in the labor force.

How can we relate the unemployment rate, then, to the employment-to-population ratio? The employment-to-population ratio is equal to the employment rate (employment as a percentage of the labor force) times the labor-force participation rate (the labor force as a percentage of the population). The employment rate and the unemployment rate add up to one. So, if the unemployment rate is going down, the employment rate must be going up. If the employment rate is going up, but the employment-to-population rate is pretty much constant, the labor force participation rate must be going down. So we find the answer to our paradox—a declining unemployment rate with a flatlining employment-to-population ratio—in a plummeting labor force participation rate.

Between the mid 1960s and 1990, the U.S. labor force participation rate (LFPR) increased from just under 60% to about 66-67%, where it hovered until 2008. (The climb was driven by women's labor force participation, which increased fast enough to offset a mild decline in men's labor force participation.) Since the onset of the Great Recession, however, the overall labor force participation

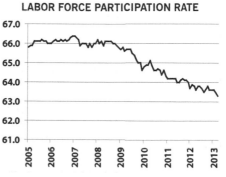

LABOR FORCE PARTICIPATION RATE

rate has dropped by about three percentage points. As economist Brad DeLong puts it, "There has been no closing of the output gap [the difference between actual and 'full employment' output] and no decline in the unemployment rate from putting a greater share of the adult population to work. All of the decline in the output gap and of the decline in the unemployment rate is from the collapse in labor force participation."

OK, Then What?

Higher labor-force participation is not automatically better. People may choose to remain out of the labor force, or to leave the labor force, for reasons that are neither personally nor socially harmful. For example, someone may decide to stay in school (or to return to school after some period in the labor force) and not seek employment "for pay or profit." That decision might enhance their future work opportunities, increase their future labor productivity, and even contribute to the general level of knowledge in society. Increases in the labor force participation rate can reflect positive changes in society (e.g., increased work opportunities for women) or negative (e.g., cuts to retirement benefits). Decreases in the LFPR, by the same token, can happen for good reasons (e.g., increased educational opportunities) or bad (e.g., despair among the unemployed of ever finding a job).

So why has the labor-force participation rate fallen like a stone in the last few years? None of the standard ways to explain away the precipitous decline is convincing:

Skills mismatch. Neoclassical economists have emphasized a supposed mismatch between the skills workers have and those employers are seeking as an explanation of high unemployment since the Great Recession, but it works equally well (that is, equally badly) for people dropping out of the labor force altogether. This view has been roundly refuted by the lack of wage growth (as we would expect if appropriately skilled workers were in short supply), the high prevalence of involuntary part-time employment (these presumably do have the necessary skills yet their employers are not desperate to increase their hours), and other observations.

Demographic changes. As the U.S. population ages, we should expect a decline in the labor force participation rate. (Remember, the definition of the working-age population does

---

Let's Do the Math!

The employment-to-population ratio (EP) is equal to the number of employed people (E) divided by the size of the working-age civilian noninstitutional population (P).

$$EP \text{ ratio} = E/P$$

The equation remains true if we multiply the right side by (LF/LF), where LF is the size of the labor force, since (LF/LF) = 1. Therefore,

$$EP \text{ ratio} = (E/LF) \times (LF/P)$$

LF/P is referred to as the "labor force participation rate." E/LF, meanwhile, is the employment rate.

If the unemployment rate (UE/LF) is 10%, then, the employment rate must be 90%. If the unemployment rate is 5%, the employment rate must be 95%. In other words, the total is always equal to 1.0.

Since: (E/LF) + (UE/LF) = 1

Then: (E/LF) = 1 - (UE/LF)

Therefore,

$$EP \text{ ratio} = (1 - (UE/LF)) \times (LF/P).$$

So here we have the relationship between the employment-to-population ratio and the unemployment rate.

If (UE/LF) is declining, then (1 - (UE/LF)) must be increasing. If (1 - (UE/LF)) is increasing, but the EP ratio is constant, this means (LF/P) must be decreasing.

not have a maximum age.) As DeLong points out, however, demographic changes account for a decline of less than 0.2 percentage points per year, and so would explain maybe 0.5 points of the decline in the LFPR over the last three years. "One-tenth of our labor-market shift relative to 2007 can be attributable to demography," he concludes."[N]ine-tenths are the result of the Lesser Depression."

Cultural and political changes. A recent piece by the conservative *New York Times* columnist Ross Douthat, "A World Without Work" (Feb. 23, 2013), suggests that the decline in the LFPR reflects an increasing willingness by those at the bottom of the occupational hierarchy to just drop out of the working world altogether and scratch together a living from "disability payments and food stamps, living with relatives, cobbling together work here and there." This third explanation suffers from the same problem as the second—it's hard to imagine why there would have been such a precipitous change in the span of just a few years. It's not as if the U.S. welfare state has suddenly become more generous. Nor is there evidence of an abrupt cultural change in attitudes toward work.

The best explanation is that the decline is the fallout of a severe recession from which we have far from recovered. There simply are not enough jobs. After long spells of unemployment, many people give up on looking for work ("discouraged workers") and are reclassified as NLF. Others have entered the working-age population—turned 16 years old—or just graduated from high school or college and found few work opportunities. Some older workers retire, leaving the labor force, before they otherwise would have. The declining LFPR, however, is not restricted to younger or older workers. As Heidi Schierholz of the Economic Policy Institute puts it, "[T]he labor force participation rate of the 'prime-age' population, people age 25-54, is also at its lowest point of the downturn ... . It's the lack of job opportunities—the lack of demand for workers—that is keeping these workers from working or seeking work, not other factors."

The decline in the unemployment rate over the last few years has contributed to the complacent view that the worst is over, that most people who made it through without losing their jobs are pretty safe now (at least for the short term), and that no major policy intervention (like further fiscal stimulus) is required to improve the employment situation. It's clear from the employment-to-population and labor-force-participation data how wrong this view is, how inadequate the federal-level fiscal stimulus was, how premature its abandonment was, and how damaging the ongoing state-level austerity has been.

It's clear, in other words, how far down employment and the fates of the unemployed have ranked in the priorities of the ruling elite. ❏

Sources: Bureau of Labor Statistics (BLS), Unemployment rate, Seasonally adjusted, 16 years and over, Series ID: LNS14000000 (bls.gov); BLS, Employment-population ratio, Seasonally adjusted, 16 years and over, Series ID: LNS12300000 (bls.gov); BLS, Civilian labor force participation rate, Seasonally adjusted, 16 years and over, Series ID: LNS11300000 (bls.gov); Brad DeLong, "A Good Employment Report This Month: A Bad Labor Market," Grasping Reality with Both Hands blog (delong.typepad.com), March 8, 2013; Ross Douthat, "A World Without Work," *New York Times*, Feb. 23, 2013 (nytimes.com); Heidi Shierholz, "The unemployment rate is hugely underestimating slack in the labor market," Economic Policy Institute, April 5, 2013. (epi.org).

Article 1.3

WHY THE UNITED STATES IS *NOT* GREECE

BY JOHN MILLER AND KATHERINE SCIACCHITANO
January/February 2012

For almost two years, we've been hearing a new battle cry in the war against government spending: unless the United States slashes deficits we will become Greece, Europe's poster child for fiscal insolvency and economic crisis. The debt crisis in the eurozone, the 17 European countries that share the euro as their common currency, is held up as proof positive of the perils that await the United States if it continues its supposedly fiscally irresponsible ways.

Take the Heritage Foundation, the Washington-based think tank that specializes in providing red meat for anti-government pro-market arguments. Heritage introduces its 2011 chart on the rising level of government debt (to GDP) with this dire warning: "Countries like Greece and Portugal have suffered or are anticipating financial crises as a result of mounting debt. If the U.S. continues federal deficit spending on its current trajectory, it will face similar economic woes."

Even for those who understand that cutting deficits right now will only weaken a still-fragile recovery, and that weakening the recovery will only increase deficits, getting past the argument that "a eurozone crisis is on its way" is no easy task.

What follows is a self-defense lesson on why the United States is not Greece—or Europe. The U.S. economy is far larger and more productive than Greece. The United States has many more tools in its macro-economic policy box than countries in the eurozone. And while calls for austerity have kept the United States from undertaking government spending and investment large enough to support a robust economic recovery, at least thus far, the United States hasn't undertaken the same self-defeating austerity measures Europe has. If we learn the right lessons from what is happening in the eurozone now, we never will.

Central Banks and Deficit Spending

When economic activity plummeted during 2008 and 2009 in the United States, Europe, and throughout the world, coordinated stimulus spending of nations across the globe prevented the collapse of world output from becoming another Great Depression. Today, deficit spending remains critical as working people continue to struggle through an economic recovery that has done little to create jobs or to lift wages, but much to restore profits.

Governments finance deficit spending by borrowing. Governments sell bonds—promissory notes—to domestic and foreign investors as well as other government agencies, and then use the proceeds to pay for spending in excess of their tax revenues. In the United States, domestic investors, foreign investors, and government agencies hold near equal shares of government bonds issued by the Treasury and receive the interest paid on those bonds.

The Federal Reserve ("the Fed"), the U.S. central bank, can buy U.S. government bonds as well. The Fed can also create money (sometimes metaphorically called "printing money") simply by entering an appropriate credit on its balance sheet and spending it. When the Fed uses this newly created money to purchase bonds directly from the government, it is financing the government deficit. Economists call the Fed's direct purchase of government bonds "monetizing the deficit." By such direct purchases of bonds that finance the deficit, the Fed can fund government spending in an emergency, should it choose to do so. Monetizing the deficit also significantly expands the money supply, which pushes down interest rates, which can also help stimulate the economy.

In the current crisis, the Fed did precisely that. By purchasing government bonds, the Fed financed public-sector spending, and by pushing down interest rates, it encouraged private-sector borrowing. In doing so, the Fed supported a market recovery, but also helped to keep unemployment from rising even higher than it did.

In seeking to lower unemployment, the Fed was exercising what is known as its "dual mandate" under the law to promote both low inflation and low unemployment.

Nevertheless, the Fed's decision to inject more money into the economy has come under heavy fire from those who worry more about inflation than unemployment, and who think that "printing money" is always inflationary. Neither continued low inflation rates nor persistently high unemployment were enough to change the thinking of these inflation-phobes. Back in August, Rick Perry, the Texas governor and candidate for president in the Republican primary, went so far as to insist that if the Fed "prints more money between now and the election" (in November 2012) it would be "almost treasonous."

The central banks of most other countries have much the same abilities as the Fed has to inject money into their economies and to buy government debt. As with the Fed, they may or may not choose to use this power. But the power is unquestionably there.

Europe's Central Bank Is Different

The 17 countries in the eurozone, however, relinquished their ability to print money, expand their money supplies, and lower interest rates when they adopted the euro as their common currency. Only the European Central Bank—known as the ECB—can authorize the "printing of euros," and the ECB maintains control over the money supply of the eurozone.

Unlike the Fed, the ECB does not have a dual mandate to pursue low employment as well as low inflation. The ECB's authority is limited to maintaining low inflation, known as "price stability," which the ECB defines as an inflation rate below 2%.

And the ECB is prohibited from directly buying government bonds. The ECB is authorized to buy government bonds only on the "secondary" bond market, when original purchasers resell them.

The result of these policies is that eurozone countries must sell their bonds on the open market. That leaves them entirely dependent on private bond buyers (i.e., lenders), whether from their own country or other countries, to finance their government deficits. Governments must offer their bonds for sale with rates of returns (or interest rates) that will attract those bonds buyers. Each uptick in the interest rate adds to the debt burden of these countries, and makes deficit spending to stimulate the economy that much more expensive.

Another way a country can stimulate its economy is by increasing exports. Typically, individual countries' currencies (when not fixed to the value of a dominant currency such as the U.S. dollar) lose value, or "depreciate," when an economy falls into a crisis, such as the crisis Greece is in now. As the value of its currency depreciates, a country's exports become cheaper, and that boosts export sales and domestic production and aids recovery. While currency fluctuations can open the door to speculative excesses, the falling value of a country's currency is yet another way to help turn around a flagging economy not available to the eurozone economies. The problem is that all countries in the eurozone have the same currency. So individual countries can't let their currencies depreciate. Nor can they take steps countries outside the eurozone can take to intentionally lower their exchange rates to become more competitive, known as devaluing.

Similarly, central banks outside the eurozone routinely stimulate economies by pushing down key interest rates at which banks lend to each other. This helps lower other interest rates in the economy, such as rates for business and consumer loans, and can lead to the expansion of borrowing and spending. But the ECB targets one interest rate for lending between banks for the whole eurozone. It is not possible to set one interest rate for Germany to fight inflation, and a second, lower, rate in Greece or Italy to stimulate growth.

Without the ability to use separate exchange rates or interest rates to stimulate lagging economies, the crisis-ridden eurozone had but one public policy left to get their economies going again: expansionary fiscal policy. But even that remaining policy option was constrained. The ECB was not about to ease the burden of increased government spending (or the cost of tax cuts) by directly buying government bonds. Eurozone guidelines prohibit budget deficits that exceed 3% of GDP, or national debt in excess of 60% of their GDP. And there is no central fiscal authority with deep pockets to turn to. Contrast this with the United States, where states also share the same currency and the Fed targets one interest rate, but where states can turn to the federal government for assistance in times of economic stress.

In effect, the eurozone countries were left to confront the global downturn and the sovereign debt crisis with one policy hand tied behind their back, and a couple of digits lopped off the other. Market pressure on interest rates made it yet more difficult for eurozone countries to get out of trouble by undertaking countercyclical, or stimulus, spending when economies slowed.

In the few cases where eurozone authorities have provided loans to indebted countries, they have insisted on austerity measures ranging from slashing government spending to public- and private-sector wage cuts as the pre-condition for providing relief. But since cutting government spending in a downturn leads to both a fall in demand and rise in unemployment, this emergency lending is making it even harder for eurozone countries to recover.

No wonder the global downturn hit the most vulnerable eurozone countries so hard, turning their sovereign (or government) debt as toxic as the mortgage-based securities that sparked the initial global downturn. This is what we're seeing played out with the Greek debt crisis.

Greek Austerity

When the 2008-2009 global collapse pushed down GDP and trade, and pushed up budget deficits around the world, Greece already had a large trade deficit and high government debt. Greece had consistently run government deficits greater than 5% of its GDP, and had carried government debt that just about matched its GDP for nearly a decade, both clear violations of eurozone guidelines. Nonetheless, Greek banks, and then banks elsewhere in Europe (including Germany and France), readily lent money to the Greek government, buying their bonds, which regularly yielded a handsome 5% rate of return (the rate of interest on a ten-year government note), and which presumably carried limited risk as the sovereign debt of a developed country unlikely to default.

But as the Greek economy tumbled downward, Greece had to raise its interest rates to above 12% to sell the additional debt it needed to stay afloat. By the summer of 2010, Greece was pushed to the point of default—not being able to pay its lenders.

The European Union and the IMF gave Greece a $140 billion loan so debt payments to the banks could continue. But both the IMF and the European Union insisted on austerity to reduce deficits and ensure repayment. Greece was forced to agree to sharp cuts in government spending, public employment, and wages and benefits of public employees; to tax increases; and to privatization of government assets. The banks that had happily lent Greece money well beyond the allowable eurozone limits escaped without having to write down the value of their loans to the Greek government.

The Greek economy, on the other hand, dropped like a stone. In the year that followed, Greece lost more output than the United States had during the Great Recession. Unemployment rates reached 18.4%, over one-third of young people were unemployed, and more than one-fifth of the population was poverty stricken. The austerity measures did trim the Greek budget deficit. Nonetheless the ratio of public debt to GDP continued to rise as Greek output plummeted.

One year later, Greece was on the brink of default again. The interest rate on Greek government bonds had skyrocketed to above 20% on ten-year government bonds, only adding to Greece's already unsustainable debt burden.

In October 2011 the IMF and the European Union granted an additional $173 billion loan to Greece in return for a new round of austerity measures. More public-sector workers lost their jobs, public pensions were cut further, and the privatization program expanded. The austerity measures were "equivalent to about 14 percent of average Greek take-home income," according to the *Financial Times*, the authoritative British newspaper, or an impact about "double that brought about by austerity measures in the other two eurozone countries subject to international bail-out programmes, Portugal and Ireland."

Also as part of the price for its debt reduction, Greece would have to accept monitoring of its fiscal affairs by the European Union. Greek Prime Minister George Papandreou, forced to cancel a referendum on the second round of austerity cuts, resigned in favor of a "government of national unity" headed by Lucas Papademos, a former banker sure to listen to the markets.

This time, banks and other holders of Greek government bonds seemed not to have escaped unharmed. The value of their bonds were to be written down to 50% of their face value, meaning they could still insist on repayment of half the amount lent, although the market value of those bonds was surely far less than that. In addition, the agreement was "voluntary," and it is yet to be seen if the agreement will be enforced.

As 2011 came to a close with this second round of austerity measures and the near collapse of the Greek economy, the Greek government was paying out a crippling 35% interest rate to attract buyers for their ten-year bonds.

Vortex Europe

European banks are the main buyers of European debt. French and German banks hold large quantities of Greek bonds.

So does the ECB, which began buying Greek bonds and other sovereign debt on the secondary (or resale) market in 2010. It resumed the practice in late 2011 to ease pressures on interest rates. Ordinarily, this bond-buying would also stimulate the economy by increasing the money supply, since the ECB creates the money it uses to buy the bonds. But the ECB also "sterilizes" its bond buying by contracting the money supply in the same amount as its purchases. This eliminates any possibility of inflation, but also negates the stimulus effect.

The bottom line is that because of the extensive holdings of Greek and other government debt within the European banking system, a Greek default would cause substantial losses in the European banking system and destabilize it.

In the last weeks of 2011, the ECB did extend a financial lifeline to banks – exactly what it had refused to give to the Greek government. To help buffer them against sudden losses, the ECB offered the banks $638 billion in three-year loans with the bargain basement interest rate of 1%. The majority of eurozone banks, some 523 of them, took out loans. The ECB's backdoor bailout, as a Wall Street Journal editorial called it, was twice the combined size of the two rescue packages for Greece. The banks, unlike governments, would not have to turn to the bond markets for funding if a Greek default occurred. And like banks bailed out in the United States, no requirements were placed on them to continue lending—in Europe's case, to continue lending to governments.

While the ECB move shored up the banks for now, it won't protect them from the large losses that will come with an outright default by Greece or another of the crisis-ridden southern eurozone countries. Such large losses would in turn force countries to bail out banks again, as they did in 2008, to avoid the prospect of cascading banking failures. Because the ECB is prohibited from directly buying European government debt, a new round of bailouts would raise the specter of increasing government deficits, of rising interest rates, and of additional countries defaulting, a sequence that could induce a depression-like downturn.

As a result, private lenders are now insisting on higher interest rates on government bonds not just in Greece, but throughout much of Europe. These interest rate rises began in weaker economies with higher debt levels, including the Italian and Spanish economies, both of which are far larger than the Greek economy. Interest-rate hikes have even spread to France and (very briefly) to Germany, the eurozone's two largest economies. The spikes in rates not only increase the likelihood of default, they put real roadblocks in the way of the spending and investment needed for recovery and long-term growth.

The danger is not only to Europe. The European Union is the largest economy in the world, accounting for nearly 20% of global economic activity. Every region of the world that trades with Europe will be affected by a slowdown there. The eurozone is the largest export market for both the United States and China. The default of any European country would cause losses and instability throughout the global economy. The U.S. financial system would also be sharply affected, for European global banks provide much of the credit for the U.S. economy.

To stem the bleeding, many in Europe and beyond have urged and continue to urge the ECB to step up and find a way to act as most normal central banks would in the situation: inject money into these economies by buying government debt in unlimited quantities. That in turn would lower interest rates, and give countries time to rebuild and restart growth. Germany, the largest and the dominant economy in Europe, continues to block this option on the grounds that printing money is not only inflationary but a "moral hazard" and makes borrowing too easy. At the last European summit, Germany successfully insisted instead on a "fiscal stability union" that will require balanced budgets (before taking interest payments into account). In other words, austerity for workers.

Rejecting Austerity

Austerity won't work for Europe: Europe needs growth, and austerity can't produce growth. Austerity also can't work because the proposed cure—budget cuts—assumes the disease is government spending. But excessive social spending by its government did not cause Greece's debt problems. In 2007, the year before the crisis hit, Greece's social expenditures relative to the size of its economy stood at 21.3% of GDP, lower than the social expenditures in France (28.3% of GDP) and Germany (25.2% of GDP), the two countries most responsible for orchestrating the austerity measures that have slashed social spending in Greece.

Europe didn't have a government debt crisis before the subprime collapse of 2008. It had countries like Germany in the north with large permanent trade surpluses, and countries in the south like Greece with large permanent trade deficits. Fixing these trade deficits and imbalances can't be done by pushing down wages. In fact, repressive wage and labor policies, especially as practiced in Germany, are what lie at the heart of those imbalances that made the weaker southern eurozone countries so vulnerable to the crisis that followed.

Rather, what's needed is government investment and coordination throughout Europe. A public investment program could modernize the infrastructure of the southern eurozone economies and boost the productivity of their workforce by improving workers' health and education.

A recession—or worse—in Europe will slow down growth and raise budget deficits in the United States as well. It will create political pressure for austerity exactly when we need more investment and more stimulus spending.

If this happens, it will be more important than ever to remember that Europe is in the position it is in, first, because it insisted on austerity for Greece and, second, because Europe has a central bank that is prohibited from financing government deficits and whose sole policy mandate is to limit inflation. Without the insistence on austerity, and without having relinquished these basic tools of economic policy—both of which the United States retains—the mess in Europe could never have happened. The United States is not and will never be Greece.

Yet like the crisis in Europe, the crisis in the United States isn't temporary or fleeting. The outcome will determine what kind of jobs and economic security people will have for a long time to come. It will have a huge effect on public-sector unions. And it will affect democracy itself, especially if we stay silent. Austerity in Europe is being imposed from above. There's no reason to let it be imposed here. ❑

Sources: C. Lapavitsas, et al., "Breaking Up? A Route Out of the Eurozone Crisis," Research on Money and Finance, RMF Occasional Report, November 2011; Heiner Flassbeck and Friederike Spiecker, "The Euro—A Story of Misunderstanding," Intereconomics, 2011; "The ECB's Backdoor Bailout," *Wall Street Journal*, December 24, 2011; George Irvin and Alex Izurieta, "Fundamental Flaws in the European Project," Economic & Political Weekly, August 6, 2011; C.P. Chandrasekhar, "The Crisis in Europe," *The Frontline*, Jul. 30-Aug. 12, 2011; Robert Skidelsky, "The Euro in a Shrinking Zone," Project Syndicate, December 12, 2011; David Enrich, "European Banks Rush to Grasp Lifeline," *Wall Street Journal*, December 22, 2011; Paul Krugman, "Bernanke's Perry Problem," *New York Times*, August 25, 2011; Paul Krugman, "Currency Warnings that Europe Ignored," Krugman & Co., November 22, 2011; Andre Leonard, "The Republican plot to turn the U.S. into Greece," Salon.com, July 18, 2011; Sally Giansbury et al.," Greek austerity plans threaten growth," *Financial Times*, October 17, 2011; James Bullard, "The Fed's Dual Mandate: Lessons of the 1970s," The 2010 Annual Report of the Federal Reserve Bank of St. Louis, April 2011.

Article 1.4

COLLAPSING INVESTMENT AND THE GREAT RECESSION

BY GERALD FRIEDMAN
July/August 2013

I nvestment in real inputs—structures and machinery used to boost future output and productivity—is one of the ways that an economy grows over time. In a capitalist economy, such investments are also crucial for macroeconomic stability and full employment because they provide an "injection" of demand to balance the "leakage" caused by personal and institutional savings. The Great Recession that began in 2007 was marked by a collapse of investment unprecedented since the Great Depression, as well as a dramatic drop in overall production and a sharp jump in unemployment. Since 2009, overall output has been growing again, but we have seen a much slower recovery of investment than after other recessions since 1947. The worst economic crisis since the 1930s, the Great Recession came after a long period of declining investment, and a break in the linkage between corporate profits and new investment.

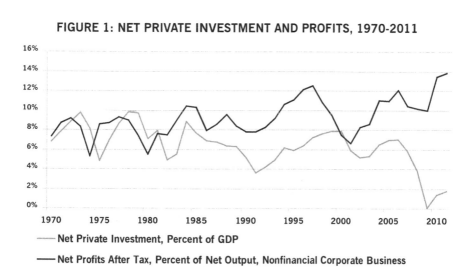

FIGURE 1: NET PRIVATE INVESTMENT AND PROFITS, 1970-2011

——Net Private Investment, Percent of GDP

——Net Profits After Tax, Percent of Net Output, Nonfinancial Corporate Business

The share of national income going to investment (net of depreciation of existing plant and machinery) has been declining since the beginning of the "neoliberal" era, around 1980. Since the start of the Great Recession, net investment as a share of GDP has plummeted to its lowest level since the 1930s. This sharp drop in investment comes despite sharply rising profits.

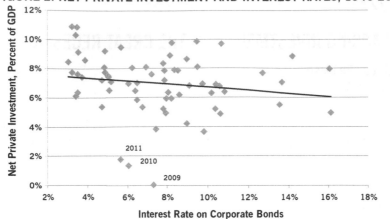

FIGURE 2: NET PRIVATE INVESTMENT AND INTEREST RATES, 1946-2011

The Federal Reserve has helped to shorten past recessions by driving down interest rates to lower the cost of borrowing and so spur investment. During the current crisis, the Fed has conducted an aggressive monetary policy, raising the money supply to lower interest rates. But it has had little effect on investment. While lower interest rates have had only a weak effect on investment in the past, monetary policy has had no discernible effect in the last few years, as investment rates are dramatically lower than would have been expected given the level of interest rates. Substantial excess capacity, weak expectations of future sales, and corporate strategies to shift production outside the United States all may be contributing to the lack of investment demand.

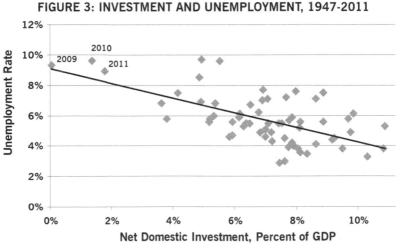

FIGURE 3: INVESTMENT AND UNEMPLOYMENT, 1947-2011

In one respect, the current recession resembles past experience. Low rates of investment are associated with high rates of unemployment, just as in previous economic downturns. The difference is that, three years after the official end of the Great Recession, the unemployment rate remains persistently high, and investment remains dramatically lower than in past recoveries.

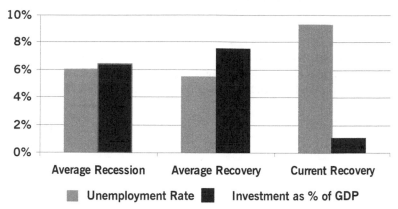

FIGURE 4: WHAT RECOVERY?

During the current "recovery" (2009-present), the unemployment rate has remained higher and investment as a share of GDP has remained lower than the average not only for past recoveries, but even for past recessions (since 1947). No wonder the current situation seems more like a continuation of the Great Recession than a genuine recovery.

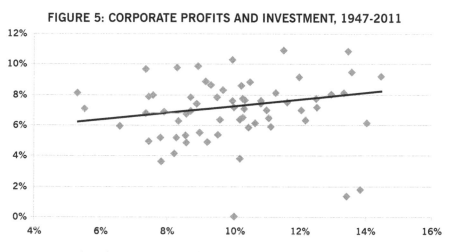

FIGURE 5: CORPORATE PROFITS AND INVESTMENT, 1947-2011

Net Profits After Tax, Percent of Net Output, Nonfinancial Corporate Business

Note: Trendline excludes years 2009-2011.

In the past, higher corporate profits were associated with higher rates of investment, as businesses have rushed to take advantage of profitable opportunities. In the current crisis, however, the link between profit and investment has been broken and investment rates have been very low despite high rates of profitability (especially in 2010 and 2011). Businesses are holding back on investing, either because they anticipate continued low levels of demand (perhaps due to high unemployment and low wages) or because they plan to shift more production outside the United States. ❑

Sources: Investment: Bureau of Economic Analysis (BEA, bea.gov), Table 5.2.5, Gross and Net Domestic Investment by Major Type; GDP: BEA, Current-Dollar and "Real" Gross Domestic Product; Profits: BEA, Table 1.15, Price, Costs, and Profit Per Unit of Real Gross Value Added of Nonfinancial Domestic Corporate Business; Unemployment: Bureau of Labor Statistics, Unemployment rate, 16 years and over, Not seasonally adjusted, Series ID LNU04000000; Interest rate: St. Louis Federal Reserve, Moody's Seasoned Baa Corporate Bond Yield.

Article 1.5

VICE VERSA: INEQUALITY AND OUR ECONOMIC PROBLEMS

BY JOHN MILLER
November/December 2013

> ...President Obama and his supporters have been talking about "an economy that grows from the middle out"...
>
> The key causal factor of the middle-out view is that a wider income distribution slows economic growth by lowering consumption demand. The data for the recovery since mid-2009 do not support this view.
>
> Moreover, data do not support the view that tax cuts in the past 30 years are responsible for the widening income distribution.
>
> —John B. Taylor, "The Weak Recovery Explains Rising Inequality, Not Vice Versa," *Wall Street Journal*, Sept. 9, 2013.

Vice versa back at you, John Taylor. Rising inequality is not just bad for us, but is the root cause of today's economic problems.

A Stanford economist and senior fellow at the conservative Hoover Institute, Taylor readily admits that inequality is on the rise. But he never spells out the degree to which the widening gulf between the best off and the rest of us has concentrated economic gains nearly exclusively among the super rich. Had he done so, he would have found it far harder to dismiss the role pro-rich economic policies and worsening inequality have played in causing today's economic maladies.

The most recent data, drawn from a variety of highly credible sources, show what the concentration of income "more at the upper end," as Taylor puts it, has meant in practice. As of 2012, the richest 1% of families, all with incomes above $394,000, received more than one-fifth of the income of the nation, some 22.5%, according to the latest data compiled by economists Emmanuel Saez and Thomas Piketty. That's nearly equal to their 23.5% share of income in 2007, before the onset of the Great Recession, and their 24% share during the late 1920s, on the eve of the Great Depression—the two highest concentrations of income since 1913. And, as Saez and Piketty document, a stunning 95% of what income gains there have been during the current recovery (from 2009 to 2012) have gone to the richest 1%.

Not surprisingly, by 2012 only the income of the top 5% had returned to its pre-recession level in 2007, as the latest figures from the Bureau of the Census confirm. The inflation-adjusted income of the median family, on the other hand, was still 8.3% below its pre-recession level, and no higher than in 1989, nearly a generation earlier.

College Grads and the Super-Rich

What accounts for today's staggering inequality? Taylor claims that changes in the private economy have driven up the wages of the well-educated and have left those with fewer years of education behind.

The distance between the economic position of workers with college degrees and those without has, indeed, widened considerably over the last three decades. In 1979, the "college premium" was 1.41. That is, the median wage of a college graduate was 41% greater than that of a worker with only a high-school diploma. By 2007, the college premium had reached 1.75. In addition, since the onset of the Great Recession in December 2007, the number of jobs held by college graduates has increased, while the number of jobs held by those without a college degree has fallen.

But that is hardly enough evidence to support Taylor's claim. First off, nearly all of the increase in the college premium occurred before the last decade, but inequality has continued to worsen. In addition, the inequality among wage earners, especially between the top wage earners and the rest of the workforce, a large and increasing number of whom hold a college degree, is far greater than the college premium data suggest. For instance, looking at the ranking of wage and salary earners between 1979 and 2007, the wages and salaries of the top 1% rose by 156%, while those of the bottom 90% went up by just 17%. At the end of that period, the ratio of the wages and salaries of the top 1% to those of the bottom 90% stood at over 20-to-1, more than double the 9.7-to-1 ratio in 1979.

When investment income is added to wage and salary income, the economic gulf between the elites and the vast majority becomes even greater and increases even more quickly than the wage gap alone. Over the same 1979-to-2007 period, the ratio of total income of the top 1% to that of the bottom 90% tripled from 14-to-1 to 42-to-1. And even among the richest 1% income became considerably more concentrated. In 1979, the ratio of income of the top one-tenth of 1% to that of the top 1% was 3.4-to-1 in 1979 but reached 5.2-to-1 by 2007.

These vast differences cannot be attributed solely, or even primarily, to differences in years of education among wage earners.

Pro-Rich Tax Cuts and Inequality

Taylor also emphatically disagrees with the "middle-out view" that the pro-rich tax cuts and economic policies that began in the early 1980s are the cause of the ever widening gulf between the haves and the have-nots. But the very evidence he uses to support his position suggests otherwise.

Taylor's argument rests on data published by the Congressional Budget Office (CBO) showing that, "the distribution of market income before taxes widened in the 1980s and '90s by about as much as the distribution of income after taxes." But that hardly makes his case.

Rather, the fact that after-tax income and before-tax income are widening at about the same rate offers powerful testimony to how pro-rich tax cuts have wiped out whatever government taxing policies had done in the past to mitigate the effects of widening economic differences in the private sector. "Market income inequality rose almost continually over the period [from 1979 to 2009]," write CBO tax analysts Ed Harris and Frank Sammartino. "Taxes and transfers did not offset market inequality."

Federal taxes are considerably less progressive than in the past and no match for three decades of ever widening inequality. In 1979, the richest 1% paid an effective federal tax rate of 35%—handing over a little over one-third of their total income in federal taxes. By 2009, the effective tax rate of the top 1% had fallen to 28.9%, according to the CBO. And when a less progressive federal tax code was combined with regressive state and local tax codes, taxes could no longer combat widening inequality.

Inequality and Economic Growth

Finally, there are also several reasons to reject Taylor's claim that inequality is not the cause of the weak recovery and sluggish economic growth since the official end of the Great Recession in June 2009.

Taylor's argument is that inequality has not retarded spending because today's savings rate of 5.4% is not especially high by historical standards. That's true. But after the 1980s, the saving rate dropped steadily as consumption, boosted by a stock market boom, rose during the 1990s and, fueled by a housing bubble, rose still more during the last decade. Today's savings rate is considerably higher than the 3% savings rate that prevailed in the middle of the last decade.

While spending by the rich, if high enough, could hypothetically power economic growth, several prominent economists are convinced that the redistribution of income toward the upper end has diminished spending and stood in the way of more rapid economic growth. Alan Krueger, current chair of the Council of Economic Advisors, thinks the drag on spending from this upper redistribution "could be substantial." He estimates that, by 2007, increased income inequality put an additional $1.1 trillion a year into the hands of the top 1%, who spend only about one-half of additional income. Had that $1.1 trillion remained in the hands of the bottom 99%, who have a general savings rate of about 10%, Krueger calculates that total consumption spending would have been 5% higher.

On top of its retarding effect on consumer spending, the concentration of income enhanced the political power of the super rich. Political scientists Adam Bonica, Nolan McCarty, Keith Poole, and Howard Rosenthal report that the share of individual campaign contributions made by the richest 0.01% rose from about 15% in 1980 to 40% in 2012.

And the political outcomes of the last three decades have surely conformed to the political interests of the most well to do—from the deregulation of the financial sector to pro-rich taxes to constraints on federal spending since the end of the Great Recession. Government spending and investment has been falling since 2010. Cuts in discretionary spending have reduced economic growth by 0.7 percentage points since 2010 and raised the unemployment rate by 0.8 percentage points, according to a recent report prepared for the conservative Peter G. Peterson Foundation.

Taylor claims that three decades of rising inequality are explained by market forces. The lesson here, as Joseph Stiglitz has argued, is that "market forces don't exist in a vacuum—we shape them." In the last three decades, the very policies Taylor is determined to absolve have, in fact, shaped market forces in a way that has brought us ever-widening economic inequality, economic crisis, and now unrelenting economic stagnation. ❏

Sources: Lawrence Mishel and Josh Bivens, "Occupy Wall Streeters Are Right About Skewed Economic Rewards in the United States," Economic Policy Institute Briefing Paper, Oct. 26, 2011; Congressional Budget Office, "The Distribution of Household Income and Federal Taxes, 2008 and 2009," July 2012; Adam Bonica, Nolan McCarty, Keith T. Poole, and Howard Rosenthal, "Why Hasn't Democracy Slowed Rising Inequality?" *Journal of Economic Perspectives*, Summer 2013; Emmanuel Saez, "Striking it Richer," University of California-Berkeley, Sept. 3, 2013; Ed Harris and Frank Sammartino, "Trends in the Distribution of Household Income, 1979-2009," Congressional Budget Office, Aug. 6, 2012; Jonathan James, "The College Wage Premium," *Economic Commentary*, Aug. 8, 2012; Carmen DeNavas-Walt, Bernadette D. Proctor, Jessica C. Smith, Income, Poverty, and Health Insurance Coverage in the United States: 2012, September 2013; Paul Krugman, "The Damage Done," *New York Times*, Oct. 17, 2013; Joseph Stiglitz, "Inequality Is Holding Back the Recovery," *New York Times*, Jan. 19, 2013; Dean Baker, "Krugman versus Stiglitz on Inequality and Economic Growth," Center For Economic and Policy Research, Jan. 20, 2013; Macroeconomic Advisers, LLC, The Cost of Crisis-Driven Fiscal Policy, Peter G. Peterson Foundation; Alan Krueger, "The Rise and Consequence of Inequality in the United States," White House Council of Economic Advisors, Jan. 12, 2012.

Chapter 2

DEFICITS AND FISCAL POLICY

Article 2.1

GOVERNMENT "LIVING WITHIN ITS MEANS"?

Claims about budget balancing are baloney.

BY JOHN MILLER
November/December 2011

> "Government has to start living within its means, just like families do. We have to cut the spending we can't afford so we can put the economy on sounder footing, and give our businesses the confidence they need to grow and create jobs."
> —President Barack Obama, weekly radio address, July 2, 2011

> "If the US was a business, it would be a failing business. That's the problem. You have to spend less than you make. Business 101."
> —Boston-area car dealer Ernie Boch, Jr., quoted in "From some of the richest, two cheers for higher taxes," *Boston Globe*, August 21, 2011

Turn on any of the television or radio gab shows and it won't be long before you hear someone proclaim that government must live within its means just as families do and businesses must.

Barack Obama gave this analogy the presidential seal of approval in a radio address in early July. In August, Ernie Boch, Jr., the Boston-based auto dealership magnate, added his two cents to Warren Buffett's call to hike taxes on the rich: he would pay more taxes only if the government balanced its budget just as his and every other business must do.

But the truth is neither families nor businesses balance their books in the sense of forgoing borrowing. And even if they did, to insist that government do the same would extinguish whatever remains of economic growth and job creation, not ignite them.

Family and Business Red Ink

Few families balance their budgets the way the guardians of financial rectitude are now demanding of government. Nearly all families spend more than they earn and borrow to do so. When a family takes out a car loan, a student loan, or a mortgage on a house, it's spending money it doesn't have.

Is borrowing the road to ruin? Not if the debt is affordable. That depends not just on the size of the debt relative to the income available to service that debt, but also on how the family spends the borrowed money. For instance, assuming the size of the debt is manageable, borrowing to pay for education is justified if the education improves the family's earning potential and so helps provide the income necessary to service the debt.

The same holds true of businesses. They borrow to invest and operate, especially in the United States where corporations finance the bulk of their investments by borrowing rather than by issuing stock. While exact numbers are not available about the privately held Boch auto dealerships, rest assured that Boch's company borrows to put the cars on his lot that he sells to the public or to build yet another dealership. That borrowing allows Boch's and other businesses to spend more than they are taking in—Business 101.

Families and businesses in the United States do quite a bit of borrowing and quite a bit more borrowing than they had in the past. Today families rely on credit to meet their needs—for everything from food to fuel, from education to entertainment, and especially housing. Total household debt stood at 92.5% of GDP in 2010, more than thirty percentage points higher than its level two decades earlier, 60.2% in 1990. And as their debt rose, families shelled out more and more of their income to make payments on that debt. In the first quarter of 2011, household payments on consumer and mortgage debt consumed 11.5% of disposable personal income.

Businesses, too, have increased their reliance on debt to finance their operations. Total debt of non-financial businesses was 53% as great as GDP in 1980, but reached 74.3% in 2010.

Those figures surely put the lie to the claim that families and businesses balance their budgets year in and out without relying on borrowing to spend beyond their income.

Government's Red Ink

Still it's true that federal government debt has increased steadily and rapidly over the last decade as the government has consistently run budget deficits. The ratio of the outstanding debt of the federal government to the country's GDP rose from 32.5% in 2001 to 62.1% in 2010.

However, payments on that rising debt are less of a burden on the federal government budget than debt payments are on family budgets. The U.S. government can perpetually refinance its debt in ways that are not open to the richest family or the largest business. Its debt burden, then, consists of the net interest payments on its debt, which will amount to 9.5% of federal revenues in 2011. That's two percentage points less than the proportion of their income that families devoted to making their debt payments— interest payments and payment on the principal—in the beginning of 2011.

Moreover, a good share of federal spending has gone to investments that are aimed at increasing its (and U.S. families') future income—similar to a household taking out an education loan or a business borrowing to expand its operation. A recent study conducted by the Brookings Institution, the Washington-based think tank, found that in 2008 the federal government spent $253.8 billion on non-defense investments in infrastructure, mostly transportation, research and development, and education and training, all expenditures that will boost the productivity of the economy and help to provide the tax revenue to service the debt. That investment spending equaled a little more than half of the $453.6 billion budget deficit in 2008.

Political Will

The aversion to the federal government deficits and borrowing fostered by pundits and politicians who pronounce that governments must balance their budgets like families and businesses do, even as the economy falters, is not only at odds with the facts. It has made us worse off by blocking government spending just when it is most needed. When family budgets are tight, and spending constrained with so many out of work and with the overhang of mortgage debt, it falls to government to provide the spending necessary to get the economy going. Government spending can put people to work and provide the income that will loosen tight family budgets, so they too can buy what businesses produce.

What's needed is to reverse the austerity budgets favored by conservative politicians in the United States and Europe today. More government spending and tax cuts targeted at working people, beyond what President Obama has proposed in his recent jobs bill, will surely make the budget deficit yet larger and drive up government debt. But that ratio of government debt to GDP, currently 62.1%, is still far below the 1946 record peak of 109% at the end of World War II, which was followed by the two of the strongest decades of economic growth in U.S. history.

It has happened before, and during even worse economic conditions than today's stagnation. In a Pittsburgh campaign speech in October 1932, some three years into the Great Depression, presidential candidate Franklin Delano Roosevelt promised that he would slash federal expenditures by 25% and balance the federal budget. But once in office, FDR reneged on his promise to balance the budget and initiated the New Deal. When he returned to Pittsburgh during his 1936 campaign for reelection, FDR declared, "to balance the budget in 1933, or 1934, or 1935 would be a crime against the American people."

Without massive government spending and without the political will to brand balancing the government budget as a "crime against the American people," today's crisis will likely drag on for a decade as economic hardship mounts for more and more of us. ❑

Sources: Barack Obama, Weekly Radio Address, July 2, 2011; Erin Ailworth, "From some of the richest, two cheers for higher taxes," *Boston Globe*, Aug. 21, 2011; Congressional Budget Office, *The Budget and Economic Outlook: Fiscal Years 2011 to 2021*, January 2011; Emilia Istrate and Robert Puentes, "Investing for Success," Metropolitan Policy Program at Brookings, Dec. 2009; Arthur MacEwan and John Miller, *Economic Collapse, Economic Change: Getting to the Roots of The Crisis*, M.E. Sharpe, 2011; Address of Gov. Franklin D. Roosevelt, Pittsburgh, Pa., Oct. 19, 1932; Franklin D. Roosevelt, "Address at Forbes Field, Pittsburgh, Pa.," Oct. 1, 1936, The American Presidency Project.

Article 2.2

THE IDEOLOGICAL ATTACK ON JOB CREATION
Responding to Anti-Government Arguments

BY MARTY WOLFSON
May/June 2012

> "Government doesn't create jobs. It's the private sector that creates jobs."
> —presidential candidate Mitt Romney, speaking at Wofford College,
> Spartenburg, S.C., January 18, 2012

It is jarring to hear pundits say that the government can't create jobs. It is even more jarring to hear the same refrain from someone whose job was created by the government! Perhaps Mr. Romney has forgotten, or would like to forget, that he used to have a government job as governor of Massachusetts.

But surely those currently on the government payroll have not forgotten, like the chairman of the House Republican Policy Committee, Rep. Tom Price (R-Ga.). He used the same talking points, "The government doesn't create jobs. It's the private sector that creates jobs," speaking on MSNBC's "Andrea Mitchell Reports" last June.

Rep. Price apparently thinks he doesn't have a real job, but what about teachers, firefighters, police officers, and school cafeteria workers? And what about the 2 to 4.8 million jobs—in both the public and private sectors—the U.S. Congressional Budget Office estimated were created by the 2009 U.S. economic stimulus package?

The "government doesn't create jobs" mantra is part of a coordinated right-wing campaign to *prevent* the government from creating jobs and promoting the interests of working families, and to instead encourage a shift in the distribution of income towards the wealthy. It is supported by ideologically motivated arguments and theories from conservative economists and anti-government think tanks. In what follows, these arguments are addressed and criticized, in the hopes of clearing away some of the confusion undermining a vigorous government program to put people back to work.

The Argument That Government Spending Can't Increase Jobs

A Senior Fellow at the Cato Institute says the idea that government spending can create jobs "has a rather glaring logical fallacy. It overlooks the fact that, in the real world, government can't inject money into the economy without first taking money out of the economy." This argument is wrong for several reasons.

First, the government *can* inject money into the economy. It does so whenever it finances its spending by selling bonds to the Federal Reserve. In this case, money is created by the Federal Reserve when it buys the bonds. It creates a reserve account on its books; money is thus created without any reduction in money elsewhere in the economy.

Alternatively, the government can finance its spending by taxes or by selling bonds to the public. This is the case envisioned by the Cato analysis. The argument is that the money spent by the government is exactly balanced by a reduction in money in the pockets of taxpayers of bond buyers. However, if the taxpayers' or the bond buyers' money would otherwise have been saved and not spent, then there is a net injection into the economy of funds that can put people to work.

The argument made by the Cato Institute is actually a variation of another theory, known as "crowding out." In this theory, government spending creates competition for real resources that "crowds out," or displaces, private investment; private companies are unable to obtain the workers and capital they need for investment, so that any jobs due to government spending are offset by a decrease of jobs in the private sector.

This theory is valid only when there is full employment because there would be no idle resources, labor or capital, to put to use. In that case, though, neither the government nor the private sector would be able to create net new jobs. In contrast, in a situation of unemployment, it is precisely because the government can access otherwise idle resources that it can create jobs.

And, of course, that is exactly the situation we are in. As of March, the official unemployment rate stood at 8.2 %. Adjusted for underemployment, e.g., by counting those discouraged workers who have dropped out of the labor force and those workers who are working part-time but would like to work full-time, the more accurate unemployment rate was 14.5%.

The Argument That Cutting Government Spending Creates Jobs

Consistent with anti-government ideology, conservative economics asserts not only that government spending can't create jobs, but also that cutting government spending creates jobs. Here's how the argument goes: less government spending will reduce the government deficit; smaller deficits will increase the confidence of businesses that will invest more and in that way create more jobs. According to John B. Taylor, an economist affiliated with Stanford's conservative Hoover Institution, "Basic economic models in which incentives and expectations of future policy matter show that a credible plan to reduce gradually the deficit will increase economic growth and reduce unemployment by removing uncertainty and lowering the chances of large tax increases in the future." (Interestingly, an analysis by economist Robert Pollin of the Political Economy Research Institute at the University of Massachusetts-Amherst finds that Taylor's empirical model concludes that the stimulus bill was ineffective—but only because it included too much in tax cuts as opposed to direct government spending.)

This assertion is based more on wishful thinking than empirical validity, and has been criticized by Paul Krugman as depending on belief in a "confidence fairy." But it is not just liberal economists like Krugman who are critical of this theory. A confidential report prepared for clients by the investment bank Goldman Sachs concluded that a $61 billion cut in government spending from a bill passed by the House of Representatives in February 2011 (but not enacted into law) would lead to a decline in economic growth of 2%. And economist Mark Zandi, formerly an advisor to Republican presidential candidate John McCain, concluded that this $61 billion reduction in government spending could result in the loss of 700,000 jobs by 2012.

Ben Bernanke, chairman of the Board of Governors of the Federal Reserve System, stated that "the cost to the recovery [of steep reductions in government outlays now] would outweigh the benefits in terms of fiscal discipline." Even the International Monetary Fund, in its semiannual report on the world economic outlook, concluded that "the idea that fiscal austerity triggers faster growth in the short term finds little support in the data."

Also, in a review of studies and historical experience about the relationship between budget-cutting and economic growth, economists Arjun Jayadev and Mike Konczal concluded that countries historically did not cut government spending and deficits in a slump and that there is no basis to conclude that doing so now, "under the conditions the United States currently faces, would improve the country's prospects."

The Argument That Private Spending Is Always Better than Public Spending

Another way that right-wing economics tries to discredit the idea that the government can create jobs is to assert that private spending is always to be preferred to public spending. There are several rationalizations for this view.

One is that private spending is more efficient than public spending. This ideological refrain has been repeated consistently, and gained a following, over the past thirty years. But repetition does not make it correct. Of course, the proponents of this argument can point to examples of government mismanagement, such as that following Hurricane Katrina. However, government bungling and inefficiency by an administration that did not believe in government does not prove the point. A much more grievous example of inefficiency and misallocation of resources is the housing speculation and financial manipulation—and eventual collapse that brought us to the current recession—due to a deregulated private financial system. Yet for free-market ideologues, this somehow does not discredit the private sector.

Some people think that economists have "proven" that "free" markets are efficient. The only thing that has been proven, however, is that you can arrive at any conclusion if your assumptions are extreme enough. And the assumptions that form the basis for the free-market theory are indeed extreme, if not totally unrealistic and impossible. For example: orthodox free-market economics assumes perfectly competitive markets; perfect information; no situations, like pollution, in which private decision-makers do not take account of the societal effects of their actions; even full employment. But none of these assumptions hold true in the real world. Also, the distribution of income is irrelevant to the conclusions of this theory. The distribution of income is simply taken as given, so that the results of the theory are consistent with a relatively equal distribution of income as well as a very unequal distribution. As economist Joseph Stiglitz has said, "Today, there is no respectable intellectual support for the proposition that markets, by themselves, lead to efficient, let alone equitable outcomes."

A second reason for supposing that private spending is to be preferred to public spending is the notion that public spending is less worthwhile than private spending. This means, for many people, reducing government spending as much as possible. For example, Grover Norquist, founder and president of Americans for Tax Reform and author of the anti-tax pledge signed by many members of Congress, said that he wanted to "shrink [the government] down to the size where we can drown it in the bathtub." The anti-tax, anti-spending crusade has in many cases been successful in reducing government budgets, on the national as well as the local level. This has resulted in a significant decrease in government services. Although some people are attracted to the view that government spending should always be reduced, they probably at the same time don't want to drive on roads and bridges that aren't repaired and they probably want fire trucks to arrive if their house is on fire. Perhaps, too, they wouldn't automatically prefer twelve kinds of toothpaste to schools, parks, and libraries.

The Argument That Government Spending Is Wasteful

Another argument contends that public spending is wasteful. Discussions of government accounts generally do not take account of public investment, so all public spending is essentially treated as consumption. As such, it is considered unproductive and wasteful by those who wish to disparage government spending. In other words, the government budget does not make a distinction between long-term investments and other spending as corporate budgets do.

One implication of treating all government spending as consumption is the notion that the federal government should maintain a balanced budget. To put this in accounting terms, on this view government accounts are considered to only have an income statement (which shows current revenues and current expenditures), not a balance sheet (which shows assets and liabilities).

Corporations, in contrast, maintain balance sheets. They don't balance their budgets in the way that the budget hawks want the government to do. Private investment in plant and equipment, for example, is accounted for on the asset side of the balance sheet; borrowing to finance this investment is accounted for on the liability side. Interest on the debt is accounted for on the income statement, and it is only the interest, not the outstanding debt balance, that has to be covered by current revenues. The assumption behind this accounting is that borrowing to finance productive investment will generate the revenue to pay off the borrowing.

The Ryan Budget: A Path to Prosperity?

On March 29, the House of Representatives passed Rep. Paul Ryan's budget proposal, called the "FY2013 Path to Prosperity Budget." It would be a disaster for working Americans. It shreds the safety net; according to the Center for Budget and Policy Priorities, 62% of Ryan's trillions in spending cuts come from programs affecting low-income Americans. The vast majority of tax cuts would go to corporations and upper-income Americans. Yet Ryan claims that his budget brings the "size of government to 20 percent of [the] economy by 2015, allowing the private sector to grow and create jobs." But an independent analysis by Ethan Pollack, a researcher at the Economic Policy Institute, concludes that Ryan's budget would result in the loss of 4.1 million jobs by 2014.

In other words, corporations borrow on a regular basis to finance investment. So they only attempt to balance their current expenditures and revenues and not their capital budget.

Much confusion about private and public spending, and also about budget deficits, could be avoided if discussion focused on a federal government balance sheet. In that way, current spending that needs to be balanced with current revenue could be separated from long-term investments that will increase the productivity of the American economy. Such investments, in areas like infrastructure and education, can increase future economic growth and income, and thus generate more tax revenue to pay off the debt. Just like a private company's investments, they are legitimately financed by borrowing.

Government Can Indeed Create Jobs

The main point, though, is this: whether financed by borrowing or taxes, whether consumption or investment, government spending that increases the demand for goods and services in the economy is not wasteful. It has the ability to employ underutilized resources and create jobs.

Ultimately, a job is a job, whether created by the private or public sector. A job has the potential to enable workers to support themselves and their families in dignity. We should not let ideological arguments keep us from using every available means to promote the basic human right of employment. ❏

Sources: Congressional Budget Office, "Estimated Impact of the American Recovery and Reinvestment Act on Employment and Economic Output From April 2010 Through June 2010," August 2010; Daniel J. Mitchell, "The Fallacy That Government Creates Jobs," The Cato Institute, 2008; John B. Taylor, "Goldman Sachs Wrong About Impact of House Budget Proposal," Economics One blog, February 28, 2011; Paul Krugman, "Myths of austerity," *The New York Times.* July 1, 2010; Jonathan Karl, "Goldman Sachs: House Spending Cuts Will Hurt Economic Growth," The Note, 2011; Mark Zandi, "A federal shutdown could derail the recovery," Moody's Analytics, February 28, 2011; Pedro da Costa and Mark Felsenthal, "Bernanke warns against steep budget cuts," Reuters, February 9, 2011; International Monetary Fund, *World Economic Outlook: Recovery, Risk, and Rebalancing,* 2010; Arjun Jayadev and Mike Konczal, "When Is Austerity Right? In Boom, Not Bust," *Challenge,* November-December 2010, pp. 37-53; Joseph Stiglitz, Foreword, in Karl Polanyi, *The Great Transformation: The Political and Economic Origins of Our Times,* 2001; David Aschauer, "Is Public Expenditure Productive?" *Journal of Monetary Economics,* 1989, pp. 177-200; Robert Pollin, "US government deficits and debt amid the great recession: what the evidence shows, *Cambridge Journal of Economics,* 2012, 36, 161-187; Kelsey Merrick and Jim Horney, "Chairman Ryan Gets 62 Percent of His Huge Budget Cuts from Programs for Lower-income Americans," Center on Budget and Policy Priorities, March 23, 2012; Paul Ryan, The Path to Prosperity, March 20, 2012; Ethan Pollack, "Ryan's Budget Would Cost Jobs," The Economic Policy Institute, March 21, 2012.

Article 2.3

WHY DO THEY OPPOSE MORE STIMULUS?

BY ARTHUR MacEWAN
January/February 2011

> Dear Dr. Dollar:
> Why are conservatives, especially wealthy conservatives, against stimulating the economy through the government's deficit spending? Don't businesses' profits and the incomes of the wealthy depend on economic growth?
> —*Andy Druding, Richmond, Calif.*

As it turns out, business profits are already doing pretty well in spite of—or perhaps because of—the poor economic conditions for most people. Corporate profits have been expanding at a good clip since the beginning of 2009. In the third quarter of 2010, profits of domestic corporations were running at an annual rate of $1.27 trillion—not back up to their peak of $1.40 trillion four years earlier, but well on the way to that high mark. Even after an adjustment for inflation, current profits are in relatively good shape.

So it is not too hard to see why the people whose incomes are tied to profits are not eager to see a dramatic shift of policy. Still, you might think that more economic growth would provide even more profits.

Profits, however, depend on two things: the amount of value that gets created (output) and the share of that value that goes to profits. With a high level of unemployment, workers are in a poor position to demand higher wages—i.e., a larger share of that value. So businesses, and the wealthy who get their income from owning businesses, do not want unemployment to fall too low—low enough to give workers more bargaining power.

The weak position of workers in the current economic situation affects more than wages. While a recession lasts, businesses are able to implement changes more readily than in "normal" times. For example, they can change work rules, get rid of older workers, and bring in new technology more easily, as workers are in a poorer position to resist change. Also, the "shock" imposed on society by bad economic conditions can be used in the political sphere, making it possible for businesses and the wealthy to obtain concessions from government—the tax incentives state governments offer, for example, in the hope of generating some local growth. (However, an economic crisis also opens up possibilities for changes in the other direction. Consider, for example, the progressive changes in the United States that came out of the Great Depression of the 1930s.)

From the perspective of the wealthy, then, perhaps a bit more growth would be better, but not so much as to weaken their positions. Most important, if that growth required the government to spend a lot more by running deficits, the wealthy are not interested. They fear that high deficits now mean more taxes down the line. In part, higher taxes could be needed to pay off the debt the government would incur when it ran those deficits. Perhaps more important, upping government spending today threatens to entrench a long-run higher level of government activity, which would require higher taxes on a permanent basis. The wealthy might be able to push the tax obligations onto lower income groups. Yet, with income inequality as great as it is, it's hard to get much more out of anyone but the wealthy. You can't get blood from a stone.

These concerns about higher taxes generate a strong anti-big-government ideology, and the ideology can trump common sense. There are plenty of people who because they oppose "big government" oppose the spending that would be involved in any program that would provide significant economic stimulus through deficit spending. Of course not all of these people are among the wealthy, but they share the anti-government, anti-tax ideology. After all, they cannot improve their incomes by voting for higher wages, but they can—or think they can—improve their incomes by voting against taxes, which means voting against "big government," which means voting against deficits.

All this said, most of today's large federal budget deficit is not the result of spending designed to stimulate the economy. In fiscal year 2009, the budget deficit was about $1.4 trillion. Yet the February 2009 "stimulus package" accounted for a small share of that deficit. In 2001, the Congressional Budget Office (CBO) estimated the government was on course for a 2009 surplus of $700 billion. Why this $2.1 trillion difference between the CBO estimate and reality?

Slow economic growth in the early 2000s followed by severe downturn in 2008 and 2009 accounted for over 40% of the difference, as tax income declined sharply and some spending automatically increased (e.g., unemployment compensation). About 50% of the difference resulted from legislation enacted in the Bush years—over half of which was war spending, tax breaks for the wealthy, and the bank bailout. The stimulus package of the Obama administration accounted for only about 8% of the difference, a pretty small share.

Businesses and the wealthy who rail against the deficit do have real interests that they are protecting. But they are also using the deficit issue to attack the Obama administration's stimulus efforts, which turn out not to have been all that big. ❑

Article 2.4

BEYOND DEFICIT SCARE-MONGERING

BY ELLEN FRANK
March/April 2013

U.S. politics seems stuck in an endless debate about the size of the federal deficit and federal debt. Congressional Republicans' refusals to lift the debt ceiling, fears of the "fiscal cliff," disputes about the "sequestration" and its automatic federal-spending cuts, and upcoming debates on a new federal budget and the need for so-called entitlement reform (primarily cuts to Social Security, Medicare, and Medicaid)—all hinge on the presumed need to get the U.S. budget in balance and curb deficit spending.

In a February appearance on ABC's "This Week," Rep. Paul Ryan (R-WI), the chair of the House Budget Committee and his party's vice-presidential nominee in 2012, repeatedly raised fears of an imminent "debt crisis" if the government deficit and debt were not cut quickly and dramatically. "We want economic growth. We want job creation," Ryan argued. "We want people to go back to work. We want to prevent a debt crisis from hurting those who are the most vulnerable in society, from giving us a European-like economy. In order to do that, you've got to get the debt and deficit under control and you've got to grow the economy."

There is no question that the debt and deficit have grown since the economy tumbled in 2008, though the deficit has been shrinking more recently and is projected to continue declining as the economy slowly recovers. The federal deficit—the amount by which federal-government spending exceeds federal revenue for a particular year—currently stands at about $1.1 trillion. That amounts to less than 7% of gross domestic product (GDP), the total market-based output of the economy in a year. The federal debt—the total amount that the federal government owes (accumulated over many years of running deficits)—is now $16 trillion. That is approximately equal to the United States' annual GDP. Some of this debt, however, is held by the Federal Reserve and some by federal agencies. When we look at only the debt held by "members of the public," total federal debt amounts to less than 75% of GDP. (See Figure 1.)

Is this a sustainable level of federal debt? What is the maximum sustainable level? Harvard economists Carmen Reinhart and Kenneth Rogoff made headlines in 2010 with research claiming that the debt should not exceed 90–100% of GDP, lest it doom future economic growth. That number, however, seems as if it has been pulled out of a hat. The argument appears to be that deficit spending will cause inflation, high interest rates, and a debased currency. But none of that has happened. Since the deficit and debt started rising, the U.S. inflation rate has fallen to 1.3%. U.S. government Treasury bills (short-term borrowing) currently pay interest of less than 0.5%. Since that is lower than the rate of inflation, it means that, in effect, creditors are paying the U.S. government to take their money. Meanwhile, longer-term bonds pay interest of only around 2%. Clearly, investors are happy to hold U.S. government debt, the safest of all financial assets.

FIGURE 1: FEDERAL GOVERNMENT DEBT AS A PERCENTAGE OF GDP (1940-2011)

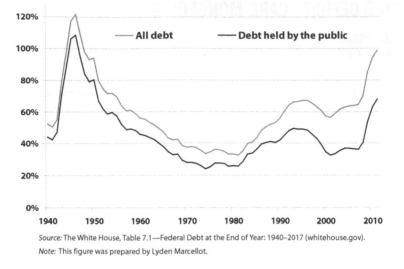

Source: The White House, Table 7.1—Federal Debt at the End of Year: 1940–2017 (whitehouse.gov).
Note: This figure was prepared by Lyden Marcellot.

It is true that the value of the dollar has fallen slightly against the euro, but this is a good thing from the standpoint of a U.S. economic recovery, since it promotes American exports. Recent export growth has been one of the few bright spots in an otherwise grim economic environment.

How Much Can the Government Borrow?

What are the limits on borrowing before it creates economic problems? The answer is that nobody really knows. The Japanese government has a national debt equal to more than twice its GDP, yet is fighting both deflation and an over-valued currency, rather than inflation and a collapsing currency. Interest rates are close to zero. Overall, the country's economic situation is certainly not good. But by borrowing heavily, Japan has been able to keep its unemployment rate between 4% and 5%, one of the lowest among the industrialized countries. This suggests that the U.S. government could more than double its debt without causing inflation, raising interest rates, or devaluing its currency.

Deficit scolds often claim that households must balance their budgets and limit their debt, and that the government should too. This reasoning is not exclusive to conservative politicians and pundits. Back in 2010, as part of the administration's pivot away from fiscal stimulus and toward deficit reduction, President Obama said, "At a time when so many families are tightening their belts," the administration "would make sure that the government continues to tighten its own." What's wrong with this idea? First, most U. S. households take on heavy debt. Including credit-card debt, home mortgages, student loans, and auto loans, most American households have debts substantially higher than their incomes. Of course, households can't continuously take on debt, and must make plans to pay their debt off (or face bankruptcy). That brings us to the second point. Debt taken on by the federal government is unlike household debt, because, unlike households or businesses, the government can print money to pay its debt. People's willingness to lend to the government reflects the understanding that the U.S. government can always repay debt, as it comes due, by printing money.

Wouldn't "running the printing press" cause inflation, though? That depends on the overall state of the economy. The Federal Reserve, in recent years, has added nearly $2 trillion dollars to the banking system. Conservative economists and commentators have been long predicting that this would lead to accelerating inflation. Arthur Laffer, a former economic advisor to Ronald Reagan and one of the progenitors of "supply side" economics, for example, argued back in 2009: "[P]anic-driven monetary policies portend to have even more dire consequences [than large fiscal deficits]. We can expect rapidly rising prices and much, much higher interest rates over the next four or five years, and a concomitant deleterious impact on output and employment not unlike the late 1970s." Since then, far from the predicted runaway inflation, the inflation rate has tumbled, and currently stands well below the Federal Reserve's own target rate of 2.0%. When unemployment is high and growth slow, inflation rates fall, almost no matter how much money is added to the economy.

By borrowing money in a recession, the government puts to use resources that would otherwise sit idle in the private sector. Recessions and depressions, after all, are not caused by lack of resources. The labor force still exists, as do all the buildings and equipment that existed before growth slowed. What is lacking is a willingness by private businesses to employ these resources. This is where governments can step in, borrowing funds that would otherwise languish in the banking system, spending them, and putting people to work. Indeed, during hard times, the government should substantially increase its deficit to get the economy back on track. This causes GDP to grow and, as it grows, helps to bring down the ratio of debt to GDP.

Why then is there so much angst and dissent in Congress over federal deficits and debts? Since the Reagan administration, federal deficits have been used by conservatives as a bludgeon to attack social programs and "starve the beast" of government spending. (The phrase, coined by an anonymous aide to Ronald Reagan, has become a conservative mantra.) Under the Reagan and George W. Bush administrations, massive tax cuts benefiting primarily the top 1% resulted in massive deficits. The deficits were then decried, as an excuse to demand cuts in federal spending. Since cutting the defense budget is renounced by Democrats and Republicans alike, conservatives demand that social programs be cut instead.

The programs in most immediate danger now are food stamps, the cost of which has more than doubled since the economy tanked in 2008, and unemployment insurance, on which the federal government now spends $110 billion. Also under assault is Medicaid, the health-care program for the poor. Spending on all these programs would drop significantly if the government just made concerted efforts to put people back to work.

Social Security and Medicare

But conservatives' real targets are the two largest non-defense programs—Social Security, which includes not only retirement pensions, but also disability and

FIGURE 2: SOCIAL SECURITY TRUST FUND, NET INCREASES, INFLATION ADJUSTED (1940-2012)

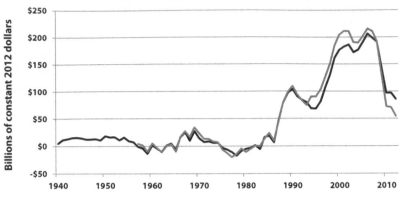

Source: Social Security Administration, Old-Age and Survivors Insurance Trust Fund, 1937-2012 (ssa.gov); Social Security Administration, Disability Insurance Trust Fund, 1957-2012 (ssa.gov); Bureau of Labor Statistics, Consumer Price Index, All Urban Consumers (CPI-U), U.S. city average, All items (bls.gov).

Note: This figure was prepared by Lyden Marcellot.

survivors' benefits, and Medicare, the health program for the elderly. Yet Social Security and Medicare are financed by payroll taxes and should not even be counted as part of general federal spending.

Social Security is largely a self-financing system. It is funded by a 12.4% dedicated tax on payrolls. This tax is highly regressive. Every dollar in wage and salary income is taxed at 12.4%, up to a maximum of $113,700 dollars in income. Wages above this maximum are not taxed, meaning that lower-income earners pay the full 12.4%, while high earners stop being charged payroll taxes once the maximum is reached. Though half of the payroll tax is formally paid by employers, economists generally concur that workers ultimately pay the whole tax, in the form of lowered wages, according to the Tax Policy Center. Thus, the effective tax rate (total tax paid divided by total income) is 12.4% for those with incomes up to the cap, then falls as one's income exceeds the cap. Earnings other than wages and salaries—such as dividends, capital gains, and interest, all of which are concentrated among high-income individuals—are not taxed at all.

As a result of the laws setting taxes and benefits, trends in employment and wages, and demographics (current earners who pay the tax relative to current retirees and others who draw benefits), the Social Security system has run surpluses since the early 1980s. (See Figure 2.) These surpluses were then lent to and spent by the United States Treasury and replaced with non-negotiable bonds. The surpluses plus interest accrued by the Social Security Administration on these bonds now add up to a $2.5 trillion trust fund. These bonds, like those issued to any other creditor, represent a promise on the part of the U.S. government to eventually raise revenue (by taxation or otherwise) and pay back this debt.

Why then, if the program has (unlike the rest of the federal budget) produced massive surpluses over the years, is Social Security a target for the "entitlement reform" that conservatives insist upon? For the past two years, benefits paid out by the Social Security Administration have exceeded payroll taxes collected. The difference, a mere $66 billion, has to be made up by the Treasury in the form of actual interest payments owed to the trust fund. In the past, the interest owed by the Treasury on the bonds in the trust fund didn't entail any cash outlay by the Treasury. These sums were merely credited to the Social Security Administration and added to the trust fund. In effect, the promise implied by the bonds—that the Treasury would someday pay the amount owed to the SSA—was deferred by a further promise (more bonds for the trust fund).

Paying out this interest now seems to be a promise that conservatives have no intent on honoring. To honor these promises would require that general revenue, primarily from the more progressive federal income tax, which mostly hits high earners who have little need for Social Security benefits, would be used to pay benefits to poorer elders—an explicitly redistributive policy which conservatives vehemently oppose. Indeed, the cuts they are now proposing to Social Security benefits exceed the interest needed to meet current benefit obligations, suggesting that conservatives would like to divert funds from the regressive payroll tax to the Treasury (this time, without bonds going into the trust fund in return) to finance other government operations.

The attack on Social Security is bipartisan, with many Democrats acceding to a cut in benefits by reducing the annual cost-of-living adjustment to benefits in the future. Social Security and Medicare have determined enemies, but they have few principled defenders.

Progressives should be intransigent here: Hands off Social Security. The system is mostly self-financed. For the next 20 years, it will need only a relatively small infusion of cash—cash that it is owed and has been promised—from the Treasury. Lifting the payroll cap and making the tax less regressive would solve most of Social Security Administration's shortfall. Paying the promises made to Social Security by past Congresses will keep the program solvent until 2035.

Medicare is also financed by a payroll tax, amounting to 2.9% of wages and salaries, with no limit on earnings. As of this year, as a result of the Affordable Care Act (a.k.a. Obamacare), high-income individuals (those above $200,000) will pay an additional 0.9% tax and the tax will be extended to non-wage income. In the past though, the Medicare tax has, like the Social Security tax, also been regressive, since it did not apply to non-wage income. For years, this regressive tax was levied in excess of what was needed to fund the program, with the balance lent to the Treasury. Medicare has accumulated a trust fund now worth $270 billion. Currently, the benefits being paid out exceed revenues, and Medicare began collecting actual interest (as opposed to interest simply credited to the fund, as in the case of Social Security) a couple of years ago. Soon, it will need to begin dipping into the trust fund itself. As with Social Security, keeping the promises made to Medicare will keep the system solvent through 2024. Containing health-care costs would keep the system solvent much further into the future.

So What's the Solution?

The answer is that we don't need a solution because there isn't a problem. There are good reasons to raise taxes on the wealthy and to raise the tax rates on dividends, capital gains, and carried interest, all of which would help close the deficit. Doing so and using the proceeds to fund social programs would go a long way to reducing inequality in the United States. But balancing the federal budget and retiring the debt now—that is, undertaking the same kind of fiscal austerity currently being imposed in Europe—will do the economy more harm than good. The deficit is simply a weapon used by conservatives in the prolonged battle to curb entitlement programs and social supports.

Attacks on entitlement programs and income supports raise a troubling question. Why are conservatives so intent on cutting them? To be sure, there is the general conservative hostility against government spending, and against those they look down on as "dependent" on the government. Entitlements, however, also place a floor under wages and substantially reduce the pain of unemployment. Pulling this floor out from under American workers would almost certainly cause wages to fall precipitously for most working-class people. A cynic might wonder whether this isn't, after all, the real goal of conservative deficit hawks and their big-business backers. ❏

Sources: Paul Ryan, ABC "This Week," Feb. 17, 2013; Arthur Laffer, "Get Ready for Inflation and Higher Interest Rates," *Wall Street Journal,* June 11, 2009; Peter Nicholas, "Obama nominates an new budget director," *Los Angeles Times,* July 14, 2010; Marty Wolfson, "Myths of the Deficit," *Dollars & Sense,* May/June 2010; John Miller, "Government 'Living Within Its Means'?" *Dollars & Sense,* November/December 2011; John Miller, "The 'Obamacare' Tax Hike and Redistribution," *Dollars & Sense,* May/June 2010.

Article 2.5

MYTHS AND REALITIES OF GOVERNMENT SPENDING

BY GERALD FRIEDMAN
March/April 2013

Conservatives claim that massive government spending threatens the economy. The corporate-funded Fix the Debt coalition, for example, warns that, under President Obama, wasteful government spending includes "unsustainable entitlement costs." Swelling government debt, Fix the Debt contends, will force the United States to pay ruinous interest rates that will drive down living standards. While these charges serve the political interests of those who oppose government social programs, they confuse the real fiscal issues in America: the effects of the Great Recession on government revenues and the inadequacy of current levels of government spending to deal with massive unemployment..

FIGURE 1: FEDERAL SPENDING AND REVENUE AS SHARE OF GDP, 1963-2012

As a share of national income, federal spending peaked during the Reagan administration. There was a brief jump in spending as a share of Gross Domestic Product (GDP) in 2009 due to the fall in national income as well as the Obama stimulus program. Since then, however, spending has fallen sharply as a share of GDP. Large federal deficits since 2001 have been the result of declining revenues, first due to the Bush tax cuts and then due to falling incomes in the Great Recession.

FIGURE 2: FEDERAL SPENDING GROWTH

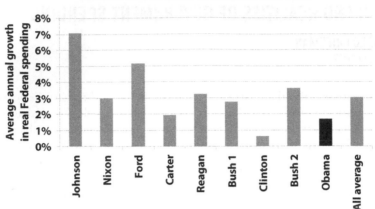

Despite the stimulus program and demands for aid to the unemployed and to distressed local and state governments, inflation-adjusted spending has increased only half as fast under President Obama as under George W. Bush. Spending under Obama has risen at the slowest rate of any presidential administration since the 1960s, except Clinton's. In past administrations, spending increased with higher unemployment. Had federal spending increased with high unemployment as fast under Obama as in the past, spending would have risen two percentage points faster each year. This increase, over $70 billion dollars a year or nearly $300 billion by the end of four years, would be enough to enact another stimulus program leading to over 2.5 million additional jobs.

FIGURE 3: ANNUAL GROWTH IN REAL FEDERAL REVENUE

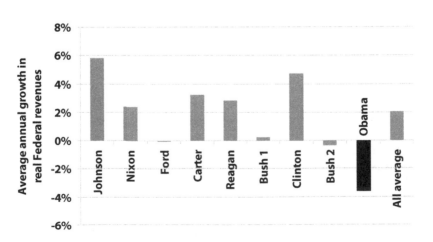

Contrary to the conservative drumbeat about "out of control" spending, it is the decline in revenues, not rising spending, that accounts for the swelling federal deficit under Presidents Bush and Obama. Revenues have fallen dramatically due to the Great Recession because laid off workers and shuttered businesses do not pay income or payroll taxes, and because tax cuts, whether to favor the rich under President George W. Bush or to stimulate the economy under President Obama, have further reduced revenues. The shortfall in revenues compared with earlier administrations explains all of the increase in the federal deficit between the last year of the Bush administration (2008) and the last year of Obama's first term (2012). ❏

Sources: "Citizens' Petition," Fix the Debt (fixthedebt.org); Economic Report of the President, 2012; United States Treasury, "Joint Statement on Budget Results for Fiscal Year 2012," Feb. 12, 2012 (treasury.gov); Bureau of Labor Statistics, "Employment Situation, 2012" Feb. 1, 2013 (bls. gov); Bureau of Economic Activity, "Gross Domestic Product: Fourth Quarter and Annual 2012," Feb. 28, 2013 (bea.gov).

Chapter 3

TAXATION

Article 3.1

NO FOOLING—CORPORATIONS EVADE TAXES
Forbes finally notices what has been obvious for years.

BY JOHN MILLER
May/June 2011

WHAT THE TOP U.S. COMPANIES PAY IN TAXES

Some of the world's biggest, most profitable corporations enjoy a far lower tax rate than you do—that is, if they pay taxes at all.

The most egregious example is General Electric. Last year the conglomerate generated $10.3 billion in pretax income, but ended up owing nothing to Uncle Sam. In fact, it recorded a tax benefit of $1.1 billion.

Over the last two years, GE Capital [one of the two divisions of General Electric] has displayed an uncanny ability to lose lots of money in the U.S. (posting a $6.5 billion loss in 2009), and make lots of money overseas (a $4.3 billion gain).

It only makes sense that multinationals "put costs in high-tax countries and profits in low-tax countries," says Scott Hodge, president of the Tax Foundation. Those low-tax countries are almost anywhere but the U.S. "When you add in state taxes, the U.S. has the highest tax burden among industrialized countries," says Hodge. In contrast, China's rate is just 25%; Ireland's is 12.5%.

　　—Christopher Helman, "What the Top U.S. Companies Pay in Taxes," *Forbes*, April 1, 2011

When *Forbes* magazine, the keeper of the list of the 400 richest Americans, warns that corporations not paying taxes on their profits will raise your hackles, you might wonder about the article's April 1 dateline. If it turns out *not* to be an April Fool's joke, things must be *really* bad.

And indeed they are. As *Forbes* reports, General Electric, the third largest U.S. corporation, turned a profit of $10.3 billion in 2010, paid no corporate income taxes, and got a "tax benefit" of $1.1 billion on taxes owed on past profits. And from 2005 to 2009, according to its own filings, GE paid a consolidated tax rate of just 11.6% on its corporate rates, including state, local, and foreign taxes. That's a far cry from the 35% rate nominally levied on corporate profits above $10 million.

Nor was GE alone among the top ten U.S. corporations with no tax obligations. Bank of America (BofA), the seventh largest U.S. corporation, racked up $4.4 billion in profits in 2010 and also paid no corporate income taxes (or in 2009 for that matter). Like GE, BofA has hauled in a whopping "tax benefit"—$1.9 billion.

For BofA, much like for GE, losses incurred during the financial crisis erased it tax liabilities. BofA, of course, contributed mightily to the crisis. It was one of four banks that controlled 95% of commercial bank derivatives activity, mortgage-based securities that inflated the housing bubble and brought on the crisis.

And when the crisis hit, U.S. taxpayers bailed them out, not once but several times. All told BofA received $45 billion of government money from the Troubled Asset Relief Program (TARP) as well as other government guarantees. And while BofA paid no taxes on their over $4 billion of profits, they nonetheless managed to pay out $3.3 billion in bonuses to corporate executives. All of that has made BofA a prime target for US Uncut protests (see p. 6) against corporate tax dodging that has cost the federal government revenues well beyond the $39 billion saved by the punishing spending cuts in the recent 2011 budget deal.

These two corporate behemoths and other many other major corporations paid no corporate income taxes last year, even though 2010 U.S. corporate profits had returned their level in 2005 in the midst the profits-heavy Bush expansion before the crisis hit.

An Old Story

But why is *Forbes* suddenly noticing corporate tax evasion? After all, corporations not paying taxes on their profits is an old story. Let's take a look at the track record of major corporations paying corporate income before the crisis hit and the losses that supposedly explain their not paying taxes.

The Government Accounting Office conducted a detailed study of the burden of the corporate income tax from 1998 to 2005. The results were stunning. Over half (55%) of large U.S. corporations reported no tax liability for at least one of those eight years. And in 2005 alone 25% of those corporations paid no corporate income taxes, even though corporate profits had more than doubled from 2001 to 2005.

In another careful study, the Treasury Department found that from 2000 to 2005, the share of corporate operating surplus that that U.S. corporations pay in taxes—a proxy for the average tax rate—was 16.7% thanks to various corporate loopholes, especially three key mechanisms:

- Accelerated Depreciation: allows corporations to write off machinery and equipment or other assets more quickly than they actually deteriorate.

- Stock Options: by giving their executives the option to buy the company's stock at a favorable price, corporations can take a tax deduction for the difference between what the employees pay for the stock and what it's worth.

- Debt Financing: offers a lower effective tax rate for corporate investment than equity (or stock) financing because the interest payments on debt (usually incurred by issuing bonds) get added to corporate costs and reduce reported profits.

Corporate income taxes are levied against reported corporate profits, and each of these mechanisms allows corporations to inflate their reported costs and thereby reduce their taxable profits.

And then there are overseas profits. U.S.-based corporations don't pay U.S. corporate taxes on their foreign income until it is "repatriated," or sent back to the parent corporation from abroad. That allows multinational corporations to defer payment of U.S. corporate income taxes on their overseas profits indefinitely or repatriate their profits from foreign subsidiaries when their losses from domestic operations can offset those profits and wipe out any tax liability, as GE did in 2010.

Hardly Overtaxed

Nonetheless, Scott Hodge, the president of the right-wing Tax Foundation, steadfastly maintains that U.S. corporations are overtaxed, and that that is what driving U.S. corporations to park their profits abroad (and lower their U.S. taxes). Looking at nominal corporate tax rates, Hodge would seem to have a case. Among the 19 OECD countries, only the statutory corporate tax rates in Japan surpass the (average combined federal and state) 39.3% rate on U.S. corporate profits. And the U.S. rate is well above the OECD average of 27.6%.

But these sorts of comparisons misrepresent where U.S. corporate taxes stand with respect to tax rates actually paid by corporations in other advanced countries. Why? The tax analyst's answer is that the U.S. corporate income tax has a "narrow base," or in plain English, is riddled with loopholes. As a result U.S. effective corporate tax rates—the proportion of corporate profits actually paid out in taxes—are not only far lower than the nominal rate but below the effective rates in several other countries. The Congressional Budget Office, for instance, found that U.S. effective corporate tax rates were near the OECD average for equity-financed investments, and below the OECD average for debt-financed investments. And for the years from 2000 to 2005, the Treasury Department found the average corporate tax rate among OECD countries was 21.6%, well above the U.S. 16.7% rate.

Current U.S. corporate tax rates are also extremely low by historical standards. In 1953, government revenue from the U.S. corporate income taxes were the equal of 5.6% of GDP; the figure was 4.0% of GDP in 1969, 2.2% of GDP from 2000 to 2005, and is currently running at about 2.0% of GDP.

By all these measures U.S. corporations are hardly over-taxed. And some major corporations are barely taxed, if taxed at all.

Closing corporate loopholes so that corporate income tax revenues in the United States match the 3.4% of GDP collected on average by OECD corporate income taxes would add close to $200 billion to federal government revenues—more than five times the $39 billion of devastating spending cuts just made in the federal budget in 2011. Returning the corporate income tax revenues to the 4.0% of GDP level of four decades ago would add close to $300 billion a year to government revenues.

The cost of not shutting down those corporate loopholes would be to let major corporations go untaxed, to rob the federal government of revenues that could, with enough political will, reverse devastating budget cuts, and to leave the rest of us to pay more and more of the taxes necessary to support a government that does less and less for us. ❏

Sources: Jane G. Gravelle and Thomas L. Hungerford, "Corporate Tax Reform: Issues for Congress," CRS Report for Congress, October 31, 2007; "Treasury Conference On Business Taxation and Global Competitiveness," U.S. Department of the Treasury, Background Paper, July 23, 2007; Chuck Marr and Brian Highsmith, "Six Tests for Corporate Tax Reform," Center on Budget and Policy Priorities, February 28, 2011; Chuck Marr and Brian Highsmith, "Tax Holiday For Overseas Corporate Profits Would Increase Deficits, Fail To Boost The Economy, And Ultimately Shift More Investment And Jobs Overseas," Center on Budget and Policy Priorities, April 8, 2011; "Comparison of the Reported Tax Liabilities of Foreign and U.S.-Controlled Corporations, 1998-2005," Government Accounting Office, July 2008.

Article 3.2

TRANSACTION TAX: SAND IN THE WHEELS, NOT IN THE FACE

Why a transaction tax is a really good idea.

BY JOHN MILLER
March/April 2010

Why Taxing Stock Trades Is a Really Bad Idea

[S]urely it is "socially useful" to let free people transact freely, without regulators and legislators micromanaging them. ... It's Economics 101 that the free actions of market participants cause supply and demand to reach equilibrium. And isn't that what investors—indeed even speculators—do? Can they do it as well when facing the dead-weight costs of a transaction tax?

If not, then trading volume in our stock markets will fall. Beyond the tax, everyone—investors and speculator, great and small—who buys or sells stocks will pay more to transact in markets that are less liquid. In such a world, markets would necessarily be more risky, and the cost of capital for business would necessarily rise. The consequence of that is that innovation, growth, and jobs would necessarily fall. That would be the full and true cost of the trading tax.

—Donald L. Luskin and Chris Hynes, "Why Taxing Stock Trades Is a Really Bad Idea," *Wall Street Journal*, January 5, 2010

"**S**ome financial activities which proliferated over the last 10 years were socially useless," Britain's Finance Service Authority Chairman Adiar Turner told a black-tie gathering of financial executives in London in September 2009. That is why he had proposed a transaction tax for the United Kingdom and why British Prime Minister Gordon Brown would propose an international transaction tax at the November G-20 summit.

The gathered bankers "saw red," as one report described their reaction. Investment bankers Donald L. Luskin and Chris Hynes are still irate.

In some ways their reaction is surprising. A financial transaction tax is nothing other than a sales tax on trading stocks and other securities. Transaction taxes are already in place in about 30 countries, and a transaction tax applied to the sale of stock in the United States from 1914 to 1964.

In addition, the transaction tax rates on a single trade are typically quite low. For instance, the "Let Wall Street Pay for the Restoration of Main Street Act of 2009," proposed by U.S. Representative Peter DeFazio (D-Ore.), would assess a one quarter of one percent (.25%) tax on the value of stock transactions, and two one hundredths of one percent (.02%) tax on the sale on a variety of derivative assets—including credit default swaps, which played such a large role in the mortgage crisis. To target speculators, the bill exempts retirement accounts, mutual funds, education and health savings accounts, and the first $100,000 of transactions annually.

In other ways, Luskin's and Hynes's reaction is not surprising at all. At its heart, a transaction tax is a radical measure. Its premise is that faster-acting financial markets driven by speculation don't bring relief to the economy—instead, they loot the economy. Its purpose, as Nobel Prize-winning economist James Tobin put it when he proposed his original transaction tax on international money markets during the 1970s, is to "throw sand in the wheels" of our financial markets.

Also, while its tax rate is low, the burden of a transaction tax adds up as securities are repeatedly traded, as is the practice on Wall Street today. For instance, even after accounting for its exemptions and allowing for a sizable decline in trading, the DeFazio bill would still raise $63.5 billion annually, according to the estimates of Dean Baker, co-director of the Center for Economic Policy Research.

Luskin and Hynes have two main objections to the transaction tax. The first is that a transaction tax would affect every single person who owns and invests in stocks, not just speculators. Customers would not have to pay a tax to buy or sell mutual funds, but, as Luskin and Hynes emphasize, the mutual funds themselves would have to pay a tax every time they trade stocks. So everyone holding mutual funds would still end up paying the tax.

What Luskin and Hynes don't say is this: Mutual funds that actively trade stocks would pay three times the transaction taxes of an average fund, as the Investment Company Institute, the fund industry trade group, reports. And stock index funds, which hold a sample of all stocks but seldom trade them, are taxed the least. Those funds have historically outperformed other mutual funds. So a transaction tax would work to push mutual fund customers to invest their savings more wisely, providing some with higher rates of return with a transaction tax than their previous funds provided without it. And that would mean fewer broker fees and lower profits for the fund industry.

But what really sticks in Luskin's and Hynes's craw is the assertion that financial trading is not socially useful. That claim flies in face of the long-held contention, buttressed by much of finance theory, that the equilibrium outcomes of financial markets are efficient. And if financial markets are efficient, there is no need for a tax that will reduce trading.

But much of what Luskin and Hynes have to say is not right. First, as anyone who *paid attention* in Economics 101 would know, reaching an equilibrium is not in and of itself desirable. To endorse the outcomes of today's speculative financial markets as desirable because they reach an equilibrium is the equivalent of describing a gambler in a poker game raking in a big pot as desirable because it clears the table. And the gamblers in our financial markets did rake in some awfully big pots betting that subprime borrowers would default on their loans. The last few years show us just how undesirable that equilibrium turned out to be.

Second, speculation dwarfs financing investment in U.S. stock markets. During the 1970s, for every dollar of new investment in plants and equipment, $1.30 in stocks were traded on the U.S. exchanges, reports Robert Pollin, co-director of the Political Economy Research Institute. But from 1998 to 2007, $27 in stocks were traded on the U.S. exchanges for every dollar of corporate investment in plant equipment. Such a rapid stock turnover has diverted the attention of managers of enterprises from long-term planning. Whatever damage that churning caused on Main Street, it paid off handsomely on Wall Street. From 1973 to 2007, the size of the financial (and insurance) sector relative to the economy doubled, financial sector profits went from one-quarter to two-fifths of domestic profits, and compensation in the finance industry went from just about average to 180% of the private industry average.

By counteracting these trends, a transactions tax can actually enhance, not diminish, the efficiency of financial markets. If it forces the financial sector to fulfill its function of transferring savings to investment with less short-term churning, then the tax will have freed up resources for more productive uses.

A transaction tax would surely be a step in the right direction toward reducing the bloat of the finance industry, righting the balance of speculation over enterprise, and restoring the focus on long-term planning and job-creation in the economy.

None of that will happen unless every last grain of the decades' worth of sand the bullies on Wall Street have kicked in our faces gets thrown into the wheels of finance. That is a tall order. But as DeFazio's and Turner's example shows, some of today's policymakers are up to the task. ❏

Sources: Dean Baker, "The Benefits of a Financial Transaction Tax," Center For Economic and Policy Research, December 2008; Robert Pollin and Dean Baker, "Public Investment, Industrial Policy, and U.S. Economic Renewal," Political Economy Research Institute, December 2009; Caroline Binham, "Turner Plan on 'Socially Useless' Trades Make Bankers See Red," Bloomberg. com; Yaiman Onaran, "Taxing Wall Street Today Wins Support for Keynes Idea (Update 1)," Bloomberg.com; Dean Baker, Robert Pollin, Travis McArthur, and Matt Sherman, "The Potential Revenue from Financial Transactions Taxes, Political Economy Research Institute, Working paper no. 212, December 2009; Donald L. Luskin and Chris Hynes, "Why Taxing Stock Trades Is a Really Bad Idea," *Wall Street Journal*, January 5, 2010; John McKinnon, "Lawmakers Weigh A Wall Street Tax," *Wall Street Journal*, December 19, 2009; Tobin Tax, freerisk.org/wiki/index. php/Tobin_tax; text of HR 4191—"Let Wall Street Pay for the Restoration of Main Street Act of 2009," www.govtrack.us.

Article 3.3

WHAT'S WRONG WITH A FLAT TAX?

BY ARTHUR MacEWAN
September/October 2012

> Dear Dr. Dollar:
> Today a minister asked me why a flat tax, where "everybody pays their fair share," is not the best idea. I did not have a short, convincing explanation. Can you help?   —*Arthur Milholland, Silver Springs, MD*

Although flat tax proposals differ, they have one basic thing in common: they would all reduce the tax rates for people with high incomes. Thus they would either shift the tax burden to people with lower incomes or lead to a reduction in government services or both.

Currently, the federal personal income tax is quite progressive on paper and somewhat progressive in fact. A "progressive" income tax system is one where people with higher incomes pay a larger percentage of their income as taxes than do people with lower incomes. (A "regressive" system is one where people with lower incomes pay a higher share of their income as taxes; a "proportional" system is one where everyone pays the same proportion of their income as taxes. A flat tax and a proportional tax are the same.)

The justification for a progressive tax system is fairness: people with higher incomes have a greater ability to pay taxes and therefore should be subject to a higher tax rate. For example (to take an extreme case), a family with an income of $2 million can pay $200,000 in taxes more easily (i.e., with less impact on their circumstances) than a family with an income of $20,000 can pay $2,000 in taxes. Also, the principle of fairness suggests that high-income families should pay higher rates to support a system that provides so well for them. These concepts of fairness have been long-established in the U.S. personal income-tax system.

Even today, with rates for high-income people lowered from earlier years, the system still has a significant element of progressivity. For example, a family with taxable income of $20,000 would supposedly pay $2,150 (10.75%), while a family with taxable income of $1 million would supposedly pay $320,000 (32%). Of course many people, especially those with high-incomes, find various "loopholes," and do not end up paying as much in taxes as they otherwise would. Many loopholes are in the deductions that allow people to keep their taxable income—and therefore their taxes—down. At the same time, many people with low incomes have their taxes greatly reduced—sometimes resulting in payments *from* the government rather than tax payments *to* the government.

The Tax Policy Center has estimated that in 2010 people in the lowest 40% of the income distribution on average got money back from the government (because of the Earned Income Tax Credit and the Child Tax Credit), while people in the highest-income 20% on average paid taxes at a rate of 13.6%. People at the very top, the highest-income 1%, paid on average 18.6%.

Conservative ideologues like to jump on the fact that many low-income people pay no federal income tax at all. Yet federal income taxes are only part of the tax story. Low-income people still pay Social Security and Medicare taxes, sales taxes at the state level, and various other taxes. Overall, the U.S. tax system is hardly progressive at all, and may even be regressive.

Advocates of a flat tax claim it would be better to get rid of all the complications in the federal income tax—the adjustments, the credits, the deductions, etc.—and just charge everyone the same rate. Also, they argue that a flat tax would boost the economy because the current high rates on people with high incomes harm the incentive to invest and to work. Yet there is no way around the simple arithmetic: to lower the top rate and to obtain the same amount of revenue from a flat tax as from the current system, people below the top would have to have their tax rates increased. (While advocates of a flat tax generally reject the principles of fairness on which the progressivity of the U.S. tax code has long been based, it would be possible to introduce an element of progressivity into a flat tax by exempting all income below a certain level. Still, except for those people near the bottom, tax rates would have to be raised for most people—though not for those at the top.)

Furthermore, the claim that with a flat tax all the adjustments, credits, deductions, etc. would be eliminated is not credible. Indeed, since a flat tax would increase the after-tax income of those at the top, it would increase the amount of money they would have to buy influence to get their favorite "complications" reinstated (as if they didn't have enough influence already!). As to the argument that reducing the tax rate on people with high incomes would boost the economy, well, we have seen how well that has worked since the Bush tax cuts for the wealthy were put in place in 2001.

So a flat tax would be one more break for the rich, increasing their income on the backs of the great majority of the populace. Not fair at all. That's what's wrong with a flat tax. ❏

Article 3.4

THE "OBAMACARE" TAX HIKE AND REDISTRIBUTION

BY JOHN MILLER
May/June 2010

OBAMACARE'S WORST TAX

Opponents [of ObamaCare] should go down swinging, and that means exposing such policy debacles as President Obama's 11th-hour decision to apply the 2.9% Medicare payroll tax to "unearned income."

That's what savings and investment income are called in Washington, and this destructive tax wasn't in either the House or Senate bills, though it may now become law with almost no scrutiny.

For the first time, the combined employer-worker Medicare rate would be extended beyond wages to interest, dividends, capital gains, annuities, royalties and rents for individuals with adjusted gross income above $200,000 and joint filers over $250,000.

Earning even a single dollar more than $200,000 in adjusted gross income will slap the tax on every dollar of a taxpayer's investment income, creating a huge marginal-rate spike that will most hurt middle-class earners, as opposed to the superrich.

—*Wall Street Journal* editorial, March 17, 2010

There are plenty of legitimate complaints about "Obamacare," but its tax hike on unearned income is surely not one of them.

The new tax does take a bite out of the income of the rich. It adds 0.9 percentage points to the current hospital-insurance tax on most wage-income above $200,000. It also levies a 3.8% tax on investment income (e.g., dividends and capital gains). Only the richest 5% of taxpayers, with 2009 incomes above $231,179, will pay the new tax. And the richest 1%, with incomes in excess of $624,396 in 2009, will pay 85% of the tax hike.

That is a good thing, doing a bit to reduce the great income inequalities that have developed in recent decades. But the new tax hardly constitutes soaking the rich. Even after the tax, the rich will hand over a smaller portion of their income in federal income taxes than they did before three decades of pro-rich tax cutting. According to the Tax Policy Center, the new tax would push up the tax burden of the richest one percent by 1.3 percentage points, to 33.6% of their income, still well below their 37.0% effective tax rate in 1979. In any case, the rich can surely afford it. The incomes of the top 1% roughly doubled from 1979 to 2009 (after correcting for inflation).

Beyond that, the new tax was a compromise. It replaced the 5.4% tax on any income above $1 million in the House healthcare bill. That tax would have been paid exclusively by the richest 1%. So the *WSJ* editors should be happy that its friends got off as well as they did. Also the new tax postponed the start date for the excise tax on high-cost healthcare plans in the Senate bill, but didn't eliminate it. When it goes into effect in 2018, the tax on "Cadillac" healthcare plans will fall mostly on better-off households, but nonetheless will collect one-third of its taxes from individuals who currently have incomes between $50,000 and $100,000.

What really has the *WSJ* editors in a lather is levying hospital-insurance taxes on non-wage, or "unearned," income. They claim that middle-income taxpayers, not the super-rich, will ultimately bear the burden of the tax. Why? Because by taxing savings and investment income, the new tax will put a stopper in "trickle-down economic growth" (not that we have seen much trickling down over recent decades).

But economic evidence suggests that they are just plain wrong. First, unearned income is not the same thing as savings and investment. Take stock-trading, the source of most capital gains. From 1998 to 2007, $27 in stocks was traded on the U.S. exchanges for very dollar corporations invested in plant and equipment, according to a recent study by economists Robert Pollin and Dean Baker. The bulk of the gains of financial investors, therefore, comes from trading existing assets, not financing investment in new assets. Second, there is no solid evidence that lower taxes on unearned income do much to spur economic growth. Economist Joel Selmrod, director of the Office of Tax Policy Research at the University of Michigan, reports: " I know of no evidence that establishes a connection between prosperity and the rate we tax capital gains." Finally, the *WSJ* editors fail to take into account that the new tax hike will go to expand health insurance coverage for families with incomes below four times the poverty level.

Health-care reform surely could have done more to redistribute income and economic power, by squeezing out private insurers' massive overhead costs and profits, and relying on the House tax on income over $1 million. But even as is, Obamacare should do more than any legislation in many years to help generate the bottom-up economic growth that could replace the "trickle-down" economic growth that has rewarded so few with so much. ❏

Sources: David Leonhardt, "In Health Bill, Obama Attacks Wealth Inequality," *New York Times*, March 23, 2010; Robert Pollin and Dean Baker, "Public Investment, Industrial Policy, and U.S. Economic Renewal," Political Economy Research Institute, December 2009; Tax Policy Center, "The Medicare Tax as Proposed in H.R. 3590 (Senate Health Bill) and H.R 48723 (Reconciliation Act of 2010)," March 19, 2010.

Article 3.5

SECOND COMING OF THE ESTATE TAX NOT SO RAPTUROUS

BY JOHN MILLER
January/February 2013

> For all the worry in Washington and Wall Street about the January tax cliff,
> almost no one is paying attention to the impending reincarnation of the death
> tax. The death tax is a long-term revenue loser. ... How is this possible?
>
> Most important, because the estate tax is a penalty on saving and capital
> investment, the economy grows more slowly over time.
>
> The strongest case against the death tax is moral. The levy ... is on top
> of the property and income taxes and other assessments that owners pay year
> after year. What is truly unfair is when a family-owned enterprise has to be
> sold at auction to pay the death tax to the IRS.
>
> —"Death Tax Resurrection," *The Wall Street Journal*, October 28, 2012

Just as the *Wall Street Journal* editors feared, the New Year's Day "fiscal cliff" deal resurrected the estate tax and made it once again a permanent part of the U.S. tax code. But this second coming of the so-called "death tax" is hardly the calamity for wealth accumulation the editors envisioned. Nor does it usher in the era of equality for which supporters might have hoped.

The estate tax that emerged from the fiscal-cliff deal, known more formally as the American Taxpayer Relief Act of 2012, was no match for today's pernicious inequality. It exempts up to the first $5 million in assets and imposes a tax rate of just 40% on the value of estates after that large exemption and various other deductions.

For the *Wall Street Journal* editors, however, bringing back the estate tax, even this enfeebled one, is not only bad for the economy, it is immoral. As they see it, the estate tax stands in the way of wealth accumulation, retards economic growth, and taxes income for a second or third time. At its worst, they claim, it destroys small family businesses and farms. But these claims have been debunked time and time again by government agencies such as the Congressional Budget Office and Congressional Research Service.

Let's look at what's wrong with the *WSJ* editors' claims about the estate tax, and how an estate tax of consequence could help reduce the scourge of inequality.

Resurrected, or Just Undead?

For nearly a decade, the Bush tax cuts have chipped away at the estate tax. Without the Bush tax cuts, the estate tax would have had a $1 million exemption and a top rate of 55%. With the Bush tax cuts, tax rates fell and the exemption rose year after year after 2001. The estate tax was gone altogether in 2010, but slated to return to its pre-Bush rate the next year, when the tax cuts were to expire. Late in 2010, the Obama administration accepted congressional Republicans' demand that the Bush tax cuts be extended for two more years—and agreed to an estate tax featuring an exemption of $5 million and a tax rate of 35% for 2011 and 2012.

The fiscal cliff deal includes an estate tax that is very similar to the 2011-2012 version. The $5 million exemption was kept and is indexed to inflation. The tax rate was raised five percentage points, to 40%. At these new rates, the government will lose $369 billion in tax revenues over the next ten years, compared to its revenues if the Bush tax cuts had been allowed to expire. That also amounts to 95% of the projected revenue loss if 2012's bargain-basement estate tax had been kept in place.

On top of that, no one will pay the statutory tax rate of 40%. Effective rates (the estate tax paid as proportion of the gross value of the estate) are far lower. The statutory rate is levied against taxable assets—the gross value of the estate minus any portion left to a spouse, any charitable gifts, and any expenses associated with administering and settling the estate, including funeral costs. With the first $5 million of taxable assets exempt from taxation, in addition to these deductions, the average effective tax rate in 2013 will be just over 14%.

The estate tax provided the lion's share of the tax relief in the fiscal-cliff agreement, and that relief went almost exclusively to the rich and the super-rich. Without the fiscal-cliff deal (and so with the return of the $1 million exemption from before the Bush tax cuts) fewer than 50,000 estates would have paid any estate tax in 2013. The fiscal cliff agreement, with its $5 million exemption, reduced that number to under 4,000, or less than 0.15% of all estates.

The Estate Tax's "Immorality"

The *Journal* editors would bring up even this enfeebled estate tax on morals charges. Its most grievous offense, they argue, is forcing heirs to liquidate the family business or farm to pay their estate taxes.

But there's little or no evidence to support the charge that estate taxes destroy small businesses or family farms. The Congressional Budget Office found that, in 2005, when the estate tax exemption was just $1.5 million, estate tax returns were required for less than 2.5% of the small-business owners and farmers who died. The same study showed that, if an exemption of $1.5 million had been in place in 2000, all but 27 of the farms and 82 of the small businesses subject to the estate tax would have had sufficient liquid assets (such as bank accounts, stocks, bonds, and insurance) to pay the tax without having to touch the farm or business itself. In addition, small businesses, farms, and landowners can spread their estate tax payments over a 15-year period at low interest rates.

With an estate tax exemption of $5 million, practically no small businesses or farms will owe estate taxes. The Tax Policy Center (a joint project of the Urban Institute and the Brookings Institution) studied estates with a value of less than $5 million, at least half of which was either small-business or farm assets. Just 20 such estates, the organization projected, will have to pay estate taxes in 2013.

The *WSJ* editors' other morals charge against the estate tax is that it subjects taxpayers to "double taxation." The rich have already paid income taxes on their earnings and property taxes on their assets, so according to the editors, they should be able to leave their wealth to their heirs without paying further taxes. But double taxation is a fact of life for everyone, not just the rich. For instance, workers pay payroll taxes and income taxes on their wages, and then sales taxes when they spend what remains of their paychecks. The important issue is not how often we pay taxes, but how much we pay. In 2009 the richest 1% of U.S. families paid well under one-third of their incomes (28.9%) in federal taxes of all kinds, far less than the two-fifths they paid in 1977, despite the fact that their real incomes have nearly tripled since then.

Beyond that, much inherited wealth has never even been taxed once, much less twice. Suppose that a Mr. One Percenter purchases a share of stock for $200, holds it as it appreciates to $1000, and then passes that stock on to one of his sons, One Percenter, Jr., when he dies. Junior then sells the stock one year later for $1100. Under current tax law, the "step-up basis" provision for capital gains, the son would pay income taxes only on the $100 capital gain since he inherited the stock. The $800 unrealized capital gain from its original purchase price to its value at the elder One Percenter's death would escape the income tax. This tax loophole cost the federal government $61.5 billion of revenues in fiscal year 2012, and its benefits go almost exclusively to the well-to-do.

These untaxed gains are no small portion of estates. Economists James Poterba and Scott Weisbenner estimate that these gains make up 56% of estates worth more than $10 million. The estate tax is the only way, under current law, to tax these capital gains that escape the income tax. So much for the double-taxation complaint.

An Obstacle to Growth?

The estate tax may be a penalty on saving and capital investment, as the *Journal* editors claim, but it is far too small to impose much of a penalty. That alone makes it highly unlikely that the estate tax, especially one as watered down as the 2013 version, could slow the growth of the economy. Beyond that, as economist Jane Gravelle of the Congressional Research Service (CRS) put it in her 2005 memo to Congress, "neither economic theory nor empirical evidence clearly indicate that the estate tax reduces savings."

Part of the reason the economic impact of the estate tax is murky is that the tax has two quite different effects on how much people save and how much effort they put into work. On the one hand, a lower estate tax makes it cheaper for people to leave money to their heirs. That might encourage them to work harder and save more. On the other hand, a lower estate tax allows people to make the same after-tax bequest with a smaller amount of savings, which might persuade them to work and save less.

This "paucity of empirical evidence" leads CRS's Gravelle and Steven Maquire to conclude that "the effect on savings and output would be negligible."

Estate-Tax End Times

Putting a dent into today's inequality is admittedly a tall order. But enacting an estate tax with real teeth surely would help.

It would not have taken much to enact an estate tax with some real punch. All Congress (and the Obama Administration) had to do was nothing—that is, allow the Bush tax cuts to expire. The estate tax would then have reverted to the $1 million exemption and 55% top tax rate in place in 2001.

A return to the 2001 estate tax would have obligated no more than 2% of 2013 decedents to pay estate taxes, and their effective tax rate would have been just 19.2%, due to the $1 million exemption and various deductions. But to take on the worst U.S. inequality since the 1920s, it would be better still to eliminate the step-up basis loophole on capital gains—in addition to, not instead of, resurrecting the 2001 estate tax.

Now, that combination would be a far more rapturous second coming of the estate tax than the one we will see in 2013. ❑

Sources: "Federal Estate and Gift Taxes," Congressional Budget Office, Dec. 18, 2009; Jane Gravelle, "Economic Issues Surrounding the Estate and Gift Tax: A Brief Summary," Congressional Research Service Report to Congress, April 14, 2005; Jane Gravelle and Steven Maguire, "Estate and Gift Taxes: Economic Issues," Congressional Research Service, Dec. 4, 2009; Chye-Ching Huang and Nathaniel Frentz, "Myths and Realities About the Estate Tax," Center on Budget and Policy Priorities, Nov. 5, 2012; "Revenue Impacts of the Fiscal Cliff Deal," Citizens for Tax Justice, Jan. 3, 2013; The Tax Policy Center, Table T12-0321, Table T12-0323.

Article 3.6

THE GREAT TAX-CUT EXPERIMENT

Has cutting tax rates for the rich helped the economy?

BY GERALD FRIEDMAN
January/February 2013

Since the late 1970s, during the Carter Administration, conservative economists have been warning that high taxes retard economic growth by discouraging productive work and investment. These arguments have resonated with politicians, who have steadily cut income taxes, especially those borne by the richest Americans. The highest marginal tax rate, which stood at 70% by the end of the 1970s, was cut to less than 30% in less than a decade. (The marginal rate for a person is the one applied to his or her last dollar of income. A marginal rate that applies to, say, the bracket above $250,000, then, is paid only on that portion of income. The portion of a person's income below that threshold is taxed at the lower rates applying to lower tax brackets.) Despite increases in the early 1990s, the top marginal rate remained below 40%, when it was cut further during the administration of George W. Bush. These dramatic cuts in tax rates, however, have not led to an acceleration in economic growth, investment, or productivity.

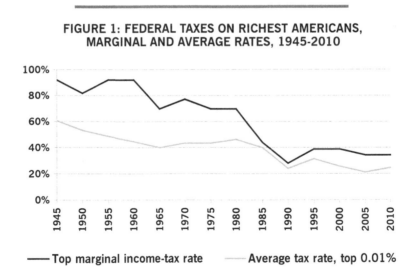

**FIGURE 1: FEDERAL TAXES ON RICHEST AMERICANS,
MARGINAL AND AVERAGE RATES, 1945-2010**

—— Top marginal income-tax rate   —— Average tax rate, top 0.01%

The federal government has been cutting taxes on the richest Americans since the end of World War II. The average tax paid by the richest taxpayers, as a percentage of income, is typically less than the top marginal rate. Some of their income (the portion below the threshold for the top marginal rate, any capital-gains income, etc.) is taxed at lower rates. Some is not subject to federal income tax because of deductions for state and local taxes, health-care costs, and other expenses. The decline in the average tax rate for the richest, however, does follow the cuts in the top marginal income-tax rate.

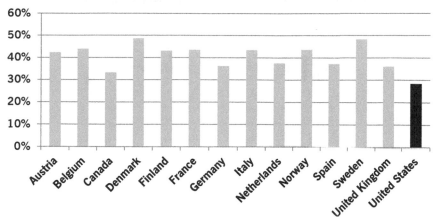

FIGURE 2: TAX REVENUE AS A PERCENTAGE OF GDP, 2008

Americans pay a smaller proportion of total income in taxes than do people in any other advanced capitalist economy. As recently as the late 1960s, taxes accounted for as high a share of national income in the United States as in Western European countries. After decades of tax cuts, however, the United States now stands out for its low taxes and small government sector.

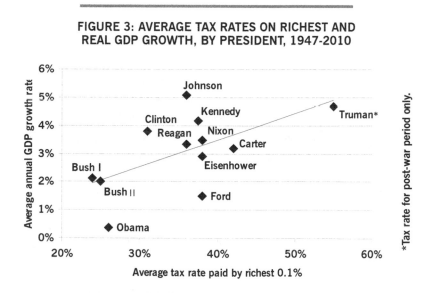

FIGURE 3: AVERAGE TAX RATES ON RICHEST AND REAL GDP GROWTH, BY PRESIDENT, 1947-2010

On average, the economy has grown faster during presidential administrations with higher tax rates on the richest Americans. Growth was unusually slow during George W. Bush's two terms (Bush II) and during Obama's first term, when the Bush tax cuts remained in effect. On average, every 10 percentage-point rise in the average tax rate on the richest has been associated with an increase in annual GDP growth of almost one percentage point.

FIGURE 4: TOP MARGINAL TAX RATE AND INVESTMENT,1963-2011

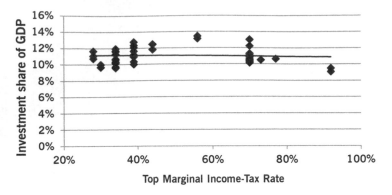

Cutting taxes on the richest Americans has not led them to invest more in plant and equipment. Over the past 50 years, as tax rates have declined, there has been no increase in investment spending as a percentage of GDP. (The flat trend line shows that changes in the highest marginal income-tax rate have not affected investment much, one way or the other.) Instead, the investment share of the economy has been determined by other factors, such as aggregate demand, rather than tax policy.

FIGURE 5: TAX SHARE OF GDP AND PRODUCTIVITY GROWTH

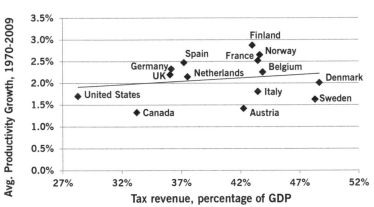

Despite lower and declining tax rates, especially on the rich, the United States has had slower productivity growth over the last several decades than other advanced economies. Overall, lower taxes are associated with slower growth in GDP per hour worked. A 10 percentage point increase in taxes as a share of GDP is associated with an increase in the productivity growth rate of 0.2 percentage points. ❑

Sources: Tom Petska and Mike Strudler, "Income, Taxes, and Tax Progressivity: An Examination of Recent Trends in the Distribution of Individual Income and Taxes" (Statistics of Income Division, Internal Revenue Service, 1997); Thomas Hungerford, "Taxes and the Economy: An Economic Analysis of the Top Tax Rates Since 1945" (Congressional Research Service, 2012); *Economic Report of the President, 2012*; Bureau of Economic Analysis (bea.gov); Organization of Economic Cooperation and Development, OECD STAT.

Chapter 4

MONEY, BANKING, AND FINANCE

Article 4.1

ABOLISHING THE FED IS NO SOLUTION TO A REAL PROBLEM

BY ARTHUR MacEWAN
July/August 2012

> Dear Dr. Dollar:
> Is the Federal Reserve, the Fed, as important to the operation of the economy as it seems? How does it work? If it is so important, how can anyone take seriously politicians such as Ron Paul, who calls for the Fed's abolition?
> —*Tom Prebis, Cleveland, Ohio*

Yes, the Federal Reserve, the central banks of the United States, is a powerful institution, important to the operation of the economy. By regulating the supply of money and influencing (if not fully determining) interest rates, the Fed has a major impact on the overall level of production, employment, and inflation. Also, the Fed has a large role (along with some other agencies) in regulating the operations of banks.

Yet the Fed is structured in a very undemocratic way. Although it derives its authority from Congress, its actions do not have to be approved by Congress, the president or any other segment of the government. Its funding is not set by Congress, and the members of its Board of Governors (the controlling group), though appointed by the president and approved by Congress, have terms that span multiple presidential and congressional terms. Also, while the Fed regulates the banks, bankers have a special role in the operation of the Fed. Some seats on the boards of directors of the twelve regional branches are reserved for bankers, giving them formal capacity to influence the Fed's policies, including its regulation of the banks.

Not surprisingly, the Fed has exercised its regulation of the banks with "a light hand." And its overall regulation of the economy—through affecting the money supply and interest rates—has often sacrificed employment to maintain the profitability of business in general and the banks in particular.

The Banks' Man at the Fed

To get some useful insight on the undemocratic and pro-business bias of the Fed, consider:

Jaimie Dimon, the head of JPMorgan Chase, is a member of the Board of Directors of the Federal Reserve Bank of New York. Cheek by jowl with Wall Street, the N.Y. Fed plays a major role in the dealings between the Fed and the large private banks. As the financial meltdown became apparent in 2008, the N.Y. Fed was fully involved in the actions that the Fed and the Treasury took in their efforts to manage the crisis.

Dimon's bank is one of the country's largest, with $19 billion in after-tax profits in 2011. In 2008, the bank received $25 billion in the government's bank bailout. Perhaps the bailout saved the economy from a more severe economic crisis, but it also saved the bankers—Dimon and the others—along with their absurd salaries. Other means of saving the system—such as temporary nationalization of the big banks (to say nothing of a permanent nationalization)—were never on the Fed's agenda.

Dimon has become one of the most vociferous and aggressive opponents of bank regulation. In 2012, he has frequently been in the news because his bank experienced a huge loss—at least $3 billion and perhaps as much as $9 billion—in a complex and risky operation, exactly the kind of banking activity that regulation is supposed to prevent, and exactly the kind of activity that could generate another financial crisis. Dimon has not moderated his opposition to regulation.

Does anyone see anything wrong here? Does the metaphor "fox guarding the henhouse" seem appropriate?

It is only a slight simplification to say that the Fed is run by and for the country's banks. If one believes that the interests of the banks are the same as the interests of the rest of us, no problem. This is the line that Dimon peddles, claiming that the banks play a crucial role in allocating funds to the most productive activity, supporting economic growth and jobs. More regulation, he claims, would prevent banks from doing this good work. In the wake of the financial crisis, it is impressive that anyone can spew such nonsense with a straight face.

Regulating the Economy

The Fed plays its role of affecting the money supply and interest rates by, in part, loaning money to the banks and then regulating the extent to which the banks can use this money to make loans to the businesses and public. More loans means more money in circulation; more money in circulation tends to reduce interest rates (i.e., the price of money), which tends to induce economic expansion. Also, in regulating the banks' activities, the Fed is supposed to maintain economic stability—preventing the banks from undertaking excessively risky activities, which, by endangering the banks themselves, would undermine the operation of the whole economy.

In the period leading up to the financial crisis that emerged in 2007-2008, the Fed certainly operated "with a light hand" in regulating the banks. Indeed, Fed Chairman Ben Bernanke took a "what, me worry?" approach, denying the existence of the housing bubble and turning a blind eye to the signs of impending crisis.

Having failed to use its power to prevent the financial crisis, the Fed has in subsequent years attempted to push economic growth by acting to increase the money supply and to keep interest rates low. Its success in this direction has been limited partly because it has not pushed as hard as it could. Right-wing congressmen and others of their ilk have accused the Fed of encouraging inflation, and perhaps Bernanke and others on the Fed's Board of Governors share this inflation fear. In earlier periods, the Fed has often given attention to maintaining low inflation at the expense of higher unemployment.

The Fed's lack of success in promoting economic growth in the current period also results from the fact that private non-financial firms have been reluctant to make new investments, even with low interest rates. So instead of making new loans for productive, job-generating investment, banks have used the low-cost money from the Fed for their own speculative activity—the sort of activity that led to JPMorgan Chase's multi-billion dollar loss, but which can also make lots of money for the banks.

The Appeal of "End the Fed"

Given the Fed's history of frequently sacrificing employment in the name of preventing inflation, its support of banks and the role of bankers in affecting its operations, its failure to prevent the recent financial crisis, its role in bailing out the banks and the bankers, and its failure to act strongly enough in the current period, there is a good deal of animosity towards the country's central bank. Ron Paul and others have been able to use this popular animosity to promote a broader agenda of reducing government regulation of the economy. Their call to "end the Fed" is one more effort to push the idea that the economy works best when the government works least. One would think that this is a pretty hard line to swallow in light of recent experience, when the "light hand" of government regulation was a key element in generating our current economic malaise. Yet it seems to have appeal.

In advocating an end to the Fed, Paul has called for a return to the gold standard as a means to regulate the money supply without government involvement. Ironically, at the center of Paul's right-wing attack on the Fed has been the claim that it has debased our currency and is generating inflation; the gold standard would supposedly prevent this debasement. The argument is ironic because reality has often been the opposite of Paul's claim—at many times in its history Fed policies have kept inflation in check but generated high unemployment, which tends to keep wages down.

In any case, the problem with the Fed is not the existence of a government authority that regulates the country's money. Before the Fed started operating in 1914, economic crises had been at least as frequent and severe as in later years. The gold standard (which the U.S. abandoned in steps, especially in the 1930s and ultimately in 1971) certainly did not provide stability and general economic well-being. The problem is the *nature* of the regulatory authority, run as it is in the interests of the banks and bankers, in particular, and of business, in general. The right's effort to "end the Fed," however, would likely throw us into an era of even greater economic instability, having us jump out of the frying pan and into the fire.

What to Do?

So what should be done about the Fed? Unfortunately, the Fed is part of the general economic and political problems of the country, and we should not expect to have a central bank that serves people's real needs until we have a more democratic society, a society in which money does not dominate politics and in which economic policy is not organized around the idea that maintaining profits is always the first priority.

Still, doing something about the Fed could be one step in doing something about those general problems. To begin a process of change, Dimon and other bankers should be removed from their positions of authority within the Fed. The removal of bankers from their positions of special influence would need to be followed by larger changes in the way members of the boards of directors of the regional Federal Reserve banks are chosen, and ultimately also the way members of the Board of Governors of the Fed are selected. Also, the Fed could be given a stronger mandate to act in ways that would reduce unemployment. Most generally, the goal should be to subject the Fed to democratic control.

At the end of the day, changing the Fed—changing how the U.S. economy is controlled—is a part of the larger struggle to change power in the United States so that it is in the hands of most people instead of the very few. ❏

Article 4.2

HOW HAVE BANKS MANAGED TO REPAY THE BAILOUT?

BY ARTHUR MacEWAN
May/June 2012

Dear Dr. Dollar:
Many of the banks that were bailed out by the Bush and Obama admin-istrations—to the tune of some trillions of dollars (no one seems to know exactly how much)—have, according to news reports, already paid back the huge sums of money they were loaned to avoid bankruptcy. How is this possible if, as the news reports also tell us, the banks have been extremely reluctant to loan money in these recessionary times? Since banks only make money by making loans, how were they able to pay off their huge debts to the U.S. Treasury in so short a period of time?
—*Clifford Anderson, Sacramento, Calif.*

Actually, banks make money in lots of ways, and for the big banks, making loans is not the main way that they make money.

Which raises the question: What is a bank? Consider the infamous Wall Street firm of Goldman Sachs, generally viewed as a bank and a recipient of substantial bail-out funds from the federal government. In 2010, Goldman Sachs had revenues of $39.2 billion, but a tiny fraction of this was interest income from loans. The largest share of its revenues, $21.8 billion, came from "Institutional Client Services," fees for handling financial transactions for institutional clients (other firms, investment funds, and governments). Activity involving "Investment and Lending" provided Goldman with $7.5 billion, but this does not mean making new loans; it means mainly buying and selling existing loans—for example, those packages of mortgages, called "collater-alized debt obligations," which were so important in the financial meltdown of 2008.

Another example is provided by JPMorgan Chase, which differs from Goldman Sachs in that its operations include a large amount of what we usually view as bank-ing—that is, commercial banking operations of holding checking and savings deposits and making loans to individuals and businesses. Still, in 2010 slightly more than half of the firm's $102.7 billion revenue was non-interest revenue. (And much of the interest revenue, we may assume, was not from making new loans.) The largest component of JPMorgan Chase's 2010 non-interest revenue, $13.5 billion, is listed in its annual report as "Asset management, administration and commissions."

In 2010, Goldman reported $8.3 billion in after-tax profits and JPMorgan Chase reported $17.4 billion. So they had a good deal of money with which to reward their stockholders, pay something back to the U.S. Treasury, and provide bonuses to executives—though bonuses would come as expenses, not deductions from profits. (It appears that these firms and large banks generally did not do so well in 2011, but final figures are not yet available).

There is a good deal of controversy over how much money was actually provided to the banks and other financial firms. So it is difficult to figure out how much has been paid back. In a December 6, 2011, letter to Congress, Ben Bernanke, chairman of the Federal Reserve Bank, wrote:

> ... one article asserted that the Federal Reserve lent or guaranteed more than $7.7 trillion during the financial crisis. Others have estimated the amounts to be $16 trillion or even $24 trillion. All of these numbers are wildly inaccurate. As disclosed on the Federal Reserve's balance sheet, published weekly and audited annually by independent auditors, total credit outstanding under the liquidity programs was never more than about $1.5 trillion; that was the peak reached in December 2008.

There is not necessarily a conflict between Bernanke's $1.5 trillion and the larger estimates. If the Fed provided $1 trillion in ten other months—money which was paid back each month— and $1.5 trillion in December 2008, the total provision of funds would be $11.5 trillion, but the peak, as Bernanke says, would still be $1.5 trillion.

Also, in what is called "quantitative easing," the Fed bought a large amount of long-term securities form the banks, which put money into the banks' hands—another way of keeping them afloat, but not through providing loans to the banks.

How does one count all this? It all depends on how you want to spin it.

However, if Bernanke's claim is correct, this means that, while a lot more than $1.5 billion was provided to the banks, the great majority of it was short term and was paid back—so the peak never rose above that $1.5 trillion.

The bottom line? The Fed provided several trillion dollars to the banks at very low interest rates. These funds allowed many banks, most of the big ones in particular, to stay in operation, make lots of money by pursing their investment strategies (but not much by making new loans), and pay back a large share of what they borrowed from the Fed.

Did this save us from an even worse financial crisis? Probably yes. Were there other ways to do it that would have bailed out the banks but not the bankers who led us into this crisis? Other ways that would have put conditions on the banks, preventing them from enriching their executives and leading us towards another crisis? Probably yes again. ❏

Article 4.3

PRIVATE EQUITY MOGULS AND THE COMMON GOOD

Can Wall Street corporate raiders cure creaking capitalism?

BY JOHN MILLER
July/August 2012

[In May], the Obama administration unveiled an attack ad against Mitt Romney's old private equity firm, Bain Capital.... But the larger argument is about private equity itself, and about the changes private equity firms and other financiers have instigated across society. Over the past several decades, these firms have scoured America looking for under-performing companies. Then they acquire them and try to force them to get better.

Most of the time they succeed. Research from around the world clearly confirms that companies that have been acquired by private equity firms are more productive than comparable firms.... [And] the overall effect on employment is modest.... Private equity firms are not lovable, but they forced a renaissance that revived American capitalism.

—"How Change Happens," by David Brooks, *New York Times*, May 21, 2012

The Obama campaign may have launched an attack against Romney's record at Bain Capital, but Vice President Biden and President Obama have been careful not to challenge the legitimacy of the private equity (PE) business or to take on Brooks' larger argument that the PE business has been good for the U.S. economy, not just its owners.

But is the private equity business legitimate? Do private equity moguls create wealth, or do they merely transfer wealth to the richest of the richest 1% by sucking dry the companies they take over? And has creating wealth for themselves and their investor revived American capitalism as Brooks maintains?

Before we can assess the record of these PE firms, we need to look more closely at how they go about making their money.

Inside Private Equity

Private equity is the new name for what used to be called "leveraged buyout" firms. PE firms are private partnerships that raise money from large investors, including pension funds, other investment funds, and wealthy individuals.

PE firms then use that money to purchase other companies, typically with the intention of selling them off within three to five years. That's the "buyout" part of a leverage buyout. But PE firms also borrow money, usually lots of it, from investment banks to pay for the companies they buy up. (The investment banks in turn package the loans into commercial mortgage-backed securities and sell them to other institutions.) PE firms' extensive reliance on debt is the "leveraged" part of the buyout.

But taking out so much debt comes with a twist. PE firms make the companies they take over responsible for repaying the loans. That way, the PE firm and the investors in its funds risk only the money they put up as a down payment.

As the defenders of private equity tell the story, PE firms acquire underperforming firms and make them more efficient by jettisoning a company's bad investments, cutting costs, and pushing the company into more productive investments. PE moguls, including Romney, like to think of themselves as engaged in an act of "creative destruction," the phrase famed Austrian-born Harvard economist Joseph Schumpeter used for breaking the eggs necessary to make the omelet of innovation.

The result, when it works, is a more valuable company. The PE firm then sells the company back to the public, paying off its debt and making a profit. In addition to the profits from selling off a company, the PE firm partners collect a 2% to 3% management fee paid to the investors in the fund, as well as 20% of any returns to the limited investors that exceeded an agreed upon standard, usually about 7% or 8% a year.

This sounds plausible. But in fact,the story of Wall Street takeover artists whipping self-indulgent Main Street managers into shape to the benefit of all of us has some awfully big holes in it.

Holes in the PE Story

To begin with, it is not at all clear that PE firms take over "underperforming corporations." For instance, average employment growth was actually stronger in businesses acquired by private equity in the five-year period prior to a buyout than in similar businesses, according to the very study that Brooks uses to argue that the effects on these takeovers on employment is modest. Similarly, economists Bo Becker and Joshua Pollet found that more profitable public firms are more likely to be taken over than less profitable public firms.

Nor is it clear that a PE takeover boosts the productivity of the companies PE firms acquire in a sustained way. Several studies confirm that labor productivity of companies after they have been taken over by PE firms is higher than in other similar companies. Also these companies under PE management are much more likely to close divisions of their business with lower productivity than were similar companies not taken over. But as economists Eileen Appelbaum and Rosemary Batt rightly maintain in their thoroughgoing primer on PE firms, it is not possible in these studies to distinguish productivity increases due to greater investments in employee skills and new technology from those due to management's intensification of work for fear of their company being downsized or closed.

Beyond that, these findings pertain to the time period when the target firms are managed by the PE firm, and have not assessed if those productivity gains are sustained after the firms are sold off.

There are real reasons to doubt that is the case. With a heavy debt burden and pressure from their PE owners to boost profits in the near term, managers have every incentive to downsize jobs and to forego investments in new technology and employee skills. Two well-known studies of U.S. leveraged buyouts during the 1980s, one conducted by economists at the Brookings Institution and another by economists at the National Science Foundation, found that research and development expenditures in post-takeover corporations declined at the same time as research and development expenditures in other large corporations increased. That pattern surely seems to be at odds with a management strategy that would boost productivity for the long haul.

But the issue that most of us care about is whether PE firms create or destroy jobs. While PE firms surely create some jobs and destroy others, the net effect of PE takeovers in job destruction is hardly modest, as Brooks claims in his column.

Brooks bases this claim on the widely cited large-scale study conducted by Steven J. Davis and four other economists. Their study, "Private Equity and Employment," surveyed private-equity transactions between 1980 and 2005. They conclude that, "employment shrinks by less than 1 percent at target firms relative to controls [comparable firms not taken over] in the first two years after private equity buyouts."

But a closer look at the study suggests that the effect of PE takeovers on employment is far less benign than what Brooks and even Davis and his co-authors maintain.

For instance, their study also reports a "clear pattern of slower growth at [private equity] targets post buyout"—a difference of 3.2% of employment in the first two years post-buyout and 6.4% over five years. In the words of *BusinessWeek* reporter Peter Coy, that means "having your company acquired by a private equity firm is like living through a national recession."

So how do Davis and company nonetheless reach the conclusion that employment growth at private equity-owned firms is only slightly slower than at other similar companies? They include in their jobs total not only the net effect of employees hired and fired by the private equity owned company, but also add in any employees in businesses that the company acquired while the PE firm owned it.

Counting jobs created by PE investment in new ventures is reasonable enough. But the authors of the paper also add in the jobs in already-established companies the PE firm acquires. Those jobs might be new to the PE firm, but, as economists Appelbaum and Batt emphasize, they are not new jobs for the economy, and should not be included in any accurate tally of the jobs created by PE takeovers.

Despite their dubious employment record, PE partners benefit from the "carried interest" tax loophole, which will cost the federal government $13.5 billion in tax revenues over the next ten years, according to Obama administration estimates. This provision allows private equity capital managers (and hedge fund and other financial managers as well) to have their fees and share of profits treated as capital gains and therefore taxed at the 15% marginal tax rate, versus the 35% top tax bracket for wage and salary income.

But unlike the profits of other investors, carried interest is profit paid to PE partners for putting other people, not their own money, at risk. In addition, much of the earnings of PE firms, the majority of their earnings according to some studies, come from their management fees, paid to them by investors regardless of performance. And to its credit, the Obama administration has proposed repealing the carried interest tax loophole.

PE vs. the Public Interest

The truth is that the record of private equity managers is long on cost cutting, amassing debt, and destroying jobs as they enrich themselves, and short on creating jobs, fostering innovation for over the long haul, and paying taxes on the millions they accumulate.

If being good for the economy and in that way serving the common interest is what makes a business legitimate, then not just Romney's Bain Capital but the PE business as a whole has failed the test. ❏

Sources: Eileen Appelbaum and Rosemary Batt, "A Primer on Private Equity at Work Management, Employment, and Sustainability," Center for Economic and Policy Research, February 2012; Orlando Segura, Jr., "Private Equity Exposed," *Dollars & Sense*, July/August 2008; "Private Equity: Fact, Fiction and What Lies in Between," Knowledge@Wharton, February 08, 2012; Peter Coy, "Private Equity: Hero or Villain?" *Bloomberg BusinessWeek*, January 11, 2012; Steven J. Davis et al., "Private Equity and Employment," National Bureau of Economic Research, September 2011; "Private equity under scrutiny: Bain or blessing?" *The Economist* January 28, 2012; John Gilligan and Mike Wright, Private Equity Demystified: An Explanatory Guide, 2nd edition, ICAEW, April 2010; Bo Becker and Joshua Pollet, "The Decision to Go Private," working paper for the Goizueta Business School, Emory University, June 2008; James Crotty and Don Goldstein, "Do U.S. Financial Markets Allocate Credit Efficiently? The Case of Corporate Restructuring in the 1980s," Working Group on Monetary and Financial Restructuring, Economic Policy Institute, December 1992.

Article 4.4

VULTURES IN THE E.R.
Private-equity firms target the U.S. health-care industry.

BY NICOLE ASCHOFF
January/February 2013

Public anger over increasing economic polarization and frustration with the seemingly unassailable power of big finance coalesced for a brief moment last summer in the public shaming of Bain Capital, the private-equity firm formerly run by Mitt Romney. Popular journalists like *Rolling Stone*'s Matt Taibbi turned their attention to the activities of powerful, secretive private equity firms, connecting the dots between private-equity investment and job loss, and people got mad. But, as with the leveraged-buyout kings of the 1980s, after the election furor subsided, Bain and its privateequity brethren dropped back under the radar, returning to business as usual.

However, the nature of "business as usual" for private equity warrants another look. Private-equity (PE) firms like Bain, Cerberus, Blackstone, Warburg Pincus, and Kohlberg, Kravis and Roberts (KKR) operate in nearly every sector of the economy, including manufacturing, business and financial services, food, entertainment, and health care. Cutthroat tactics, job loss, and bankruptcy are common themes in the PE world (see John Miller, "Private Equity Moguls and the Common Good," *Dollars & Sense*, July/August 2012).

Health care is a particularly popular sector for PE firms. After a decline following the 2008 financial crisis, PE investment in health care has rebounded, both in the United States and globally. In particular, medical technology, pharmaceuticals, and medical services (like hospitals and nursing homes) are seeing sharp increases in PE investment. According to a recent report by Bain, the value of global private-equity deals in health care was over $30 billion in 2011, double the investment of 2010.

Growing PE interest in low-profit, or no-profit, sectors like hospitals may come as a surprise to many who assume that private investors prefer to channel their money toward industries with rapid growth or high profit potential, like medical technology and pharmaceuticals. But private-equity firms are not like most investors. Unlike venture capitalists, who bet their own money on the success of a company, in most cases private-equity firms put very little of their own capital into their investments, and instead arrange for outside investors (like pension funds) and the firm being taken over to fund the investment. The PE firms make their money from fees and dividends, which are often debt-financed by the acquired firm. This unique feature of private-equity firms means that any company with steady cash flow (or even just a substantial potential cash flow) is a possible target for acquisition.

The growing appetite for hospital takeovers by PE firms has its roots in the ongoing struggle for survival experienced by many hospitals. Hospitals— particularly small, community hospitals and those serving poor populations—are under intense pressure due to declining Medicare/Medicaid reimbursement rates, new government demands for technological upgrades, increasing numbers of under- and uninsured patients, and restricted access to credit markets. According to the American Hospital Association (AHA), roughly 30% of non-profit hospitals are operating at a loss. Many more hospitals find themselves breaking even each year, but unable to borrow and make investments to keep up with increasing costs and regulation.

The precarious financial situation of many community hospitals has led to a wave of mergers and acquisitions in recent years by for-profit hospital corporations and larger non-profit systems. Community hospitals believe that being absorbed by a larger hospital or hospital chain will result in improved access to capital to make necessary upgrades and maintain their patient base. Meanwhile, big, for-profit, and non-profit hospitals view the acquisition of smaller, community hospitals as an easy way to increase market share and improve economies of scale.

This consolidation trend is similar to the one that occurred in the hospital sector in the 1990s, but with one significant difference—the increasing role of PE investors. PE investors are betting that the growing needs of the baby-boomer generation, in combination with the Affordable Care Act, which will dramatically expand health-insurance coverage (an estimated 15-20 million new insured by 2014, and an additional 15 million by 2016), will create new profit opportunities. For example, in 2006, KKR, Bain, and Merrill Lynch acquired the mammoth Hospital Corporation of America (HCA), a for-profit hospital chain that owns hundreds of hospitals in the United States and England, for $31.6 billion. PE firms are also snapping up non-profit, community hospitals. In December 2010, Vanguard Health (owned at the time by Blackstone), bought the Detroit Medical Center for $1.3 billion. In the same year, Cerberus Capital Management paid $830 million to acquire the Caritas Christi chain of hospitals from the Archdiocese of Boston, folding the hospitals into a new, for-profit entity called Steward Health Care System. Although the AHA estimates that less than 20% of community hospitals are investor-owned, the number is growing rapidly. Josh Kosman, an expert on PE investment, estimates that half of the biggest for-profit hospital chains are now owned by private-equity firms.

One of the strategies followed by PE-backed, forprofit hospital chains like Vanguard and Steward is to gain control over urban market share by aggressively acquiring hospital groups. This strategy is a departure from earlier, more scattered, and somewhat opportunistic, acquisition patterns by for-profit hospital chains like HCA and Essent. Vanguard's purchase of Detroit Medical Center gave it control over 13.4% of Detroit's total market, while its 2010 purchase of Westlake Hospital and West Suburban Medical Center in Illinois gave it 47% of acute care inpatient beds in the immediate health planning area. Steward's recent acquisitions, including its purchase of the Caritas chain, give it control over a quarter of eastern Massachusetts acute care beds.

What's the Difference?

All hospitals are facing similar market conditions and are concerned with minimizing costs and increasing revenues. So what is the difference between not-forprofit systems like Partners, for-profit hospital chains such as Tenet and LifePoint, and

PE-owned hospital chains like Steward? A recent report issued by the Congressional Budget Office suggests that there is little difference in the behavior of non-profit and forprofit hospitals. The report found that not-for-profit hospitals on average provide slightly higher levels of uncompensated care than for-profit hospitals, while for-profit hospitals, on average, serve poorer populations with higher rates of people living with little or no health insurance.

However, Jill Horwitz, a professor at the University of Michigan, argues that nonprofit hospitals and forprofit hospitals exhibit important differences in the types of care they offer. For-profit firms emphasize surgical and acute care services, and cardiac and diagnostic services, while non-profit hospitals often provide less lucrative care such as mental health services, drug-and-alcohol treatment programs, and traumaand- burn centers. When non-profit hospitals are converted into for-profits, they often discontinue or decrease these crucial, but less-profitable, services.

PE-backed hospital firms are particularly likely to jettison less-profitable services given their shorter investment timelines. Like most PE investments, PE firms' hospital acquisitions tend to last a short period (around five years). Then, the PE firm either takes the acquired firm public (offers stock for sale to the general public) or re-sells to other PE firms. For example, HCA was owned by two PE firms (KKR and Bain) for five years before a March 2011 initial public offering of stock (IPO), while Vanguard was owned by Morgan Stanley and Blackstone before going public in June 2011. The PE owners' goal during this period of time is to quickly increase profits and cash flow, enabling the PE firm to collect its fees and dividends, often by accessing credit and bond markets.

This investment timeline pushes PE firms to look for simple, and relatively fast, ways to increase revenues, such as eliminating less-profitable services. For example, in 2004, Vanguard's Weiss Hospital in Chicago failed a spot inspection for maternity-ward security. Staff failed to stop undercover inspectors from removing a baby (actually, for the purpose of the inspection, just an infant doll) from the ward without authorization. Rather than resolve the issue through increased staffing and a reexamination of hospital policy, Vanguard simply closed the maternity wing in 2007, eliminating a vital service for the surrounding community.

At the Vanguard-acquired Phoenix Memorial Hospital, located in a predominately urban, poor area of Phoenix, the company announced the closure of the emergency room despite earlier promises to the contrary. After a public outcry, Vanguard shelved the plan, but just a few years later closed the entire hospital and leased out the space. In the meantime, Vanguard invested heavily in surgical and ambulatory services at a nearby hospital in Phoenix's wealthier western suburbs.

In addition to reducing less-profitable services, PE-owned hospitals look for other ways to increase profits. These include centralizing and improving billing, records management, and financial services, and reducing staff, particularly registered nurses. In late 2011, nurses organized by the Massachusetts Nurses Association (MNA) gathered at Cerberus headquarters in New York to protest cuts of registered nurses on duty at Steward's Morton Hospital in southeastern Massachusetts. Since Steward's creation in 2010, the MNA and Steward have been at loggerheads. The MNA argues that Steward has cut the level of registered nurses to dangerously low levels at a number of its hospitals, including psychiatric units like the one at Carney Hospital in Boston, and has cut back on basics for patients. Nurses at Holy Family Hospital in northeastern Massachusetts complained that they were not allowed to give patients even a cup of coffee, while nurses at Norwood Hospital (in Norwood, Mass., south of Boston) brought loaves of bread to their floor to protest decreased food for patients. Nurses at Merrimack Valley Hospital, also in northeastern Massachusetts, claimed that administrators were turning down the temperature of electric blankets for chemotherapy patients to save pennies. The MNA and Steward are also fighting an ongoing battle over the MNA's pension plan. The MNA argues that Steward has refused to honor the pension agreement the union made with Caritas Christi, the former owner of the Steward chain, prior to the PE firm's 2010 acquisition.

PE-owned hospitals also engage in less-visible strategies to boost profits such as increasing lucrative surgical procedures. In 2005, the former chief compliance officer at the PE-owned Iasis hospital chain filed a complaint under the False Claims Act, alleging that doctors at St. Luke's Medical Center in Phoenix were installing a specific kind of heart implant—the intra-aortic pump—at ten times the normal rate. The alleged motive? Iasis could bill patients an additional $1000. In a 2012 exposé, the New York Times reported that an internal HCA memo showed that the company performed 1,200 cardiac procedures on patients without significant heart disease. The whistleblower, a registered nurse at a Florida HCA hospital, was fired for reporting the abuse.

The Biggest Difference: The Debt Trap

While service and staffing cuts, deteriorating patient care, and potentially unethical medical practices are easy to find at PE-owned hospitals and deserve urgent attention, they are not uniformly present at all PE-owned hospitals, and are also present at many non-PE-owned hospitals, both for-profit and non-profit. There is, however, another much bigger problem particular to PE hospital ownership.

PE firms are often portrayed as "turnaround" specialists and are viewed by many, including the hospitals themselves, as white knights bringing desperately needed investment and credit access. The problem with this view is that PE firms do not actually earn their money by turning around companies and making them successful. A PE firm's return on investment has little relation to whether the acquired hospital succeeds through improved patient care or increased cash flow. Instead, PE firms recoup their investment through fees (management fees, transaction fees, selling fees, etc.) from both the acquired firm and outside institutional investors. In fact, unlike other kinds of investment firms, PE firms generally put only a small percentage of the total equity down themselves, instead getting outside investors to cover the bulk of the initial equity investment. So even if the PE firm's investment fails to yield the imagined profits, the PE firm still earns a profit, or loses little or no money, because the risk is shouldered by outside investors, and in many cases, the acquired firm itself.

The primary source of risk for hospitals being acquired by PE firms is the debt load that comes with PE ownership. PE firms use the acquired hospital as a vehicle to earn profits by forcing it to sell bonds or shares, or take on bank debt, to pay the

PE firm fees and dividends. For example, in January 2010, Vanguard took on $1.76 billion in debt, of which $300 million went to pay dividends to Blackstone. In June 2010, the hospital chain issued an additional $250 million in bonds and, in January 2011, the company recapitalized again. It paid a grand total of $775 million in debt-funded dividends to its PE sponsors between January 2010 and summer 2011.

When PE-backed hospital chains like Vanguard and HCA go public, they (and their PE sponsor) are able to make huge profits from their initial public offerings (IPOs). HCA raked in a record $3.8 billion at its 2011 IPO, but the money from the IPO went directly to chip away at the huge debt HCA incurred under KKR and Bain ownership. In the spring of the previous year, HCA's PE owners borrowed $2.5 billion to pay themselves a dividend, and then followed up in December with a junk-bond sale to pay themselves another nearly $2 billion dividend. As a result, under PE ownership, hospital companies like Vanguard and HCA, and all the community hospitals they have acquired along the way, become buried under a mountain of debt that stays with them long after their PE sponsor has moved on to other investments.

High levels of debt make hospitals vulnerable to changes in the industry as well as broader economic shifts. When credit markets are loose and the economy is growing, hospitals can manage their debt by issuing bonds to cover interest payments or by tapping revolving lines of credit from banks, enabling a steady inflow of funds. But these safety valves quickly disappear during broader economic downturns. A contraction in credit markets can make it difficult or impossible for hospitals to service debt by accessing new sources of liquidity. At the same time, because hospitals are saddled with so much debt, profits are channeled toward servicing the debt rather than building up cash reserves or making long-term investments in patient care or technology. This weakens the hospitals' ability to adjust to industry or economic shifts and makes them more likely to end up in bankruptcy.

The pitfalls associated with PE ownership have, in some cases, led to pushback against PE hospital acquisitions. For example, when Steward attempted to acquire Florida's non-profit Jackson Health System in 2011, it was met with public outcry from Miami residents and local politicians and was forced to back out of the deal. Unions have also been vocal opponents. In 2010, Council 31 of AFSCME in Chicago fought hard against the sale of Westlake Hospital and West Suburban Medical Center to Vanguard Health Systems, but ultimately failed to prevent the sale. Some states have attached conditions to deals involving the transformation of non-profit hospitals to forprofit, PE-owned entities. Michigan's attorney general forced Vanguard to agree to continue existing operations and services at the Detroit Medical Center for ten years after the 2010 purchase date, including commitments to charity care and research. However, the Michigan deal is exceptional, and most PE-hospital acquisitions come with few restrictions on the sale or closure of facilities.

The future of PE investment in hospitals depends on a number of factors, including the cost and availability of credit, health care legislation, and the public response to PE ownership. PE interest in the hospital sector hinges on cheap credit. If credit markets contract, and PE firms find it harder to arrange financing for their investment deals, they may lose interest in health care and instead restrict their investments to more profitable ventures. However, growing demand for health care, in the context of increased hospital obligations and restrictions as a result of the Affordable Care Act, may make community hospitals more vulnerable, and actually increase their attractiveness as takeover targets. Ultimately, the most promising avenue for restricting, or ideally, preventing PE takeovers of hospitals is to publicly scrutinize their behavior and demand alternative forms of financial support for the hospitals, doctors, and nurses struggling to provide affordable, high-quality care. ❑

Sources: Tim van Biesen and Karen Murphy, "Global Healthcare Private Equity Report 2012," Bain & Company, 2012; Advisen, "Private equity and hospitals: providence or problem," OneBeacon Professional Insurance, 2011; Lisa Goldstein, "New forces driving rise in not-for-profit hospital consolidation," Moody's Investor Service, 2012; Josh Kosman, *The Buyout of America: How Private Equity Will Cause the Next Great Credit Crisis* (New York: Portfolio, 2009); Congressional Budget Office, "Nonprofit hospitals and the provision of community benefits," Dec., 2006; Jill Horwitz, "Making Profits And Providing Care: Comparing Nonprofit, For-Profit, And Government Hospitals," *Health Affairs*, 24 (3), May 2005; Reed Abelson and Julie Creswell, "Hospital Chain Inquiry Cited Unnecessary Cardiac Work," *New York Times*, Aug. 6, 2012.

Article 4.5

BIG BANK IMMUNITY
When do we crack down on Wall Street?

BY DEAN BAKER
March 2013

The Wall Street gang must really be partying these days. Profits and bonuses are as high as ever as these super-rich takers were able to use trillions of dollars of below-market government loans to get themselves through the crisis they created. The rest of the country is still struggling with high unemployment, stagnant wages, underwater mortgages and hollowed out retirement accounts, but life is good again on Wall Street.

Their world must have gotten even brighter last week when Attorney General Eric Holder told the Senate Judiciary Committee that the Justice Department may have to restrain its prosecutors in dealing with the big banks because it has to consider the possibility that a prosecution could lead to financial instability. Not only can the big banks count on taxpayer bailouts when they need them; it turns out that they can share profits with drug dealers with impunity. (The case immediately at hand involved money laundered for the Mexican drug cartel.) And who says that times are bad?

It's hard to know where to begin with this one. First off, we should not assume that just because the Justice Department says it is concerned about financial instability that this is the real reason that they are not prosecuting a big bank. There is precedent for being less than honest about such issues.

When Enron was about to collapse in 2002 as its illegal dealings became public, former Treasury Secretary Robert Rubin, who was at the time a top Citigroup executive, called a former aide at Treasury. He asked him to intervene with the bond rating agencies to get them to delay downgrading Enron's debt. Citigroup owned several hundred million dollars in Enron debt at the time. If Rubin had gotten this delay Citigroup would have been able to dump much of this debt on suckers before the price collapsed.

The Treasury official refused. When the matter became public, Robert Rubin claimed that he was concerned about instability in financial markets.

It is entirely possible that the reluctance to prosecute big banks represents the same sort of fear of financial instability as motivated Robert Rubin. In other words, it is a pretext that the Justice Department is using to justify its failure to prosecute powerful friends on Wall Street. In Washington this possibility can never be ruled out.

However, there is the possibility that the Justice Department really believes that prosecuting the criminal activities of Bank of America or JP Morgan could sink the economy. If this is true then it make the case for breaking up the big banks even more of a slam dunk since it takes the logic of too big to fail one step further.

Just to remind everyone, the simple argument against too-big-to-fail is that it subsidizes risk-taking by large banks. In principle, when a bank or other company is engaged in a risky line of business those who are investing in the company or lending it money demand a higher rate of return in recognition of the risk.

However, if they know that government will back up the bank if it gets into trouble then investors have little reason to properly evaluate the risk. This means that more money will flow to the TBTF bank since it knows it can undertake risky activities without paying the same interest rate as other companies that take on the same amount of risk. The result is that we have given the banks an incentive to engage in risky activity and a big subsidy to their top executives and creditors.

If it turns out that we also give them a get-out-of-jail-free card when it comes to criminal activity then we are giving these banks an incentive to engage in criminal activity. There is a lot of money to be gained by assisting drug dealers and other nefarious types in laundering their money. In principle the laws are supposed to be structured to discourage banks from engaging in such behavior. But when the attorney general tells us that the laws cannot be fully enforced against the big banks he is saying that we are giving them incentive to break the law in the pursuit of profit.

Our anti-trust laws are supposed to protect the country against companies whose size allows them inordinate market power. In principle, we would use anti-trust law to break up a phone company because its market dominance allowed it to charge us $10 a month too much on our cable. How could we not use anti-trust policy to break up a bank whose size allows it to profit from dealing with drug dealers and murderers with impunity? ❏

Chapter 5

SOCIAL POLICY

Article 5.1

UNIVERSAL HEALTH CARE:
CAN WE AFFORD ANYTHING LESS?

Why only a single-payer system can solve America's health-care mess.

BY GERALD FRIEDMAN
July/August 2011

America's broken health-care system suffers from what appear to be two separate problems. From the right, a chorus warns of the dangers of rising costs; we on the left focus on the growing number of people going without health care because they lack adequate insurance. This division of labor allows the right to dismiss attempts to extend coverage while crying crocodile tears for the 40 million uninsured. But the division between problem of cost and the problem of coverage is misguided. It is founded on the assumption, common among neoclassical economists, that the current market system is efficient. Instead, however, the current system is inherently inefficient; it is the very source of the rising cost pressures. In fact, the only way we can control health-care costs and avoid fiscal and economic catastrophe is to establish a single-payer system with universal coverage.

The rising cost of health care threatens the U.S. economy. For decades, the cost of health insurance has been rising at over twice the general rate of inflation; the share of American income going to pay for health care has more than doubled since 1970 from 7% to 17%. By driving up costs for employees, retirees, the needy, the young, and the old, rising health-care costs have become a major problem for governments at every level. Health costs are squeezing public spending needed for education and infrastructure. Rising costs threaten all Americans by squeezing the income available for other activities. Indeed, if current trends continued, the entire economy would be absorbed by health care by the 2050s.

Conservatives argue that providing universal coverage would bring this fiscal Armageddon on even sooner by increasing the number of people receiving care. Following this logic, their policy has been to restrict access to health care by raising insurance deductibles, copayments, and cost sharing and by reducing access to insurance. Even before the Great Recession, growing numbers of American adults were uninsured or underinsured. Between 2003 and 2007, the share of non-elderly adults without adequate health insurance rose from 35% to 42%, reaching 75 million. This number has grown substantially since then, with the recession reducing employment and with the continued decline in employer-provided health insurance. Content to believe that our current health-care system is efficient, conservatives assume that costs would have risen more had these millions not lost access, and likewise believe that extending health-insurance coverage to tens of millions using a plan like the Affordable Care Act would drive up costs even further. Attacks on employee health insurance and on Medicare and Medicaid come from this same logic—the idea that the only way to control health-care costs is to reduce the number of people with access to health care. If we do not find a way to control costs by increasing access, there will be more proposals like that of Rep. Paul Ryan (R-Wisc.) and the Republicans in the House of Representatives to slash Medicaid and abolish Medicare.

The Problem of Cost in a Private, For-Profit Health Insurance System

If health insurance were like other commodities, like shoes or bow ties, then reducing access might lower costs by reducing demands on suppliers for time and materials. But health care is different because so much of the cost of providing it is in the administration of the payment system rather than in the actual work of doctors, nurses, and other providers, and because coordination and cooperation among different providers is essential for effective and efficient health care. It is not cost pressures on providers that are driving up health-care costs; instead, costs are rising because of what economists call transaction costs, the rising cost of administering and coordinating a system that is designed to reduce access.

The health-insurance and health-care markets are different from most other markets because private companies selling insurance do not want to sell to everyone, but only to those unlikely to need care (and, therefore, most likely to drop coverage if prices rise). As much as 70% of the "losses" suffered by health-insurance providers—that is, the money they pay out in claims—goes to as few as 10% of their subscribers. This creates a powerful incentive for companies to screen subscribers, to identify those likely to submit claims, and to harass them so that they will drop their coverage and go elsewhere. The collection of insurance-related information has become a major source of waste in the American economy because it is not organized to improve patient care but to harass and to drive away needy subscribers and their health-care providers. Because driving away the sick is so profitable for health insurers, they are doing it more and more, creating the enormous bureaucratic waste that characterizes the process of billing and insurance handling. Rising by over 10% a year for the past 25 years, health insurers' administrative costs are among the fastest-growing in the U.S. health-care sector. Doctors in private practice now spend as much as 25% of their revenue on administration, nearly $70,000 per physician for billing and insurance costs.

For-profit health insurance also creates waste by discouraging people from receiving preventive care and by driving the sick into more expensive care settings. Almost a third of Americans with "adequate" health insurance go without care every year due to costs, and the proportion going without care rises to over half of those with "inadequate" insurance and over two-thirds for those without insurance. Nearly half of the uninsured have no regular source of care, and a third did not fill a prescription in the past year because of cost. All of this unutilized care might appear to save the system money. But it doesn't. Reducing access does not reduce health-care expenditures when it makes people sicker and pushes them into hospitals and emergency rooms, which are the most expensive settings for health care and are often the least efficient because care provided in these settings rarely has continuity or follow-up.

The great waste in our current private insurance system is an opportunity for policy because it makes it possible to economize on spending by replacing our current system with one providing universal access. I have estimated that in Massachusetts, a state with a relatively efficient health-insurance system, it would be possible to lower the cost of providing health care by nearly 16% even after providing coverage to everyone in the state currently without insurance (see Table 1). This could be done largely by reducing the cost of administering the private insurance system, with most of the savings coming within providers' offices by reducing the costs of billing and processing insurance claims. This is a conservative estimate made for a state with a relatively efficient health-insurance system. In a report prepared for the state of Vermont, William Hsiao of the Harvard School of Public Health and MIT economist Jonathan Gruber estimate that shifting to a single-payer system could lead to savings of around 25% through reduced administrative cost and improved delivery of care. (They have also noted that administrative savings would be even larger if the entire country shifted to a single-payer system because this would save the cost of billing people with private, out-of-state insurance plans.) In Massachusetts, my conservative estimates suggests that as much as $10 billion a year could be saved by shifting to a single-payer system.

TABLE 1: SOURCES OF SAVINGS AND ADDED COSTS FOR A HYPTHETICAL MASSACHUSETTS SINGLE-PAYER HEALTH SYSTEM

Change in health-care expenditures	Size of change as share of total health-care expenditures
Savings from single-payer system	
Administration costs within health-insurance system	-2.0%
Administrative costs within providers' offices	-10.1%
Reduction in provider prices through reducing market leverage for privileged providers	-5.0%
Savings:	-17.1%
Increased costs from single-payer	
Expansion in coverage to the uninsured	+1.35%
Increased utilization because of elimination of copayments, balanced by improvements in preventive care	+/- 0.0%
Total increased costs:	+1.35%
Net change in health-care expenditures:	-15.75%

Source: Calculations by the author from data in OECD Health Data 2010 (oecd.org).

Single-Payer Systems Control Costs by Providing Better Care

Adoption of a single-payer health-insurance program with universal coverage could also save money and improve care by allowing better coordination of care among different providers and by providing a continuity of care that is not possible with competing insurance plans. A comparison of health care in the United States with health care in other countries shows how large these cost savings might be. When Canada first adopted its current health-care financing system in 1968, the health-care share of the national gross domestic product in the United States (7.1%) was nearly the same as in Canada (6.9%), and only a little higher than in other advanced economies. Since then, however, health care has become dramatically more expensive in the United States. In the United States, per capita health-care spending since 1971 has risen by over $6,900 compared with an increase of less than $3,600 in Canada and barely $3,200 elsewhere (see Table 2). Physician Steffie Woolhandler and others have shown how much of this discrepancy between the experience of the United States and Canada can be associated with the lower administrative costs of Canada's single-payer system; she has found that administrative costs are nearly twice as high in the United States as in Canada—31% of costs versus 17%.

The United States is unique among advanced economies both for its reliance on private health insurance and for rapid inflation in health-care costs. Health-care costs have risen faster in the United States than in any other advanced economy: twice as fast as in Canada, France, Germany, Sweden, or the United Kingdom. We might accept higher and rapidly rising costs had Americans experienced better health outcomes. But using life expectancy at birth as a measure of general health,

TABLE 2: GREATER INCREASE IN COST FOR U.S. HEALTH-CARE SYSTEM, 1971-2007

	U.S. vs. Canada		U.S. vs. 5-country average	
	Dollars	Share of GDP	Dollars	Share of GDP
Extra increase 1971-2007	$3,356	5.40%	$3,690	4.72%
Extra adjusted for smaller life expectancy gain	$4,006	5.98%	$4,480	5.73%
	As share of national health expenditures			
Extra increase 1971-2007	45%		49%	
Extra adjusted for smaller life expectancy gain	53%		59%	

Note: The first line shows how much faster health-care spending rose per person and as a share of gross domestic product in the United States compared with Canada and with the average of five countries (Canada, France, Germany, Sweden, and the United Kingdom). The second row adjusts this increase for the slower rate of growth in life expectancy in the United States than in these other countries. The third and fourth rows estimate the degree of waste in our health-care system as the proportion of total expenditures accounted for by the extra increases in health-care expenditures in the United States.

Source: Calculations by the author from data in OECD Health Data 2010 (oecd.org).

we have gone from a relatively healthy country to a relatively unhealthy one. Our gain in life expectancy since 1971 (5.4 years for women) is impressive except when put beside other advanced economies (where the average increase is 7.3 years).

The relatively slow increase in life expectancy in the United States highlights the gross inefficiency of our private health-care system. Had the United States increased life expectancy at the same dollar cost as in other countries, we would have saved nearly $4,500 per person. Or, put another way, had we increased life expectancy at the same rate as other countries, our spending increase since 1971 would have bought an extra 15 years of life expectancy, 10 years more than we have. The failure of American life expectancy to rise as fast as life expectancy elsewhere can be directly tied to the inequitable provision of health care through our private, for-profit health-insurance system. Increases in life expectancy since 1990 have been largely restricted to relatively affluent Americans with better health insurance. Since

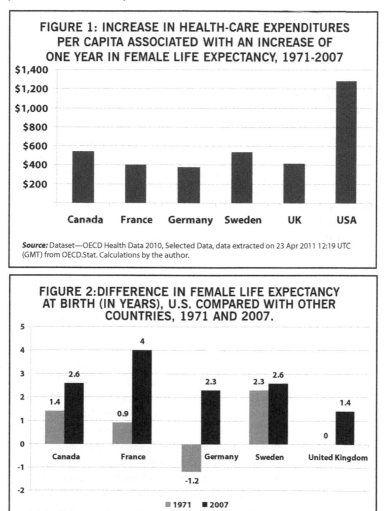

FIGURE 1: INCREASE IN HEALTH-CARE EXPENDITURES PER CAPITA ASSOCIATED WITH AN INCREASE OF ONE YEAR IN FEMALE LIFE EXPECTANCY, 1971-2007

Source: Dataset—OECD Health Data 2010, Selected Data, data extracted on 23 Apr 2011 12:19 UTC (GMT) from OECD.Stat. Calculations by the author.

FIGURE 2:DIFFERENCE IN FEMALE LIFE EXPECTANCY AT BIRTH (IN YEARS), U.S. COMPARED WITH OTHER COUNTRIES, 1971 AND 2007.

Source: Dataset—OECD Health Data 2010, Selected Data, data extracted on 23 Apr 2011 12:19 UTC (GMT) from OECD.Stat.

1990, men in the top 50% of the income distribution have had a six-year increase in life expectancy at age 65 compared with an increase of only one year for men earning below the median.

Rising health-care costs reflect in part the greater costs of caring for an aging population with more chronic conditions. As such, the United States looks especially bad because our population is aging less quickly than that of other countries because of high rates of immigration, relatively higher fertility, and the slower increase in life expectancy in the United States. Countries also buy higher life expectancy by spending on health care; rising health expenditures have funded improvements in treatment that have contributed to rising life expectancy throughout the world. Female life expectancy at birth has increased by nearly nine years in Germany since 1971, by over eight years in France, by seven years in Canada and the United Kingdom, and by six years in Sweden. By contrast, the United States, where female life expectancy increased by a little over five years, has done relatively poorly despite increasing health-care expenditures that dwarf those of other countries. In other countries, increasing expenditures by about $500 per person is associated with an extra year of life expectancy. With our privatized health-insurance system, we need spending increases over twice as large to gain an extra year of life (see Figure 1, previous page).

The international comparison also provides another perspective on any supposed trade-off between containing costs and expanding coverage. In countries other than the United States, almost all of the increase in health-care spending as a share of national income is due to better quality health care as measured by improvements in life expectancy (see Figure 2, previous page). The problem of rising health-care costs is almost unique to the United States, the only advanced industrialized country without universal coverage and without any effective national health plan.

In short, the question is not whether we can afford a single-payer health-insurance system that would provide adequate health care for all Americans. The real question is: can we afford anything else? ❏

Sources: Cathy Shoen, "How Many Are Underinsured? Trends Among U.S. Adults, 2003 and 2007," *Health Affairs*, June 10, 2008; "Insured but Poorly Protected: How Many Are Underinsured? U. S. Adults Trends, 2003 to 2007," Commonwealth Fund, June 10, 2008 (commonwealthfund.org); David Cutler and Dan Ly, "The (Paper) Work of Medicine: Understanding International Medical Costs," *Journal of Economic Perspectives*, Spring 2011; Stephen M. Davidson, *Still Broken: Understanding the U.S. Health Care System*, Stanford Business Books, 2010; P. Franks and C. M. Clancy, "Health insurance and mortality. Evidence from a national cohort," *The Journal of the American Medical Association*, August 11, 1993; Allan Garber and Jonathan Skinner, "Is American Health Care Uniquely Inefficient?" *Journal of Economic Perspectives*, Fall 2008; Jonathan Gruber, "The Role of Consumer Co-payments for Health Care: Lessons from the RAND Health Insurance Experiment and Beyond," Kaiser Family Foundation, October 2006 (kff.org); David Himmelstein and Steffie Woolhandler, "Administrative Waste in the U.S. Health Care System in 2003," *International Journal of Health Services*, 2004; "The Uninsured: A Primer: Supplemental Data Tables," Kaiser Family Foundation, December 2010; Karen Davis and Cathy Shoen, "Slowing the Growth of U.S. Health Care Expenditures: What are the Options?" Commonwealth Fund, January 2007 (commonwealthfund.org); "Accounting for the

Cost of Health Care in the United States," McKinsey Global Institute, January 2007 (mckinsey.com); "Investigation of Health Care Cost Trends and Cost Drivers," Office of Massachusetts Attorney General Martha Coakley, January 29, 2010 (mass.gov); Trends in Mortality Differentials and Life Expectancy for Male Social Security-Covered Workers, by Average Relative Earnings by Hilary Waldron, Social Security Administration, October 2007; Richard G. Wilkinson, *The Spirit Level*, Bloomsbury Press, 2010; William Hsiao and Steven Kappel, "Act 128: Health System Reform Design. Achieving Affordable Universal Health Care in Vermont," January 21, 2011 (leg.state.vt.us); Steffie Woolhandler and Terry Campbell, "Cost of Health Care Administration in the United States and Canada," *New England Journal of Medicine*, 2003.

Article 5.2

DIFFERENT ANTI-POVERTY REGIME, SAME SINGLE-MOTHER POVERTY

BY RANDY ALBELDA
January/February 2012

Four years into a period of deep recession and persistent economic crisis, only now has the p-word—poverty—finally surfaced. The Census Bureau's September 13 announcement that the U.S. poverty rate had increased to 15.1% in 2010, up from 14.3% in 2009, put the issue of poverty onto page one, albeit briefly. In fact, poverty and how to address it have not been prominent items on the national agenda since the "welfare reform" debates of the 1980s and early 1990s.

"Welfare queens" may have disappeared from politicians' rhetoric, but poor people, disproportionately single mothers and their children, are still around. Single-mother families have been and continue to be particularly vulnerable to being poor. The September report showed the poverty rate for single mothers and their children rose as well: from 32.5% in 2009 to 34.2% in 2010.

It is remarkably hard to be the primary caregiver *and* garner enough income to support a family. This reality was built into the design of the first generation of federal anti-poverty programs in the United States. Developed beginning in the New Deal era, these programs were aimed at families with no able-bodied male breadwinner and hence no jobs or wages—single mothers, people with disabilities, and elders. Putting single mothers to work was thought to be undesirable. Or, white single mothers—there was much less reluctance in the case of black single mothers, who were largely excluded from the various anti-poverty programs until the 1960s.

The most important of the anti-poverty programs for single mothers was the cash assistance program, Aid to Dependent Children (later renamed Aid to Families with Dependent Children, or AFDC), established in 1935—also commonly referred to as "welfare." Other programs developed in the succeeding decades included Food Stamps, Medicaid, and housing assistance.

Then, in 1996, with the support of President Clinton, Congress abolished AFDC, replacing it with a block grant called TANF (Temporary Assistance to Needy Families), and passed a spate of other changes to related programs. The new anti-poverty regime implied a new social compact with the non-disabled, non-elder poor, supported by both conservatives and liberals: to require employment in exchange for—and ultimately be weaned off of—government support. In other words, the new mandate for poor adults, especially single mothers, was to get a job—any job.

And, in fact, in the ensuing years the number of poor families with wages from work increased. Moreover, welfare rolls dropped. And, in the first four years following welfare "reform," the official poverty rate for single-mother families fell too. (It has been increasing since 2000, although not quite back to its 1996 level.) But despite their higher wage income, many single-mother families are no better able to provide for their basic needs today than before the mid-1990s. Even the lower poverty rate may not reflect the real material well-being of many single moms and their children, given that their mix of resources has shifted to include more of the kinds of income counted by poverty measures and less of the uncounted kinds.

While TANF and the other legislative changes promote employment in theory, they did not reshape anti-poverty programs to genuinely support employment. Key programs are insufficiently funded, leaving many without access to child care and other vital work supports; income eligibility requirements and benefit levels designed for those with no earnings work poorly for low-wage earners; and the sheer amount of time it takes to apply for and keep benefits is at odds with holding down a job.

Ironically, there has been little or no talk of revisiting these policies despite the massive job losses of the Great Recession. With job creation at a standstill, in 2010 the unemployment rate for single mothers was 14.6% (more than one out of every seven). For this and other reasons it is time to "modernize" anti-poverty programs by assuring they do what policy makers and others want them to do—encourage employment while reducing poverty. And they must also serve as an important safety net when work is not available or possible. But changes to government policies are not enough. If employment is to be the route out of poverty, then wages and employer benefits must support workers at basic minimum levels.

Ending "Welfare" And Promoting Employment

Among the changes to U.S. anti-poverty programs in the 1990s, the most sweeping and highly politicized involved AFDC, the cash assistance program for poor parents. The 1996 legislative overhaul gave states tremendous leeway over eligibility rules in the new TANF program. For the first time there was a time limit: states are not allowed to allocate federal TANF money to any adult who has received TANF for 60 months—regardless of how long it took to accrue 60 months of aid. And the new law required recipients whose youngest child is over one year old to do some form of paid or unpaid work—most forms of education and job training don't count—after 24 months of receiving benefits.

To accommodate the push for employment, Congress expanded the Earned Income Tax Credit, which provides refundable tax credits for low-income wage earners; expanded the Child Care Development Block Grant, which gives states money to help provide child care to working parents with low incomes, including parents leaving TANF; and established the State Children's Health Insurance Program (S-CHIP), in part out of a recognition that single mothers entering the workforce were losing Medicaid coverage yet often working for employers who provided unaffordable health insurance coverage or none at all. Even housing assistance programs started promoting employment: the Department of Housing and Urban Development encouraged local housing authorities to redesign housing assistance so as to induce residents to increase their earnings.

The strategy of promoting employment was remarkably successful at getting single mothers into the labor force. In 1995, 63.5% of all single mothers were employed; by 2009, 67.8% were. This rate exceeds that of married mothers, at 66.3%. So with all that employment, why are poverty rates still so high for single-mother families? The answer lies in the nature of low-wage work and the mismatch between poverty reduction policies and employment.

Single Mothers and Low-Wage Jobs Don't Mix

There are two fundamental mismatches single mothers face in this new welfare regime. The first has to do with the awkward pairing of poor mothers and low-wage jobs. In 2009 over one-third of single mothers were in jobs that are low paying (defined as below two-thirds of the median hourly wage, which was $9.06). In addition to the low pay, these jobs typically lack benefits such as paid sick or vacation days and health insurance. Many low-wage jobs that mothers find in retail and hospitality have very irregular work hours, providing the employers with lots of flexibility but workers with almost none. These features of low-wage work wreak havoc for single moms. An irregular work schedule makes child care nearly impossible to arrange. A late school bus, a sick child, or a sick child-care provider can throw a wrench in the best-laid plans for getting to and staying at work. Without paid time off, a missed day of work is a missed day of pay. And too many missed days can easily cost you your job.

Medicaid, the government health insurance program for the poor, does not make up for the lack of employer-sponsored health insurance common in low-wage jobs. Medicaid income eligibility thresholds vary state by state, but are typically so low that many low-wage workers don't qualify. Only 63% of low-wage single mothers have any health insurance coverage at all, compared to 82% of all workers. The new Patient Protection and Affordable Care Act (a.k.a. Obamacare) may help, depending on the cost of purchasing insurance, but for now many low-wage mothers go without health care coverage.

Finally, there is the ultimate reality that there are only 24 hours in a day. Low wages mean working many hours to earn enough to cover basic needs. Yet working more hours means less time with kids. This can be costly in several ways. Hiring babysitters can be expensive. Relying heavily on good-natured relatives who provide care but may not engage and motivate young children also has costs, as does leaving younger children in the care of older brothers and sisters, who in turn can miss out on important after-school learning. Long work hours coupled with a tight budget might mean little time to help do homework, meet with teachers, or participate in in- and out-of-school activities that enrich children's lives.

A New Mismatch

The first generation of anti-poverty programs were designed on the assumption that recipients would not be working outside the home. Unfortunately, their successor programs such as TANF and SNAP, despite their explicit aim of encouraging employment, still do not work well for working people.

What does it mean that these programs are not designed for those with employment? There are two important features. First, income thresholds for eligibility tend to be very low—that is, only those with extremely low earnings qualify. For example, only two states have income thresholds above the poverty line for TANF eligibility. To get any SNAP benefits, a single mother needs to have income below 130% of the poverty line. Working full-time at $10 an hour (that's about $1,600 a month in take-home pay) would make a single mother with one child ineligible for both programs in all states. Moreover, even if you are eligible, these benefits phase out sharply. With TANF (in most states), SNAP, and housing assistance, for every additional dollar you earn, you lose about 33 cents in each form of support. This means work just does not pay.

Second, applying for and maintaining benefits under these programs often takes a great deal of time. Each program has particular eligibility requirements; each requires different sets of documents to verify eligibility. While some states have tried to move to a "one-stop" system, most require separate applications for each program and, often, one or more office visits. Recertification (i.e., maintaining eligibility) can require assembling further documentation and meeting again with caseworkers. If you have ever applied for one of these programs, maybe you have experienced how time-consuming—and frustrating—the process can be.

In short, the programs were designed for applicants and recipients with plenty of time on their hands. But with employment requirements, this is not the right assumption. Missing time at work to provide more paperwork for the welfare office is just not worth it; there is considerable evidence that many eligible people do not use TANF or SNAP for that reason. Even the benefit levels assume an unlimited amount of time. Until recently, the maximum dollar amount of monthly SNAP benefits was based on a very low-cost food budget that assumed hours of home cooking.

Unlike cash assistance or food assistance, child care subsidies are obviously aimed at "working" mothers. But this program, too, often has onerous reporting requirements. Moreover, in most states the subsidy phases out very quickly especially after recipients' earnings reach the federal poverty line. This means that a worker who gets a small raise at work can suddenly face a steep increase in her child-care bill. (Of course, this is only a problem for the lucky parents who actually receive a child-care subsidy; as mentioned earlier, the lack of funding means that most eligible parents do not.)

The Earned Income Tax Credit is a notable exception. The refundable tax credit was established explicitly to help working parents with low incomes. It is relatively easy to claim (fill out a two page tax form along with the standard income tax forms), and of all the anti-poverty programs it reaches the highest up the income ladder. It even phases out differently: the credit increases as earnings rise, flattens out, and then decreases at higher levels of earnings. Most recipients get the credit in an annual lump sum and so use it very differently from other anti-poverty supports. Families often use the "windfall" to pay off a large bill or to pay for things long put off, like a visit to the dentist or a major car repair. While helpful and relatively easy to get, then, the Earned Income Tax Credit does not typically help with day-to-day expenses as the other anti-poverty programs do.

Has Employment-Promotion "Worked"?

The most striking change in the anti-poverty picture since welfare reform was enacted is that the welfare rolls have plummeted. In 1996, the last full year under the old system, there were 4.43 million families on AFDC nationwide; in 2010, amid the worst labor market in decades, the TANF caseload was only 1.86 million. In fact, when unemployment soared in 2008, only 15 states saw their TANF caseloads increase. The rest continued to experience reductions. Plus, when the TANF rolls fell sharply in the late 1990s, so did Medicaid and Food Stamps enrollments. These programs have since seen increases in usage, especially since the recession, but it's clear that when families lose cash assistance they frequently lose access to other supports as well.

Welfare reform has worked very well, then, if receiving welfare is a bad thing. Indeed, advocates of the new regime tout the rapid and steep decline in welfare use as their main indicator of its success. In and of itself, however, fewer families using anti-poverty programs does not mean less poverty, more personal responsibility, or greater self-sufficiency. During the economic expansion of the late 1990s, the official poverty rate for single mothers and their children fell from 35.8% in 1996 to 28.5% in 2000. It has risen nearly every year since, reaching 34.2% in 2010. But if a successful anti-poverty effort is measured at all by the economic well-being of the targeted families, then that slight drop in the poverty rate is swamped by the 60% decrease in the number of families using welfare over the same period. Far fewer poor families are being served. In 1996, 45.7% of all poor children received some form of income-based cash assistance; in 2009, only 18.7% did. The Great Recession pushed 800,000 additional U.S. families into poverty between 2007 and 2009, yet the TANF rolls rose by only 110,000 over this period.

Data from two federal government reports on TANF, depicted in the chart below, nicely illustrate the dilemmas of the new welfare regime. The chart shows the total average amounts of earnings and the value of major government supports ("means-tested income") for the bottom 40% of single-mother families (by total income) between 1996 and 2005. It is clear that since welfare reform, these families are relying much more on earnings. But despite the additional work effort, they find

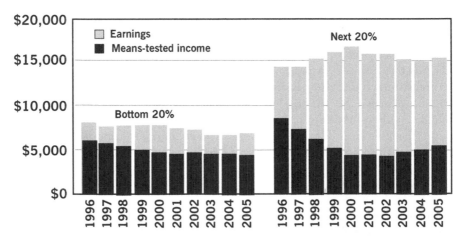

EARNINGS AND MEANS-TESTED INCOME FOR THE BOTTOM TWO QUINTILES OF SINGLE-MOTHER FAMILIES, 1996-2005 (IN 2005 DOLLARS)

Notes: Those with negative income not included. Means-tested income is the total of Supplemental Security Income, Public Assistance, certain Veteran's Benefits, Food Stamps, School Lunch, and housing benefits.

Source: U.S. Department of Health and Human Services, the Office of Assistant Secretary for Planning and Evaluation, Table 4:3 of TANF 6th Annual Report to Congress (November 2004) and Table 4:2 of TANF 8th Annual Report to Congress (June 2009), using tabulations from the U.S. Census Bureau, 1996-2005.

themselves essentially no better off. The bottom 20% saw their package of earnings and government benefits *fall*: their average earnings have not increased much while government supports have dropped off, leaving them with fewer resources on average in 2006 than in 1996. For the second quintile, earnings have increased substantially but benefits have fallen nearly as much, leaving this group only slightly better off over the period. And that is without taking into account the expenses associated with employment (e.g. child care, transportation, work clothes) and with the loss of public supports (such as increased co-payments for child care or health insurance). These women are working a lot more—in the second quintile about double—but are barely better off at all! So much for "making work pay."

More hours of work also means fewer hours with children. If the time a mother spends with her children is worth anything, then substituting earnings for benefits represents a loss of resources to her family.

What Might Be Done?

Employment, even with government supports, is unlikely to provide a substantial share of single-mother families with adequate incomes. Three factors—women's lower pay, the time and money it takes to raise children, and the primary reliance on only one adult to both earn and care for children—combine to make it nearly impossible for a sizeable number of single mothers to move to stable and sufficient levels of resources.

Addressing the time- and money-squeeze that single mothers faced in the old anti-poverty regime and still face in the new one will take thoroughgoing changes in the relations among work, family, and income.

- *Make work pay by shoring up wages and employer benefits.* To ensure that the private sector does its part, raise the minimum wage. A full-time, year-round minimum wage job pays just over the poverty income threshold for a family of two. Conservatives and the small business lobby will trot out the bogeyman of job destruction, but studies on minimum-wage increases show a zero or even positive effect on employment. In addition, mandate paid sick days for all workers and require benefit parity for part-time, temporary, and subcontracted workers. This would close a loophole that a growing number of employers use to dodge fringe benefits.

- *Reform anti-poverty programs to really support employment.* To truly support low-wage employment, anti-poverty programs should increase income eligibility limits so that a worker can receive the supports even while earning and then phase out the programs more gradually so low-wage workers keep getting them until they earn enough not to need them. Also, streamline application processes and make them more user-friendly. Many states have done this for unemployment insurance, car registration, and driver's license renewal. Why not do the same for SNAP, TANF and Medicaid?

- *Support paid and unpaid care work.* A society that expects all able-bodied adults to work—regardless of the age of their children—should also be a society that shares the costs of going to work, by offering programs to care for children and others who need care. This means universal child care and afterschool programs. It also means paid parental leave and paid time off to care for an ill relative. The federal Family and Medical Leave Act gives most workers the right to take unpaid leaves, but many can't afford to. California and New Jersey have extended their temporary disability insurance benefits to cover those facing a wide range of family needs—perhaps a helpful model.

New anti-poverty regime, but same poverty problems. Most single mothers *cannot* work their way out of poverty—definitely not without the right kinds of supplemental support. There are many possible policy steps that could be taken to help them and other low-wage workers get the most out of an inhospitable labor market. But ultimately, better designed assistance to poor and low-income families, old fashioned cash assistance, and minimal employment standards must be part of the formula. ❑

Sources: Randy Albelda and Chris Tilly, *Glass Ceilings and Bottomless Pits: Women's Work, Women's Poverty*, South End Press, 1997; U.S. Census Bureau, *Historical Tables on Poverty*; Kaiser Family Foundation, "Income Eligibility Limits for Working Adults at Application as a Percent of the Federal Poverty Level by Scope of Benefit Package," statehealthfacts.org, January 2011; U.S. Dept. of Health and Human Services, *TANF 6th and 8th Annual Report to Congress,* November 2004 and July 2009; U.S. Dept. of Health and Human Services, *Estimates of Child Care Eligibility and Receipt for Fiscal Year 2006*, April 2010; Thomas Gabe, *Trends in Welfare, Work, and the Economic Well-being of Female Headed Families with Children: 1987-2005*, Congressional Research Service Report RL30797, 2007; Randy Albelda and Heather Boushey, *Bridging the Gaps: A Picture of How Work Supports Work in Ten States,* Center for Social Policy, Univ. of Mass. Boston and Center for Economic and Policy Research, 2007; Author's calculations from the U.S. Census Bureau's Current Population Survey, various years.

Article 5.3

THE BIG LIE ABOUT THE "ENTITLEMENT STATE"

BY ALEJANDRO REUSS
November/December 2012

> In 1960, government transfers to individuals totaled $24 billion. By
> 2010, that total was 100 times as large. Even after adjusting for infla-
> tion, entitlement transfers to individuals have grown by more than 700
> percent over the last 50 years. ...
>
> There are sensible conclusions to be drawn from these facts. You
> could say that the entitlement state is growing at an unsustainable rate
> and will bankrupt the country.
>
> —David Brooks, "Thurston Howell Romney," *New York Times*,
> September 17, 2012

Is the view that "entitlements"—government programs like Social Security, Medicare, and Medicaid—"will bankrupt the country" a "sensible conclusion"? No. It's scare-mongering of the "OH MYGOD WE'RE ALL GOING TO DIE!" variety, completely unjustified by a sober look at data on government transfer payments between 1960 and 2010

New York Times columnist David Brooks starts the passage on entitlements in his September 17 column by noting that total government transfer payments have increased by an alarming-sounding 100 times over the last half-century. In the next sentence, he acknowledges that this figure is not adjusted for inflation. (Nor for population growth.) As it turns out, the "100 times" mostly reflects the increase in the general price level (more than seven-fold between 1960 and 2010) and the growth of the U.S. resident population (not quite doubled), not the growth in transfer programs specifically. Correcting for these factors, Brooks admits, the increase is just "700 percent." One can only guess that he switched to percentage terms because he's trying to sound scary, and "700 percent" sounds far scarier than "seven times." (Brooks actually describes this figure simply as "after adjusting for inflation," but it appears that he actually adjusted for both inflation and population growth.)

That's as far as Brooks gets, so he misses another crucial adjustment. The average income in the United States is far greater today than it was in 1960. Real GDP per capita grew by more than two-and-a-half times between 1960 and 2010. Now, looking at real entitlements spending per capita relative to real GDP per capita (or just real entitlements spending relative to real GDP), the growth over the last 50 years is down to less than three-fold. It makes perfect sense that cash benefits programs like Social Security—which send people checks and allow them to spend the money as they see fit—should grow with increasing incomes. These programs are meant to help people maintain something resembling the customary standards of living of today, after all, not those of the Eisenhower era.

With a few sensible adjustments, then, Brooks' alarming initial figure of "100 times" vanishes almost into thin air. That still leaves, however, an increase of a little less than three times. What accounts for that?

To begin with, over 70% of the increase in social benefits at all levels of government, over the half century between 1960 and 2010, is accounted for by three programs: Social Security, Medicare, and Medicaid. Two of these, Medicare and Medicaid, did not even exist in 1960. (Social Security, meanwhile, did not cover anywhere near the percentage of the labor force it covers today.) It is rather disingenuous to bemoan the "unsustainable growth" of certain government programs, over a certain period, when they did not even exist at the beginning of that period.

More generally, the growth in the Big Three social-benefits programs is the combined result of several different effects. Party, it reflects changes in the demographic composition of the population. Social Security and Medicare primarily benefit the elder population. This age group has grown as a percentage of the overall U.S. population because people are, on average, living longer and because the demographic "bump" of the baby-boom generation is beginning to reach retirement age. Partly, the increase reflects the growth in medical costs, which has been faster than the increase in the general price level. Finally, it reflects the expansion of benefits associated with these programs (Social Security retirement benefits, for example, are tied to lifetime earnings, so as earnings go up so do benefits).

Even aside from the numbers, Brooks is fundamentally wrong that transfer programs can "bankrupt the country." Transfer programs, like their name suggests, transfer income from one part of the population to another. Social Security, for example, is primarily an intergenerational transfer program. It taxes current workers to fund benefits for current retirees. (Most people pay taxes that fund other people's benefits, during one part of their lives, and then receive benefits paid for by other people's taxes, during another part.) The "losses" for those who are paying the taxes, at any given time, are not losses to society as a whole. They are balanced by the gains to those who are receiving the benefits.

In another sense, the benefits to everyone covered by these programs greatly exceed just the cash amount of the transfers. Social Security provides not only a retirement annuity (insurance against destitution during old age), but also disability benefits (insurance against being unable to work) and survivors' benefits (insurance for family members against the death of a financial provider). Medicare and Medicaid, meanwhile, pay for medical services and prescription medicines. These programs, in short, offer meaningful protection against many of life's possible calamities.

When we think of costs (of a government program or of something else) to "society as a whole," we need to think about the use of real resources—a part of society's total labor time, buildings, tools, etc.—that could have been used for some other purpose. The real costs of the Big Three transfer programs, in this sense, fall into two categories.

First, there are costs involved in administering the programs. The work hours and other resources (office buildings, desks, chairs, computers, electricity, pencils, paper clips, etc.) used to keep program records, send out benefits checks, and so on, could have been used for something else. So those represent real costs to society. In the case of the major transfer programs, however, the administrative costs are very small relative to the total benefits paid. The costs of administering Social Security, for example, are less than one percent.

Second, there are real costs for the goods and services for which government transfers pay. Medicare and Medicaid, for example, pay medical practices, hospitals, medical-supply companies, and pharmaceutical manufacturers to deliver medical care and medicines to program beneficiaries. Total transfer program costs, therefore, have increased along with rising medical costs. Part of the reason for rising medical costs has been that people now receive medical services they once could not. Magnetic resonance imaging (MRI) scans, for example, were not widely available two decades age. Now they are. Another is the rising real incomes of (some) medical professionals and the burgeoning profits of pharmaceutical manufacturers. Perhaps the most important, however, is that the U.S. health-care delivery system has enormous administrative costs, far above those of other high-income countries.

Advocates of single-payer (public) health insurance point out that such a system could 1) rein in pharmaceutical costs by using the government's purchasing power to negotiate lower prices and 2) dramatically reduce administrative costs by eliminating the crazy quilt of different private-insurance billing systems. (See Gerald Friedman, "Funding a National Single-Payer System," *Dollars & Sense*, March/April 2012; Gerald Friedman, "Universal Health Care: Can We Afford Anything Less?" *Dollars & Sense*, July/August 2011). Maybe David Brooks should start a clamor about that.

Two obvious ways to pay for growing transfer programs, from a public-finance standpoint, are: First, keep government revenue the same, but change its uses. For example, the United States could fight fewer wars, have a smaller military, and buy less military hardware. Or it could liberalize laws on recreational drug use, and reduce spending on police, courts, and prisons. (Or both!) It could use some of the savings to fund the Big Three and other social programs. Second, increase government revenue. Contrary to current mythology, the U.S. population is not being taxed to the very limits of its endurance. Of thirty high-income OECD countries, the United States ranks dead last in total tax revenue (for all levels of government) as a percentage of GDP, at less than 25%. The figure is 30% or more for 24 of the 30 countries, and over 40% for eight.

Brooks acts as if budget issues are one-sided: a matter only of how much a particular program or combination of programs costs. This one-sided view is especially evident in U.S. political discourse on deficits, which politicians and commentators often frame as a problem of excessive spending. A budget deficit, however, is the difference between expenditures and revenue—it is an inherently two-sided issue—so looking at the expenditures side alone doesn't help us understand the causes of deficits or the possible policy responses.

Could the U.S. government just raise more revenue, as a percentage of GDP, to pay for transfers that have grown as a share of GDP? Well, somehow a couple of dozen other countries seem to manage. So probably yes. ❏

Sources: Bureau of Economic Analysis, National Income and Product Accounts, Table 3.1.Government Current Receipts and Expenditures (bea.gov); Bureau of Labor Statistics, Consumer Price Index - All Urban Consumers (Series ID: CUSR0000SA0) (bls.gov); Bureau of Economic Analysis, National Income and Product Accounts, Table 1.1.3. Real Gross Domestic Product, Quantity Indexes (bea.gov); U.S. Census Bureau, Population Estimates (census.gov); Social Security Administration, Actuarial Publications, Administrative Expenditures (ssa.gov); OECD Tax Database, Table A. Total tax revenue as percentage of GDP (oecd.org/tax).

Article 5.4

THE CHAINED CPI IS BAD FOR SENIORS AND FOR ACCURACY

BY JOHN MILLER
May/June 2013

> The word "thuggish" comes to mind. "I'm not a number," says the older man in a television ad funded by the seniors' lobby AARP. ... "But I am a voter. So Washington, before you even think about cutting my Medicare and Social Security benefits, here's a number you should remember: 50 million."
>
> This unyielding position, undergirded by a multimillion-dollar ad campaign, is as wrongheaded as the equivalent line-drawing of Grover Norquist and the no-new-taxes crowd. ...
>
> [T]he brutal fact is that Social Security cannot pay all promised benefits, and a debt discussion is a useful place to make reasonable tradeoffs.
>
> —*Washington Post*, "Congress should reject AARP's self-centered appeals on Social Security," Nov. 4, 2011.

That AARP television ad sure raised the hackles of the *Washington Post* editors back in 2011. The editors called AARP's threat—to vote out any politician who supported a reduction in the cost-of-living adjustment (COLA) for Social Security benefits—"thuggish," "self-centered," in denial about the crisis of Social Security, and as "wrongheaded" as conservative power-broker Grover Norquist. That last one had to hurt.

Back then, the proposal to reduce the Social Security COLA by switching to the "chained" Consumer Price Index (CPI) didn't come to pass. But now it's back, this time as part of the 2014 Obama budget proposal and going by its technical economic name—the "superlative CPI." Make no mistake, though. It's the same idea now as then, and would reduce the COLAs for Social Security and veterans' benefits, as well as the inflation adjustment for income-tax brackets.

What's all the fuss about? The Social Security Administration currently uses the CPI-W, a measure of the price of a basket of goods and services typically purchased by urban wage-earners and clerical workers, to calculate COLAs for Social Security recipients. The "chained CPI-U," as it is officially designated by the Bureau of Labor Statistics (BLS), grows at a slower rate than the CPI-W. Therefore, calculating the COLAs using the chained CPI will reduce future Social Security benefits by more and more each year. If that sounds to you like a roundabout way to hold down spending on Social Security, you've got it right.

The proposal is meant to establish Obama's deficit-reduction bona fides and to lure Republicans and conservative Democrats into a "grand bargain" boosting tax revenues and cutting entitlements spending. For good measure, the Obama administration is selling the superlative CPI as just that—"a more accurate measure of the average change in the cost of living than the standard CPI." And the Washington Post is once again on board, endorsing the Obama proposal for "Social Security spending restraint" as part of the "worthy end" of entitlement reform.

Using the chained CPI to reduce future Social Security spending, however, is far from the even-handed proposal the *Post* editors suggest. In truth, it is neither fair nor accurate. Worse yet, it would fall most heavily on some of the most vulnerable in our society—older women, veterans, and the disabled.

The CPI in Chains

To understand why, we need to look at just how the COLA for Social Security benefits is calculated. In 2013, the COLA was 1.7%, equal to the increase in the CPI-W from the third quarter of 2011 to the third quarter of 2012. For the typical Social Security retiree, this translated into about $250, boosting the average retirement benefit to just over $15,000 a year in 2013.

The CPI-W is what economists call a "fixed-weight" index. It measures the price of a fixed "basket" of 211 different items. (The basket of goods is updated every two years to keep up with changes in consumers' buying patterns.)

According to the persistent complaints of conservative politicians and economists, however, that fixed basket results in the CPI-W overstating the rate of inflation. They argue that consumers typically purchase less of those goods whose prices are rising compared to those of other goods. Take the example provided by BLS: If the price of pork rises while the price of beef falls, consumers are likely to purchase less pork and more beef.

That's the supposed problem the chained CPI is intended to correct. The "U" in "CPI-U," by the way, stands for all urban consumers, a broader group than urban workers. The basket used for the chained CPI, therefore, differs from that for the CPI-W. More importantly, however, the chained CPI uses a flexible basket of goods that captures how consumers adjust their purchases in reaction to rising prices. The basket used for the final chained CPI is updated monthly. In the example of rising pork prices and declining beef prices, then, declining pork consumption means that pork prices will have less weight in the calculation of the index. By the same token, rising beef consumption means that beef will have greater weight in the index.

The long and the short of it is that the chained CPI reports a lower rate of inflation than the fixed-basket CPI-W. The Social Security Administration estimates that using the chained CPI instead of the CPI-W would reduce annual Social Security COLAs by about 0.3 percentage points per year. If the chained CPI had been used to calculate the Social Security COLA, the average retiree would have gotten $45 less in benefits this year.

Perhaps it is these small figures that have the *Post* editors convinced that AARP is "wrongheaded" about the switch. The loss of benefits, however, gets larger each year, and the cumulative effect is substantial. The average 65-year-old is now expected to live about 19 additional years. According to AARP projections, a chained-CPI

COLA would cost the average Social Security retiree more than $5,000 over the first 15 years of retirement and more than $9,000 over the first 20.

Nor is the chained CPI an accurate measure of the cost of living for most seniors. The typical senior spends a larger share of her income on medical care and housing than other consumers. The cost of both items has risen more quickly than other costs and it is hard to substitute for either item with other purchases. In addition, because seniors are less mobile than other consumers, it is harder for them to change their consumption patterns. This makes the chained CPI, whether or not it is valid for other individuals, inappropriate for calculating COLAs affecting seniors' retirement incomes.

Double and Triple Whammies

The reduction of the COLA would hit hardest on some of the most vulnerable in our society.

Older women would suffer, as the National Women's Law Center puts it, a "triple-whammy." First, the effects of the change would increase over time, and women tend to live longer than men. (A 65-year-old woman is more than 1.5 times as likely to live into her 90s as a 65-year-old man.) By age 90, a typical single woman who retired at age 65 would have lost $15,000 of benefits from the switch to a chained-CPI COLA.

Second, women rely more heavily on their Social Security benefits than men do. Among beneficiaries 80 or older, Social Security accounts for two-thirds of women's income, compared to three-fifths of men's. So any reduction in benefits will cost women a larger share of their total income than it will men.

Third, older women are more economically vulnerable than older men. Among women receiving Social Security benefits, almost 10% remain in poverty, nearly twice the rate as for men. Shifting to the chained CPI would heighten the risk of poverty for these women.

Veterans would also be hit by the switch to the chained CPI. Because veterans with twenty years of service are eligible for their pensions as early as age 50, the cumulative effect of a reduced COLA would be particularly large. Disabled veterans would face a double whammy. With a chained-CPI COLA, they would collect lower Social Security benefits and lower veterans' benefits.

The story is similar for those receiving disability benefits. The disabled typically start receiving Social Security benefits before retirement age, so their cumulative loss of future income will be much greater than retirees'. For instance, someone who began collecting disability benefits at age 30 would collect nearly 10% less in benefits at age 65 under the chained CPI, and the annual loss would get larger each year after that.

The switch to the chained CPI would also lower the inflation adjustment for income-tax brackets. While income taxes would go up across the board, more than three-quarters of the additional taxes would be paid by those with adjusted gross incomes under $200,000. Those with incomes between $30,000 and $40,000 would suffer the largest declines in their after-tax incomes, according to the Tax Policy Center.

Fair and Accurate

If accuracy were the goal of reforming the COLA, it would be far better to adopt the BLS's new CPI-E (for "elderly"). This fixed-weight experimental index is derived specifically from seniors' spending patterns, placing higher weights on housing and medical care than other indices, including the CPI-W. The BLS reports that between December 1982 and December 2011, the CPI-E added 0.2 percentage points to the annual inflation rate, compared to the CPI-W. (The difference between the two rates has shrunk recently as the rise in health-care costs has slowed.) Using the CPI-E would make it clear that the honest way to lower the COLA for seniors would be to rein in health costs and therefore slow the growth in their actual cost of living.

Finally, reducing benefits is neither right nor necessary to avoid the projected shortfall in Social Security payments starting in 2033. Currently, wage income above $113,700 is not subject to the payroll tax. Lifting this cap would eliminate the entire projected shortfall in one easy step. And unlike a reduction in the COLA, which would hurt the most vulnerable, lifting the cap would put the burden on some of those who benefited most from the lopsided economic growth of the last three decades. ❑

Sources: "Obama's 2014 budget is an offer to negotiate," *Washington Post*, April 10, 2013; Joan Entmacher and Katherine Gallagher Robbins, "Cutting the Social Security COLA by Changing the Way Inflation Is Calculated Would Especially Hurt Women," National Women's Law Center, June 2011 (nwlc.org); Tax Policy Center, "Distributional Effects of Using Chained CPI" (taxpolicycenter.org); Clark Burdick and Lynn Fisher, "Social Security Cost-of-Living Adjustments and the Consumer Price Index," *Social Security Bulletin*, Vol. 67, No. 3, 2007 (socialsecurity.gov); Alison Shelton, "Inflation Indexation in Major Federal Benefit Programs: Impact of the Chained CPI," AARP Public Policy Institute, March 2013.

Article 5.5

PUTTING THE SCREWS TO GENERATION SCREWED
Wall Street Journal *editors oppose expanded Pell grants.*

BY JOHN MILLER
September/October 2012

- Pell Grants are now so broad that more than half of all undergrads benefit.
- Better-off students often receive the large Pell Grants and apply them to more expensive schools.
- Pell Grants and other student aid are contributing to the ever-higher tuition spiral. Write 100 times on the chalkboard: Student aid raises tuition.
- Overall graduation rates were lower for students who received Pell Grants than for those who didn't.
- The best thing Mr. Obama could do for students, and taxpayers, is to get Pell Grants away from being a broad entitlement and back to their core mission of helping the poorest students.
  —Claims from "Pell Grants Flunk Out: The subsidy program has strayed far from its origins," *Wall Street Journal*, June 18, 2012.

More than $1 trillion of U.S. student debt. Better than nine of ten college graduates with student debt. Over one quarter of the repayments on those loans past due.

"A Generation Hobbled by the Soaring Cost of College" is how the *New York Times* put it in their recent exposé on college debt. And if you mix in the worst economy since the Great Depression, one that has hit those without a college degree especially hard and has left the employment prospects of even college graduates much diminished, this generation is not just hobbled but screwed. Apparently, however, not screwed enough for the editors of the *Wall Street Journal*. The editors rail against the ongoing expansion of Pell Grants, the chief form of federal aid to low- and middle-income students that can reduce the debt burden students incur.

The prospect of Pell Grants becoming an ever-more-universal entitlement must really have the *Wall Street Journal* editors spooked.

Below is a closer look at the predicament of students and former students burdened by debt and exactly why expanding Pell Grants should be supported, not opposed.

Generation Screwed

The cost of college tuition and fees has skyrocketed and student debt along with it. Since 1978, the cost of college tuition and fees has increased eleven-fold, rising faster than even the cost of medical care, and many times faster than family incomes. Since 1999, student loan debt has increased fivefold. It has eclipsed credit-card debt and is now second only to mortgage debt.

With bankruptcy not an option, borrowers can be stuck repaying their student loans long after leaving college. The federal government is now garnishing the Social Security benefits of an increasing number of retirees with student debt. The Treasury Department reports that in the first seven months of this year, the federal government withheld money from roughly 115,000 retirees' Social Security checks because they had fallen behind on federal student loans. That's nearly double the 60,000 cases in all of 2007. There were just six cases in 2000.

A college degree is now the minimum credential needed for entrance into much of today's economy. "In the mid 1970s, less than 30% of jobs in America required any education beyond high school," reports Jamie P. Merisotis, president and chief executive officer of Lumina Foundation, a private foundation dedicated to expanding higher-education opportunity. "Today, the majority of U.S. jobs require a postsecondary degree or credential." A recent study conducted by the Georgetown Center on Education and the Workforce projects that 63% of job openings in 2018 will require at least some college education.

On top of that, the penalty for not obtaining a college degree has increased dramatically over the last three decades. Beginning with the loss of manufacturing jobs beginning in the late 1970s, the gap between the earnings of college graduates and those with just high school education has steadily widened. The Georgetown study calculated that in 1980 college graduates' lifetime earnings were 44% higher than those of high-school graduates. In 2010 college graduates' lifetime earnings were nearly twice (97% more than) those of high school graduates.

At the same time, the employment prospects of even college graduates are far from bright. First off, having graduated from college is no guarantee of full-time employment. The Economic Policy Institute Briefing Paper on "The Class of 2012" found that the unemployment rate for young college graduates (ages 21 to 24) averaged 9.4% from April 2011 to March 2012. Another 19.1% of of this group was underemployed--unable to find full-time work--during that time period. Second, pay for college grads is down. On average, wages for full-time workers with four-year college degrees fell by 5.4% (adjusted for inflation) between 2000 and 2011. Finally, many graduates do not find the kinds of jobs they wanted. More than a third (37.8%) of college graduates under 25, reports a recent study by economist Andrew Sum of Northeastern University's Center for Labor Market Studies, were working at jobs that did not require a college degree.

For workers without a college degree the numbers are even worse. In May 2012 about one quarter (24%) of new high school graduates from 17 to 20 years old were unemployed, and about half (54% for April 2011 to March 212) were underemployed, unable to get a full time job. Finally, average hourly wages for young high-school graduates plummeted from 2000 to 2011, falling 11.1% after adjusting for inflation.

Pell-Mell

The *WSJ* editors stand four square against providing relief for those hobbled by student debt, especially by expanding Pell Grants to an ever-wider swath of college students. But there is plenty wrong with the editors' long list of complaints about Pell Grants.

To start with, contrary to the editors' complaints, Pell Grants are well targeted. The evidence from a report by the conservative John William Pope Center, which is the source of many of the editors' claims, shows as much. In academic year 2009-2010, a year when the median household income was $51,190, some 94.2% of Pell grant recipients had a family income less than $50,000, and the majority (58.9%) had a family income of less than $20,000.

Nor is it surprising that the graduation rates for Pell Grant recipients are lower than other students. Proportionally, nearly twice as many Pell recipients have parents with only a high school diploma and nearly twice as many come from non-English-speaking homes as other undergraduates. Even the Pope Center recognizes that these are risk factors for dropping out.

The size of Pell Grants is another reason why it is hardly surprising that the graduation rates of Pell recipients are lower than those of other undergraduates. Award amounts for Pell recipients have remained relatively flat in real terms, but covered less and less of college costs. The $5,550 maximum Pell Grant in 2011 covered just one-third of the average cost of attending a public four-year college, just one half the level it covered in 1980-81, according to the Institute for College Access and Success. [Add something like: If Pell Grants covered more of college costs, students from lower-income families would be less likely to drop out due to economic hardship--like being unable to make tuition due to tight family budgets.

In addition, better-off students do not often receive large Pell Grants, as the editors contend. The College Board reports that in academic year 2010-2011 just 1.6% of recipients from families with an income above $60,000 received the maximum Pell Grant of $5,550, well below the 33.8% of the recipients from families with incomes between $15,000 and $20,000 who got the maximum grant. While a bit more than one-fifth of those high-income recipients did apply their Pell Grants to schools that cost $30,000 or more, that amounts to less than one half of one percent of all Pell Grants going to help these high-income recipients attend "more expensive" colleges.

Finally, writing 100 times on the chalkboard "student aid raises tuition," as the editors have suggested, might convince some readers that Pell Grants are driving up tuition. But the evidence is far from conclusive. The Pope Center report states that, "most studies show at least some effect of aid on tuition," which implies that other studies show that student aid has had zero effect on tuition. Indeed they do. For instance, David L. Warren, president of the National Association of Independent Colleges and Universities, reports, "Studies conducted during three successive administrations—Bill Clinton, George W. Bush, and Barack Obama—have found no link between student aid and tuition increases."

One must also ask how Pell Grants with a maximum grant that now covers just one third of the cost of attending a public four-year college, could have fueled the rise in college tuition. What's more, the College Board reports that the average inflation-adjusted net tuition and fees (published tuition and fees minus grants from all sources and federal tax benefits) at private, nonprofit colleges and universities actually dropped from 2006-07 to 2011-12, even as total Pell Grant expenditures more than doubled after correcting for inflation.

A Universal Entitlement

The Obama administration has undertaken some positive steps to expand access to Pell Grants and toward providing debt relief for students. In 2010, the President signed legislation that converted all federally guaranteed student loans (loans issued by private banks to students, with the federal government promising to pay back the loan if the debtor failed to do so) to direct loans administered by the government. This change eliminated fees paid to the private banks that had acted as intermediaries, saving nearly $68 billion over the next 11 years, $36 billion of which is to be used to expand Pell Grants. This year, the Obama Consumer Financial Protection Bureau issued a report recommending that Congress enact legislation letting borrowers discharge their private student loans (those not backed by the federal government) through bankruptcy.

But much more needs to be done. Private student loans account for just 10% of student loans. A good first step toward genuine debt relief would be for Congress to pass the Student Loan Forgiveness Act of 2012, introduced by Representative Hansen Clarke, a Michigan Democrat, which would allow "existing borrowers" to be forgiven up to $45,000 in student debt after the borrower has made ten years of income-based payments (no more than 10% of income).

Pell Grants need to be not only a entitlement, but expanded to a near universal entitlement A recent report from the Pell Institute's newsletter, Postsecondary Education Opportunity, throws into to sharp relief the need to do yet more. Only 10.7% of students from families in the bottom fourth by family income, below $33,050, had attained a bachelor's degree by 24 years of age; among students from families in the second fourth by family income, with incomes between $33,050 and $61,600, only 15%. At the same time, 79.1% of students from the top fourth by family income, above $98,875, had a bachelor's degree by age 24.

As more and more families rely on Pell Grants to reduce the cost of a college education for their children, the more likely it is that Pell Grants will continue to withstand the budget cuts likely to come in the upcoming years. And more fulsome and the more universal Pell Grants will help make merit, not economic means, the determinant of who gets a college degree. ❏

Sources: Anthony Carnevale, Tamara Jayasundera, and Ban Cheah, "The College Advantage: Weathering the Economic Storm," Center on Education and the Workforce, Georgetown University, August 15, 2012; Jenna Ashley Robinson and Duke Cheston, "Pell Grants: Where Does All the Money Go?" John W. Pope Center for Higher Education Policy, June 2012; Rep. Hansen Clarke, The Student Loan Forgiveness Act of 2012; "Public Policy Analysis of Opportunity for Postsecondary Education," Postsecondary Education Opportunity newsletter, January 2012; Heidi Shierholz, Natalie Sabadish, and Hilary Wething, "The Class Of 2012: Labor market for young graduates remains grim," Economic Policy Institute Briefing Paper, May 3, 2012; Meta Brown, Andrew Haughwout, Donghoon Lee, Maricar Mabutas, and Wilbert van der Klaauw, "Federal Student Financial Aid: Grading Student Loans," Federal Reserve Bank of New York, March 05, 2012; Charley Stone, Carl Van Horn, Cliff Zukin, and John J. Heldrich, "Chasing the American Dream: Recent College Graduates and the Great Recession," Center for Workforce Development, May 2012.

Article 5.6

EDUCATION: NOT JUST "HUMAN CAPITAL"

BY ARTHUR MacEWAN
January/February 2013

Dear Dr. Dollar:

What's going on with the economics of education? It all seems to be about imposing "standards" to motivate and punish educators. And then there is privatization, which is supposed to force schools to shape up or die. Help me out here!

—*Nancy Hernandez, Colorado Springs, Colo.*

A great deal of the economics of education reduces schooling to the creation of "human capital." Economists tend to view education as a way of making the individual more productive—like a better-functioning machine that can generate more output. As with any piece of equipment coming off the production line, human capital is subjected to quality control—through standardized testing.

Of course, people are not machines, which presents employers with a problem. A good machine does what it is supposed to do and has no ideas about fair wages and decent working conditions. So in creating human capital, schools have the task of turning out well-behaved workers, people who follow orders and accept their employers' authority. In other words, in economists' human-capital view of education, schools need to prepare pupils for the discipline of the capitalist workplace. Thus, testing is not simply quality-control for technical skills (reading and math) but also for test-taking ability, which teaches discipline, endurance, and not asking too many questions.

Education has—or should have—goals that are much more complex than those involved in building a machine. Education is about the passing on of culture. It is about preparing people both to get the most out of and make the greatest contribution to society. Enabling people to be more economically productive, while important, is only a part of this process. Reducing schooling to its narrowest economic function obscures and undermines the larger roles of education.

But from the perspective of business executives, the narrowest economic function is the important thing, at least in the short run. Complaining that our public schools are failing, elite business groups have pushed an education agenda that would standardize the "products" of the schools, especially through high-stakes standardized testing. These groups (often private foundations, most prominently the Gates Foundation) and many economists argue that testing can create appropriate incentives for the students and their teachers. Students who fail the tests can't graduate and teachers whose students do poorly on the tests don't get raises or get fired.

Likewise, the argument continues, schools with low test scores should be closed down and replaced by other schools—just as private firms that don't produce good products are replaced by other firms. This is the root of the argument for school privatization—sometimes in the form of (formally public) charter schools and sometimes through private schools. Privatized schools eliminate the supposed causes of public schools' failures—public bureaucracy and teachers' unions.

Beyond this ideological drive for privatization, there is also money to be made. For-profit firms such as EdisonLearning, Inc., and Educational Services of America, which run schools and provide services for school systems, are cashing in on the education market. As one consultant recently told a group of potential investors in education: "You start to see entire ecosystems of investment opportunity lining up. It could get really, really big."

There are many problems with the kind of school reform being pushed by many economists and elite business groups. For example:

Our public schools are not failing. We have some marvelous public schools. We also have some terrible schools. No surprise: the good schools tend to be in wealthy areas, the terrible schools in poverty-stricken areas.

To a large extent, the poor academic performance of many kids—in both traditional public schools and charter schools—is rooted in the larger problems of economic inequality and poverty. Poverty undermines children's ability to come to school ready to learn. Poor health, overworked parents, dangerous communities—all this undermines teachers' efforts.

In states where teachers unions exist, both good schools and terrible schools are unionized. Likewise, both good and terrible public schools operate under similar—sometimes the same—bureaucratic structures.

Incentives directed toward the wrong goal (the narrowest economic function) lead people in negative directions. Teaching to the test does not create students who are effective contributors to society.

Charter schools have been operating for decades. Yet there is no evidence that they produce better outcomes than traditional public schools.

Public schools are one of the great social support programs of our society. By themselves, they cannot eliminate poverty and other social ills, but they can move things in a positive direction. However, for the public schools to be an effective social support program, they need effective social support. ❑

Chapter 6

THE ENVIRONMENT

Article 6.1

THE PHANTOM MENACE
Environmental regulations are not "job-killers" after all.

BY HEIDI GARRETT-PELTIER
July/August 2011

Polluting industries, along with the legislators who are in their pockets, consistently claim that environmental regulation will be a "job killer." They counter efforts to control pollution and to protect the environment by claiming that any such measures would increase costs and destroy jobs. But these are empty threats. In fact, the bulk of the evidence shows that environmental regulations do not hinder economic growth or employment and may actually stimulate both.

One recent example of this, the Northeast Regional Greenhouse Gas Initiative (RGGI), is an emissions-allowance program that caps and reduces emissions in ten northeast and mid-Atlantic states. Under RGGI, allowances are auctioned to power companies and the majority of the revenues are used to offset increases in consumer energy bills and to invest in energy efficiency and renewable energy. A report released in February of this year shows that RGGI has created an economic return of $3 to $4 for every $1 invested, and has created jobs throughout the region. Yet this successful program has come under attack by right-wing ideologues, including the Koch brothers-funded "Americans for Prosperity"; as a result, the state of New Hampshire recently pulled out of the program.

The allegation that environmental regulation is a job-killer is based on a mischaracterization of costs, both by firms and by economists. Firms often frame spending on environmental controls or energy-efficient machinery as a pure cost—wasted spending that reduces profitability. But such expenses should instead be seen as investments that enhance productivity and in turn promote economic development. Not only can these investments lead to lower costs for energy use and waste disposal, they may also direct innovations in the production process itself that could increase the firm's long-run profits. This is the Porter Hypothesis, named after Harvard Business School professor Michael Porter. According to studies conducted by Porter, properly and flexibly designed environmental regulation can trigger innovation that partly or completely offsets the costs of complying with the regulation.

The positive aspects of environmental regulation are overlooked not only by firms, but also by economists who model the costs of compliance without including its widespread benefits. These include reduced mortality, fewer sick days for workers and school children, reduced health-care costs, increased biodiversity, and mitigation of climate change. But most mainstream models leave these benefits out of their calculations. The Environmental Protection Agency, which recently released a study of the impacts of the Clean Air Act from 1990 to 2020, compared the effects of a "cost-only" model with those of a more complete model. In the version which only incorporated the costs of compliance, both GDP and overall economic welfare were expected to decline by 2020 due to Clean Air Act regulations. However, once the costs of compliance were coupled with the benefits, the model showed that both GDP and economic welfare would increase over time, and that by 2020 the economic benefits would outweigh the costs. Likewise, the Office of Management and Budget found that to date the benefits of the law have far exceeded the cost, with an economic return of between $4 and $8 for every $1 invested in compliance.

Environmental regulations do affect jobs. But contrary to claims by polluting industries and congressional Republicans, efforts to protect our environment can actually create jobs. In order to reduce harmful pollution from power plants, for example, an electric company would have to equip plants with scrubbers and other technologies. These technologies would need to be manufactured and installed, creating jobs for people in the manufacturing and construction industries.

The official unemployment rate in the United States is still quite high, hovering around 9%. In this economic climate, politicians are more sensitive than ever to claims that environmental regulation could be a job-killer. By framing investments as wasted costs and relying on incomplete economic models, polluting industries have consistently tried to fight environmental standards. It's time to change the terms of the debate. We need to move beyond fear-mongering about the costs and start capturing the benefits. ❏

Article 6.2

WAY BEYOND GREENWASHING

Have corporations captured "Big Conservation"?

BY JONATHAN LATHAM
March/April 2012

Imagine an international mega-deal. The global organic food industry agrees to support international agribusiness in clearing as much tropical rainforest as they want for farming. In return, agribusiness agrees to farm the now-deforested land using organic methods, and the organic industry encourages its supporters to buy the resulting timber and food under the newly devised "Rainforest Plus" label. There would surely be an international outcry.

Virtually unnoticed, however, even by their own membership, the world's biggest wildlife conservation groups have agreed to exactly such a scenario, only in reverse. Led by the World Wide Fund for Nature (WWF, still known as the World Wildlife Fund in the United States), many of the biggest conservation nonprofits including Conservation International and the Nature Conservancy have already agreed to a series of global bargains with international agribusiness. In exchange for vague promises of habitat protection, sustainability, and social justice, these conservation groups are offering to greenwash industrial commodity agriculture.

The big conservation nonprofits don't see it that way, of course. According to WWF's "Vice President for Market Transformation" Jason Clay, the new conservation strategy arose from two fundamental realizations.

The first was that agriculture and food production are the key drivers of almost every environmental concern. From issues as diverse as habitat destruction to over-use of water, from climate change to ocean dead zones, agriculture and food production are globally the primary culprits. To take one example, 80-90% of all fresh water extracted by humans is for agriculture, according to the UN Food and Agriculture Organization's "State of the World's Land and Water" report.

This point was emphasized once again in an analysis published in the scientific journal *Nature* in October 2011. The lead author of this study was Professor Jonathan Foley. Not only is Foley the director of the University of Minnesota-based Institute on the Environment, but he is also a science board member of the Nature Conservancy.

The second crucial realization for WWF was that forest destroyers typically are not peasants with machetes but national and international agribusinesses with bulldozers. It is the latter who deforest tens of thousands of acres at a time. Land clearance on this scale is an ecological disaster, but Claire Robinson of Earth Open Source points out it is also "incredibly socially destructive," as peasants are driven off their land and communities are destroyed. According to the UN Permanent Forum on Indigenous Issues, 60 million people worldwide risk losing their land and means of subsistence from palm plantations.

By about 2004, WWF had come to recognize the true impacts of industrial agriculture. Instead of informing their membership and initiating protests and boycotts, however, they embarked on a partnership strategy they call "market transformation."

Market Transformation

With WWF leading the way, the conservation nonprofits have negotiated approval schemes for "Responsible" and "Sustainable" farmed commodity crops. According to WWF's Clay, the plan is to have agribusinesses sign up to reduce the 4-6 most serious negative impacts of each commodity crop by 70-80%. And if enough growers and suppliers sign up, then the Indonesian rainforests or the Brazilian Cerrado will be saved.

The ambition of market transformation is on a grand scale. There are schemes for palm oil (the Roundtable on Sustainable Palm Oil; RSPO), soybeans (the Round Table on Responsible Soy; RTRS), biofuels (the Roundtable on Sustainable Biofuels), Sugar (Bonsucro) and also for cotton, shrimp, cocoa and farmed salmon. These are markets each worth many billions of dollars annually and the intention is for these new "Responsible" and "Sustainable" certified products to dominate them.

The reward for producers and supermarkets will be that, reinforced on every shopping trip, "Responsible" and "Sustainable" logos and marketing can be expected to have major effects on public perception of the global food supply chain. And the ultimate goal is that, if these schemes are successful, human rights, critical habitats, and global sustainability will receive a huge and globally significant boost.

The role of WWF and other nonprofits in these schemes is to offer their knowledge to negotiate standards, to provide credibility, and to lubricate entry of certified products into international markets. On its UK website, for example, WWF offers its members the chance to "Save the Cerrado" by emailing supermarkets to buy "Responsible Soy." What WWF argues will be a major leap forward in environmental and social responsibility has already started. "Sustainable" and "Responsible" products are already entering global supply chains.

Reputational Risk

For conservation nonprofits these plans entail risk, one of which is simple guilt by association. The Round Table on Responsible Soy (RTRS) scheme is typical of these certification schemes. Its membership includes WWF, Conservation International, Fauna and Flora International, the Nature Conservancy, and other prominent nonprofits. Corporate members include repeatedly vilified members of the industrial food chain. As of January 2012, there are 102 members, including Monsanto, Cargill, ADM, Nestle, BP, and UK supermarket ASDA.

That is not the only risk. Membership in the scheme, which includes signatures on press-releases and sometimes on labels, indicates approval for activities that are widely opposed. The RTRS, for example, certifies soybeans grown in large-scale chemical-intensive monocultures. They are usually genetically modified organisms (GMOs). They are mostly fed to animals. And they originate in countries with hungry populations. When, according to an ABC News poll, 52% of Americans think GMOs are unsafe and 93% think GMOs ought to be labeled, for example, this is a risk most organizations dependent on their reputations probably would not consider.

The remedy for such reputational risk is high standards, rigorous certification, and watertight traceability procedures. Only credibility at every step can deflect the seemingly obvious suspicion that the conservation nonprofits have been hood-winked or have somehow "sold out."

So, which one is it? Are "Responsible" and "Sustainable" certifications indicative of a genuine strategic success by WWF and its fellows, or are the schemes nothing more than business as usual with industrial-scale greenwashing and a social-justice varnish?

Low and Ambiguous Standards

The first place to look is the standards themselves. The language from the RTRS standards (see sidebar), to stick with the case of soy, illustrates the tone of the RTRS principles and guidance.

There are two ways to read these standards. The generous interpretation is to recognize that the sentiments expressed are higher than what is actually practiced in many countries where soybeans are grown, in that the standards broadly follow common practice in Europe or North America. Nevertheless, they are far lower than organic or fair-trade standards; for example, they don't require crop rotation, or prohibit pesticides. Even a generous reading also needs to acknowledge the crucial point that adherence to similar requirements in Europe and North America has contaminated wells, depleted aquifers, degraded rivers, eroded the soil, polluted the oceans, driven species to extinction, and depopulated the countryside—to mention only a few well-documented downsides.

There is also a less generous interpretation of the standards. Much of the content is either in the form of statements, or it is merely advice. Thus section 4.2 reads: "Pollution is minimized and production waste is managed responsibly." Imperatives, such as: "must," "may never," "will," etc., are mostly lacking from the document. Worse, key terms such as "pollution," "minimized," "responsible," and "timely" (see sidebar) are left undefined. This chronic vagueness means that both certifiers and producers possess effectively infinite latitude to implement or judge the standards. They could never be enforced, in or out of court.

The Round Table on Responsible Soy Standards

RTRS standards (version 1, June 2010) cover five "principles." Principle 1: Legal Compliance and Good Business Practices. Principle 2: Responsible Labour Conditions. Principle 3: Responsible Community Relations. Principle 4: Environmental Responsibility. Principle 5: Good Agricultural Practice.

Language typical of the standards includes, under Principle 2 (Responsible Labour Conditions), section 2.1.1 states: "No forced, compulsory, bonded, trafficked, or otherwise involuntary labor is used at any stage of production," while section 2.4.4 states, "Workers are not hindered from interacting with external parties outside working hours."

Under Principle 3 (Responsible Community Relations), section 3.3.3 states: "Any complaints and grievances received are dealt with in a timely manner."

Under Principle 4 (Environmental Responsibility), section 4.2 states: "Pollution is minimized and production waste is managed responsibly," and section 4.4 states: "Expansion of soy cultivation is responsible."

Under Principle 5 (Good Agricultural Practice), Section 5.9 states: "Appropriate measures are implemented to prevent the drift of agrochemicals to neighboring areas."

Dubious Verification and Enforcement

Unfortunately, the flaws of RTRS certification do not end there. They include the use of an internal verification system. The RTRS uses professional certifiers, but only those who are members of RTRS. This means that the conservation nonprofits are relying on third parties for compliance information. It also means that only RTRS members can judge whether a principle was adhered to. Even if they consider it was not, there is nothing they can do, since the RTRS has no legal status or sanctions.

The "culture" of deforestation is also important to the standards. Rainforest clearance is often questionably legal, or actively illegal, and usually requires removing existing occupants from the land. It is a world of private armies and bribery. This operating environment makes very relevant the irony under which RTRS members, under Principle 1, volunteer to obey the law. The concept of volunteering to obey the law invites more than a few questions. If an organization is not already obeying the law, what makes WWF suppose that a voluntary code of conduct will persuade it? And does obeying the law meaningfully contribute to a marketing campaign based on responsibility?

Of equal concern is the absence of a clear certification trail. Under the "Mass Balance" system offered by RTRS, soybeans (or derived products) can be sold as "Responsible" that were never grown under the system. Mass Balance means vendors can transfer the certification quantity purchased, to non-RTRS soybeans. Such an opportunity raises the inherent difficulties of traceability and verification to new levels.

How Will Certification Save Wild Habitats?

A key stated goal of WWF is to halt deforestation through the use of maps identifying priority habitat areas that are off-limits to RTRS members. There are crucial questions over these maps, however. First, even though soybeans are already being traded, the maps have yet to be drawn up. Secondly, the maps are to be drawn up by RTRS members themselves. Thirdly, RTRS maps can be periodically redrawn. Fourthly, RTRS members need not certify all of their production acreage. This means they can certify part of their acreage as "Responsible," but still sell (as "Irresponsible"?) soybeans from formerly virgin habitat. This means WWF's target for year 2020 of 25% coverage globally and 75% in WWF's "priority areas" would still allow 25% of the Brazilian soybean harvest to come from newly deforested land. And of course, the scheme cannot prevent non-members, or even non-certified subsidiaries, from specializing in deforestation.

These are certification schemes, therefore, with low standards, no methods of enforcement, and enormous loopholes. Pete Riley of UK GM Freeze dubs their instigator the "World Wide Fund for naïveté" and believes "the chances of Responsible soy saving the Cerrado are zero." Claire Robinson of Earth Open Source agrees: "The RTRS standard will not protect the forests and other sensitive ecosystems. Additionally, it greenwashes soy that's genetically modified to survive being sprayed with quantities of herbicide that endanger human health and the environment." There is even a website (www.toxicsoy.org) dedicated to exposing the greenwashing of GMO soy.

Many other groups apparently share that view. More than 250 large and small sustainable farming, social justice, and rainforest preservation groups from all over the world signed a "Letter of Critical Opposition to the RTRS" in 2009. Signatories included the Global Forest Coalition, Friends of the Earth, Food First, the British Soil Association and the World Development Movement.

Other commodity certifications involving WWF have also received strong criticism. The Mangrove Action Project in 2008 published a "Public Declaration Against the Process of Certification of Industrial Shrimp Aquaculture" while the World Rainforest Movement issued "Declaration against the Roundtable on Sustainable Palm Oil (RSPO)," signed by 256 organizations in October 2008.

What Really Drives Commodity Certification?

Commodity certification is in many ways a strange departure for conservation non-profits. In the first place the big conservation nonprofits are more normally active in acquiring and researching wild habitats. Secondly, these are membership organizations, yet it is hard to envisage these schemes energizing the membership. How many members of the Nature Conservancy will be pleased to find that their organization has been working with Monsanto to promote GM crops as "Responsible"? Indeed, one can argue that these programs are being actively concealed from their members, donors, and the public. From their advertising, their websites, and their educational materials, one would presume that poachers, population growth and ignorance are the chief threats to wildlife in developing countries. It is not true, however, and as WWF's Jason Clay and the very existence of these certification schemes make clear, senior management knows it well.

In public, the conservation nonprofits justify market transformation as cooperative; they wish to work with others, not against them. However, they have chosen to work preferentially with powerful and wealthy corporations. Why not cooperate instead with small farmers' movements, indigenous groups, and already successful standards, such as fair-trade, organic and non-GMO? These are causes that could use the help of big international organizations. Why not, with WWF help, embed into organic standards a rainforest conservation element? Why not cooperate with your membership to create engaged consumer power against habitat destruction, monoculture, and industrial farming? Instead, the new "Responsible" and "Sustainable" standards threaten organic, fair-trade, and local food systems—which are some of the environmental movement's biggest successes.

One clue to the enthusiasm for "market transformation" may be that financial rewards are available. According to Nina Holland of Corporate Europe Observatory, certification is "now a core business" for WWF. Indeed, WWF and the Dutch nonprofit Solidaridad are currently receiving millions of euros from the Dutch government (under its Sustainable Trade Action Plan) to support these schemes. According to the plan, 67 million euros have already been committed, and similar amounts are promised.

The Threat From the Food Movement

Commodity-certification schemes like RTRS can be seen as an inability of global conservation leadership to work constructively with the ordinary people who live in and around wild areas of the globe; or they can be seen as a disregard for fair-trade and organic labels; or as a lost opportunity to inform and energize members and potential members as to the true causes of habitat destruction; or even as a cynical moneymaking scheme. These are all plausible explanations of the enthusiasm for certification schemes and probably each plays a part. None, however, explains why conservation nonprofits would sign up to schemes whose standards and credibility are so low. Especially when, as never before, agribusiness is under pressure to change its destructive social and environmental practices.

The context of these schemes is that we live at an historic moment. Positive alternatives to industrial agriculture, such as fair trade, organic agriculture, agroecology, and the System of Rice Intensification, have shown they can feed the planet, without destroying it, even with a greater population. Consequently, there is now a substantial international consensus of informed opinion that industrial agriculture is a principal cause of the current environmental crisis and the chief obstacle to hunger eradication.

This consensus is one of several roots of the international food movement. As a powerful synergism of sustainability, social-justice, sustainability, food-quality, and environmental concerns, the food movement is a clear threat to the long-term existence of the industrial food system. Incidentally, this is why big multinationals have been buying up ethical brands.

Under these circumstances, evading the blame for the environmental devastation of the Amazon, Asia, and elsewhere, undermining organic and other genuine certification schemes, and splitting the environmental movement must be a dream come true for members of the industrial food system. A true cynic might surmise that the food industry could hardly have engineered it better had they planned it themselves.

Who Runs Big Conservation?

To guard against such possibilities, nonprofits are required to have boards of directors whose primary legal function is to guard the mission of the organization and to protect its good name. In practice, for conservation nonprofits this means overseeing potential financial conflicts and preventing the organization from lending its name to greenwashing.

So, who are the individuals guarding the mission of global conservation nonprofits? U.S.-WWF boasts (literally) that its new vice-chair was the last CEO of Coca-Cola, Inc. (a member of Bonsucro) and that another board member is Charles O. Holliday Jr., the current chairman of the board of Bank of America, who was formerly CEO of DuPont (owner of Pioneer Hi-Bred International, a major player in the GMO industry). The current chair of the executive board at Conservation International is Robert Walton, better known as chair of the board of Wal-Mart (which now sells "sustainably sourced" food and owns the supermarket chain ASDA). The boards of WWF and Conservation International do have more than a sprinkling of members with conservation-related careers. But they are heavily outnumbered by business represen-tatives. On the board of Conservation International, for example, are GAP, Intel, Northrop Grumman, JP Morgan, Starbucks, and UPS, among others.

The Nature Conservancy's board of directors has only two members (out of 22) who list an active affiliation to a conservation organization in their board CV (Prof. Gretchen Daly and Cristian Samper, head of the U.S. Museum of Natural History). Only one other member even mentions among his qualifications an interest in the subject of con-servation. The remaining members are like Shona Brown, who is an employee of Google and a board member of Pepsico, or Meg Whitman, the current president and CEO of Hewlett-Packard, or Muneer A. Satter, a managing director of Goldman Sachs.

So, was market transformation developed with the support of these boards or against their wishes? The latter is hardly likely. The key question then becomes: Did these boards in fact instigate market transformation? Did it come from the very top?

Never Ending

Leaving aside whether conservation was ever their true intention, it seems highly unlikely that WWF and its fellow conservation groups will leverage a positive trans-formation of the food system by bestowing "Sustainable" and "Responsible" stan-dards on agribusiness. Instead, it appears much more likely that, by undermining existing standards and offering worthless standards of their own, habitat destruc-tion and human misery will only increase.

Market transformation, as envisaged by WWF, nevertheless might have worked. However, WWF neglected to consider that successful certification schemes start from the ground up. Organic and fair-trade began with a large base of committed farmers determined to fashion a better food system. Producers willingly signed up to high standards and clear requirements because they believed in them. Indeed, many already were practicing high standards without certification. But when big players in the food industry have tried to climb on board, game the system and manipulate standards, problems have resulted, even with credible standards like fair-trade and organic. At some point big players will probably undermine these standards. They seem already to be well on the way, but if they succeed their efforts will only have proved that certification standards can never be a substitute for trust, commitment and individual integrity.

The only good news in this story is that it contradicts fundamentally the defeatist arguments of the WWF. Old-fashioned activist strategies, of shaming bad practice, boycotting products, and encouraging alternatives, do work. The market opportunity presently being exploited by WWF and company resulted from the success of these strategies, not their failure. Multinational corporations, we should conclude, really do fear activists, non-profits, informed consumers, and small pro-ducers all working together. ❑

Sources: Jonathan A. Foley et al. "Solutions for a Cultivated Planet" *Nature*, October 2011 (Nature.com); Jason Clay, "Economics, Behavior and Biodiversity Loss: Sustainability as a Pre-competitive Issue," March 25, 2011 (youtube.com); Food and Agriculture Organization of the United Nations, "Scarcity and degradation of land and water: growing threat to food security," November 28, 2011 (fao.org); State of the World's Land and Water Resources for Food and Agriculture (SOLAW), November 28, 2011 (fao.org); Mat McDermott, "More Dirty Deforestation: 55% of Indonesia's Logging Illegal + Cargill's Two Hidden Palm Oil Plantations," May 6, 2010 (treehugger.com); Earth Open Source (earthopensource.org); United Nations (UN; un.org); Roundtable on Sustainable Palm Oil (RSPO; rspo.org); Round Table on Responsible Soy (RTRS; responsiblesoy.org); Roundtable on Sustainable Biofuels (rsb.epfl.ch); Bonsucro (Bonsucro.com); WWF, "Save the Cerrado: What's happening in the Cerrado?" (wwf.org. uk); Gary Langer, "Behind the Label, Many Skeptical of Bio-engineered Food," June 19, 2001 (abcnews.com); Round Table on Responsible Soy, "Why certifying under the RTST Standard?" (responsiblesoy.org); Natural Resources Defense Council, "Atrazine: Poisoning the Well," May 2010 (nrdc.org); The *Capital-Journal* Editorial Board, "Time for action on rural depopulation," July 28, 2011 (cjonline.com); "State of the World's Indigenous Peoples Report, Chapter 7: Emerging Issues," January 2010 (un.org); "A Brief History of Rubber" (rainforests.mongabay.com); "Letter of critical opposition to the Round Table on Responsible Soy," April 2009 (bangmfood. org); Global Forest Coalition (globalforestcoalition.org); Public Declaration Against the Process of Certification of Industrial Shrimp Aquaculture, November 3, 2008 (mangroveactionproject. org); World Rainforest Movement, "Declarations against the Roundtable on Sustainable Palm Oil (RSPO) in Defence of Human Rights, Food Sovereignty," September 2008 (wrm.org); System of Rice Intensification (SRI-Rice; sri.ciifad.cornell.edu); Sarah Hills, "Coca-Cola snaps up first Bonsucro certified sugarcane," June 22, 2011 (foodnavigator.com); "Wal-Mart Unveils Global Sustainable Agriculture Goal," October 14, 2010 (walmartstores.com); "Largest Corporate Dairy, Biotech Firm and USDA Accused of Conspiring to Corrupt Rulemaking and Pollute Organics," January 23, 2012 (cornucopia.org); Dutch Ministry of Agriculture, "Nature and Food Quality Sustainable Food: Public Summary of Policy Document" (government.nl); Jonathan Latham and Allison Wilson, "How the Science Media Failed the IAASTD," April 7, 2008 (independentsciencenews.org).

Article 6.3

THE COSTS OF EXTREME WEATHER
Climate inaction is expensive—and inequitable.

BY HEIDI GARRETT-PELTIER
November/December 2011

Two thousand eleven has already been a record-setting year. The number of weather disasters in the United States whose costs exceed $1 billion—ten— is the highest ever. August witnessed one of the ten most expensive catastrophes in U.S. history, Tropical Storm Irene. An initial estimate put the damages from Irene at between $7 billion and $13 billion. In this one storm alone, eight million businesses and homes lost power, roads collapsed, buildings flooded, and dozens of people lost their lives. Meanwhile, Texas is experiencing its hottest year in recorded history: millions of acres in the state have burned, over 1,550 homes have been lost to wildfires as of early September, and tens of thousands of people have had to evacuate their homes. The devastation caused by the storms and droughts has left individuals and businesses wondering how they'll recover, and has left cash-strapped towns wondering how they'll pay for road and infrastructure repairs.

Extreme weather events like these are expected to become more frequent and more intense over the next century. That's just one of the impacts of climate change, which, according to the consensus of scientists and research organizations from around the world, is occurring with both natural and human causes, but mainly from the burning of fossil fuels. According to NASA, since 1950 the number of record high-temperature days has been rising while the number of record low-temperature days has been falling. The number of intense rainfall events has also increased in the past six decades. At the same time, droughts and heat waves have also become more frequent, as warmer conditions in drier areas have led to faster evaporation. This is why in the same month we had wildfires in Texas (resulting from more rapid evaporation and drought) and flooding in the Northeast (since warmer air holds more moisture and results in more intense precipitation).

In response to these dramatic weather changes, the courses of action available to us are *mitigation*, *adaptation*, and *reparation*. *Mitigation* refers to efforts to prevent or reduce climate change, for example, cutting fossil fuel use by increasing energy efficiency and using more renewable energy. *Adaptation* refers to changing our behaviors, technologies, institutions, and infrastructure to cope with the damages that climate change creates—building levees near flood-prone areas or relocating homes further inland, for example. And as the term implies, *reparation* means repairing or rebuilding the roads, bridges, homes, and communities that are damaged by floods, winds, heat, and other weather-related events.

Of these, mitigation is the one strategy whose costs and benefits can both be shared globally. Moving toward a more sustainable economy less reliant on the burning of fossil fuels for its energy would slow the rise in average global temperatures and make extreme weather events less likely. Mitigation will have the greatest impact with a shared worldwide commitment, but even without binding international agreements, countries can take steps to reduce their use of coal, oil, and natural gas.

According to the Intergovernmental Panel on Climate Change, even the most stringent mitigation efforts cannot prevent further impacts of climate change in the next few decades. We will still need to adapt and repair—all the more in the absence of such efforts. But the costs and burdens of adaptation and reparation are spread unevenly across different populations and in many cases the communities most affected by climate change will be those least able to afford to build retaining walls or relocate to new homes. Farmers who can afford to will change their planting and harvesting techniques and schedules, but others will have unusable land and will be unable to sustain themselves. Roads that are washed away will be more quickly rebuilt in richer towns, while poorer towns will take longer to rebuild if they can at all. The divide between rich and poor will only grow.

Given the high cost of damages we've already faced just this year, mitigation may very well be sound economic planning. But it is also the most humane and equitable approach to solving our climate problem. ❑

Sources: NOAA/NESDIS/NCDC, "Billion Dollar U.S. Weather/Climate Disasters 1980-August 2011"; Michael Cooper, "Hurricane Cost Seen as Ranking Among Top Ten," *New York Times*, August 30, 2011; "Hurricane Irene Damage: Storm Likely Cost $7 Billion to $13 Billion," *International Business Times*, August 29, 2011; Intergovernmental Panel on Climate Change, *Fourth Assessment Report: Climate Change 2007*, Working Group II ch. 19; NASA, "Global Climate Change: Vital Signs of the Planet—Evidence"; U.S. EPA, "Climate Change—Health and Environmental Effects, Extreme Events."

Article 6.4

KEEP IT IN THE GROUND

An alternative vision for petroleum emerges in Ecuador. But will Big Oil win the day?

BY ELISSA DENNIS
July/August 2010

In the far eastern reaches of Ecuador, in the Amazon basin rain forest, lies a land of incredible beauty and biological diversity. More than 2,200 varieties of trees reach for the sky, providing a habitat for more species of birds, bats, insects, frogs, and fish than can be found almost anywhere else in the world. Indigenous Waorani people have made the land their home for millennia, including the last two tribes living in voluntary isolation in the country. The land was established as Yasuní National Park in 1979, and recognized as a UNESCO World Biosphere Reserve in 1989.

Underneath this landscape lies a different type of natural resource: petroleum. Since 1972, oil has been Ecuador's primary export, representing 57% of the country's exports in 2008; oil revenues comprised on average 26% of the government's revenue between 2000 and 2007. More than 1.1 billion barrels of heavy crude oil have been extracted from Yasuní, about one quarter of the nation's production to date.

At this economic, environmental, and political intersection lie two distinct visions for Yasuní's, and Ecuador's, next 25 years. Petroecuador, the state-owned oil company, has concluded that 846 million barrels of oil could be extracted from proven reserves at the Ishpingo, Tambococha, and Tiputini (ITT) wells in an approximately 200,000 hectare area covering about 20% of the parkland. Extracting this petroleum, either alone or in partnership with interested oil companies in Brazil, Venezuela, or China, would generate approximately $7 billion, primarily in the first 13 years of extraction and continuing with declining productivity for another 12 years.

The alternative vision is the simple but profound choice to leave the oil in the ground.

Environmentalists and indigenous communities have been organizing for years to restrict drilling in Yasuní. But the vision became much more real when President Rafael Correa presented a challenge to the world community at a September 24, 2007 meeting of the United Nations General Assembly: if governments, companies, international organizations, and individuals pledge a total of $350 million per year for 10 years, equal to half of the forgone revenues from ITT, then Ecuador will chip in the other half and keep the oil underground indefinitely, as this nation's contribution to halting global climate change.

The Yasuní-ITT Initiative would preserve the fragile environment, leave the voluntarily isolated tribes in peace, and prevent the emission of an estimated 407 million metric tons of carbon dioxide into the atmosphere. This "big idea from a small country" has even broader implications, as Alberto Acosta, former Energy Minister and one of the architects of the proposal, notes in his new book, *La Maldición de la Abundancia* (*The Curse of Abundance*). The Initiative is a *"punto de ruptura,"* he writes, a turning point in environmental history which "questions the logic of extractive (exporter of raw material) development," while introducing the possibility of global *"sumak kawsay,"* the indigenous Kichwa concept of "good living" in harmony with nature.

Ecuador, like much of Latin America, has long been an exporter of raw materials: cacao in the 19th century, bananas in the 20th century, and now petroleum. The nation dove into the oil boom of the 1970s, investing in infrastructure and building up external debt. When oil prices plummeted in the 1980s while interest rates on that debt ballooned, Ecuador was trapped in the debt crisis that affected much of the region. Thus began what Correa calls "the long night of neoliberalism:" IMF-mandated privatizations of utilities and mining sectors, with a concomitant decline of revenues from the nation's natural resources to the Ecuadorian people. By 1986, all of the nation's petroleum revenues were going to pay external debt.

Close to 40 years of oil production has failed to improve the living standards of the majority of Ecuadorians. "Petroleum has not helped this country," notes Ana Cecilia Salazar, director of the Department of Social Sciences in the College of Economics of the University of Cuenca. "It has been corrupt. It has not diminished poverty. It has not industrialized this country. It has just made a few people rich."

Currently 38% of the population lives in poverty, with 13% in extreme poverty. The nation's per capita income growth between 1982 and 2007 was only .7% per year. And although the unemployment rate of 10% may seem moderate, an estimated 53% of the population is considered "underemployed."

Petroleum extraction has brought significant environmental damage. Each year 198,000 hectares of land in the Amazon are deforested for oil production. A verdict is expected this year in an Ecuadorian court in the 17-year-old class action suit brought by 30,000 victims of Texaco/Chevron's drilling operations in the area northwest of Yasuní between 1964 and 1990. The unprecedented $27 billion lawsuit alleges that thousands of cancers and other health problems were caused by Texaco's use of outdated and dangerous practices, including the dumping of 18 billion gallons of toxic wastewater into local water supplies.

Regardless of its economic or environmental impacts, the oil is running out. With 4.16 billion barrels in proven reserves nationwide, and another half billion "probable" barrels, best-case projections, including the discovery of new reserves, indicate the nation will stop exporting oil within 28 years, and stop producing oil within 35 years.

"At this moment we have an opportunity to rethink the extractive economy that for many years has constrained the economy and politics in the country," says Esperanza Martinez, a biologist, environmental activist, and author of the book *Yasuní: El tortuoso camino de Kioto a Quito.* "This proposal intends to change the terms of the North-South relationship in climate change negotiations."

As such, the Initiative fits into the emerging idea of "climate debt." The North's voracious energy consumption in the past has destroyed natural resources in the South; the South is currently bearing the brunt of global warming effects like floods and drought; and the South needs to adapt expensive new energy technology for the future instead of industrializing with the cheap fossil fuels that built the North. Bolivian president Evo Morales proposed at the Copenhagen climate talks last December that developed nations pay 1% of GDP, totaling $700 billion/year, into a compensation fund that poor nations could use to adapt their energy systems.

"Clearly in the future, it will not be possible to extract all the petroleum in the world because that would create a very serious world problem, so we need to create measures of compensation to pay the ecological debt to the countries," says Malki

Sáenz, formerly Coordinator of the Yasuní-ITT Initiative within the Ministry of Foreign Relations. The Initiative "is a way to show the international community that real compensation mechanisms exist for not extracting petroleum."

Indigenous and environmental movements in Latin America and Africa are raising possibilities of leaving oil in the ground elsewhere. But the Yasuní-ITT proposal is the furthest along in detail, government sponsorship, and ongoing negotiations. The Initiative proposes that governments, international institutions, civil associations, companies, and individuals contribute to a fund administered through an international organization such as the United Nations Development Program (UNDP). Contributions could include swaps of Ecuador's external debt, as well as resources generated from emissions auctions in the European Union and carbon emission taxes such as those implemented in Sweden and Slovakia.

Contributors of at least $10,000 would receive a Yasuní Guarantee Certificate (CGY), redeemable only in the event that a future government decides to extract the oil. The total dollar value of the CGYs issued would equal the calculated value of the 407 million metric tons of non-emitted carbon dioxide.

The money would be invested in fixed income shares of renewable energy projects with a guaranteed yield, such as hydroelectric, geothermal, wind, and solar power, thus helping to reduce the country's dependence on fossil fuels. The interest payments generated by these investments would be designated for: 1) conservation projects, preventing deforestation of almost 10 million hectares in 40 protected areas covering 38% of Ecuador's territory; 2) reforestation and natural regeneration projects on another one million hectares of forest land; 3) national energy efficiency improvements; and 4) education, health, employment, and training programs in sustainable activities like ecotourism and agro forestry in the affected areas. The first three activities could prevent an additional 820 million metric tons of carbon dioxide emissions, tripling the Initiative's effectiveness.

These nationwide conservation efforts, as well as the proposal's mention of "monitoring" throughout Yasuní and possibly shutting down existing oil production, are particularly disconcerting to Ecuadorian and international oil and wood interests. Many speculate that political pressure from these economic powerhouses was behind a major blow to the Initiative this past January, when Correa, in one of his regular Saturday radio broadcasts, suddenly blasted the negotiations as "shameful," and a threat to the nation's "sovereignty" and "dignity." He threatened that if the full package of international commitments was not in place by this June, he would begin extracting oil from ITT.

Correa's comments spurred the resignations of four critical members of the negotiating commission, including Chancellor Fander Falconí, a longtime ally in Correa's PAIS party, and Roque Sevilla, an ecologist, businessman, and ex-Mayor of Quito whom Correa had picked to lead the commission. Ecuador's Ambassador to the UN Francisco Carrion also resigned from the commission, as did World Wildlife Fund president Yolanda Kakabadse.

Correa has been clear from the outset that the government has a Plan B, to extract the oil, and that the non-extraction "first option" is contingent on the mandated monetary commitments. But oddly his outburst came as the negotiating team's efforts were bearing fruit. Sevilla told the press in January of commitments in various stages of approval from Germany, Spain, Belgium, France, and Switzerland, totaling at least $1.5 billion. The team was poised to sign an agreement with UNDP last December in Copenhagen to administer the fund. Correa called off the signing at the last minute, questioning the breadth of the Initiative's conservation efforts and UNDP's proposed six-person administrative body, three appointed by Ecuador, two by contributing nations, and one by UNDP. This joint control structure apparently sparked Correa's tirade about shame and dignity.

Within a couple of weeks of the blowup, the government had backpedaled, withdrawing the June deadline, appointing a new negotiating team, and reasserting the position that the government's "first option" is to leave the oil in the ground. At the same time, Petroecuador began work on a new pipeline near Yasuní, part of the infrastructure needed for ITT production, pursuant to a 2007 Memorandum of Understanding with several foreign oil companies.

Amid the doubts and mixed messages, proponents are fighting to save the Initiative as a cornerstone in the creation of a post-petroleum Ecuador and ultimately a post-petroleum world. In media interviews after his resignation, Sevilla stressed that he would keep working to ensure that the Initiative would not fail. The Constitution provides for a public referendum prior to extracting oil from protected areas like Yasuní, he noted. "If the president doesn't want to assume his responsibility as leader...let's pass the responsibility to the public." In fact, 75% of respondents in a January poll in Quito and Guayaquil, the country's two largest cities, indicated that they would vote to not extract the ITT oil.

Martinez and Sáenz concur that just as the Initiative emerged from widespread organizing efforts, its success will come from the people. "This is the moment to define ourselves and develop an economic model not based on petroleum," Salazar says. "We have other knowledge, we have minerals, water. We need to change our consciousness and end the economic dependence on one resource." ❑

Resources: Live Yasuni, Finding Species, Inc., liveyasuni.org; "S.O.S. Yasuni" sosyasuni.org; "Yasuni-ITT: An Initiative to Change History," Government of Ecuador, yasuni-itt.gov.ec.

Article 6.5

FRACKONOMICS
The Science and Economics of the Gas Boom

BY ROBERT LARSON
July/August 2013

Between 1868 and 1969, Cleveland's Cuyahoga River caught fire at least ten times, including one blaze that reached the Standard Oil refinery where storage tanks detonated. Ultimately, the seemingly impossible and unnatural phenomenon of burning water came to represent the dangers of unregulated industrial development and generated popular support for the environmental laws of the 1970s, including the Clean Water Act and the Safe Drinking Water Act.

Today the unsettling sight of burning water has returned, from a new industry that is exempt from both these laws. In homes near installations using the drilling technique known as hydraulic fracturing, or "fracking," the tap water has been known to ignite with the touch of a lighter. The industry is relatively new, so the scientific literature yields only tentative results and provisional research conclusions. But the early research suggests fracking has serious negative consequences for public health and local ecology, from flaming tap water to toxic chemicals to ground tremors. Industry spokesmen insist that the negative side-effects of fracking are insignificant. But there's one positive side-effect everyone should be able to agree upon: fracking is an ideal vehicle for explaining key economic concepts of market failure and market power, including *externalities*, *asymmetrical information*, and *regulatory capture*, along with brand-new ones, like *science capture*. Let's start with the firewater.

Liar Liar, Taps on Fire

In the fracking process, natural gas (methane) is released from shale rock strata up to a mile underground, by injecting millions of gallons of water, along with sand and a variety of synthetic chemicals. The huge pressure of the water makes new cracks in the rock, allowing the gas to dissolve and be extracted. Fracking is now responsible for 30% of U.S. electricity production and for heating half of all U.S. homes. The national and business media have breathlessly reported huge growth in gas production, and the oil-and-gas industry projects that North America will return to exporting energy by 2025. Besides the sheer growth in production, the *Wall Street Journal* reported earlier this year, the fracking boom has brought other economic benefits, "improving employment in some regions and a rebound in U.S.-based manufacturing," and "greater defense against overseas turmoil that can disrupt energy supplies."

As made notorious by the documentary *Gasland*, water supplies are a major focus of concern about fracking, especially since the emergence of dramatic footage of a number of Pennsylvania homes, near fracking pads above the Marcellus Shale formation, producing fireballs from the kitchen tap. Duke University earth scientists conducted a more rigorous exploration of this phenomenon, published in the *Proceedings of the National Academy of the Sciences*. They surveyed rural Pennsylvanian water wells for residential use, measuring concentrations of methane, the main chemical component of natural gas. Concentrations rose far above natural levels closer to drill pads, spiking within one kilometer of active gas development sites to a level that "represents a potential explosion hazard." It was also found that the specific gas chemistry in the wells matched those produced through drilling, rather than through naturally occurring compounds. As the gas boom goes "boom," the cautious scientists conclude: "Greater stewardship, knowledge, and—possibly—regulation are needed to ensure the sustainable future of shale-gas extraction."

In parts of the country where water is scarcer, the issue is more ominous. The Environmental Protection Agency (EPA) and U.S. Geological Survey have found toxic alcohols, glycols, and carcinogenic benzene in underground aquifers in Wyoming, evidence that fracking has tainted precious underground water supplies. In press accounts, local residents who requested the study "expressed gratitude to the EPA, and perhaps a bit of veiled doubt about the zeal of local and state regulators." In parched Texas, the volume of water adequate for irrigating $200,000 worth of crops can be used to frack $2.5 billion-worth of gas or oil. The *Wall Street Journal* reports that "companies have been on a buying spree, snapping up rights to scarce river water—easily outbidding traditional users such as farmers and cities." A Texan rancher relates: "They're just so much bigger and more powerful than we are…We're just kind of the little ant that gets squashed."

Top-Secret Ingredients

The heavy use of often-secret synthetic chemicals has also cast a shadow over the fracking debate. Bloomberg News reported in 2012 that energy companies and well operators were refusing to disclose the chemical formulas of thousands of substances used in the fracking process, enough to "keep [the] U.S. clueless on wells." Many states have instituted a self-reporting law, modeled on one first developed in Texas, allowing drillers to withhold the ingredients used in their chemical mixes. Bloomberg reports that drillers "claimed similar exemptions about 19,000 times" in the first eight months of 2012 alone. The congressional exemption of the industry from federal water requirements (discussed below) makes this non-disclosure possible, so that "neighbors of fracked wells … can't use the disclosures to watch for frack fluids migrating into creeks, rivers and aquifers, because they don't know what to look for."

This development is a perfect example of what economists call *asymmetric information*, where one participant in a transaction knows relevant information that is unknown to the other party. The lack of information on one side can put the other party at an advantage, like the seller of a used car who knows more about the car's problems than the prospective buyer. For example, a team of Colorado endocrinologists set out to catalogue these synthetic compounds used in wells across the country, based on regulatory filings. The survey was limited due to the "void of environmental authority" to compel chemical disclosure, and thus the data sheets and reports are "fraught with gaps in information about the formulation of the products." Many of these reports only specify the general chemical class or use the label "proprietary," providing no additional information. Ultimately, the scientists found that over 75% of the chemicals were harmful for the sensory organs, nearly half could affect the nervous and immune systems, and 25% could cause "cancer and mutations."

Another report by Colorado scientists observed that fracking development is increasingly located "near where people live, work, and play." The study used air sampling to find strongly elevated health risks within a radius of about half a mile from fracking sites. The effects ranged from "headaches and eye irritation" up to "tremors, temporary limb paralysis, and unconsciousness at higher exposures." A larger review by Pennsylvania scientists reached similar conclusions, based on local resident reporting and finding a match of over two-thirds "between known health effects of chemicals detected and symptoms reported."

The scientists caution that their findings "do not constitute definitive proof of cause and effect," but they do "indicate the strong likelihood that the health of people living in proximity to gas facilities is being affected by exposure to pollutants from those facilities." They frequently advocate the *precautionary principle*—that careful study showing that a product or process is *not* harmful should precede its use—as when they recommend "health impact assessments before permitting begins," and note that "scientific knowledge about the health and environmental impacts of shale gas development ... are proceeding at a far slower pace than the development itself." These conclusions contradict the industry's claim that fracking is both safe for public health and not in need of any further study. Especially considering the earthquakes.

Tectonic Economics

Perhaps more alarming than the burning water and secret chemicals is the association of fracking with earthquakes. An early report of this development came from the Oklahoma Geological Survey, which surveyed the timing of tremors and their proximity to fracking sites and found a "strong correlation in time and space" and thus "a possibility these earthquakes were induced by hydraulic fracturing." Earthquake epicenters were mostly within two miles of wells, and any earthquake disruption or damage caused by fracking-related activities represents an *externality*, a side effect of an economic transaction that affects parties outside the transaction.

These findings are backed up by a review in the prestigious research journal *Science*, in which cautious scientists note that fracking *itself* is not responsible for "the earthquakes that have been shaking previously calm regions." Yet they find that the induced earthquakes do arise from "all manner of other energy-related fluid injection—including deep disposal of fracking's wastewater, extraction of methane from coal beds, and creation of geothermal energy reservoirs." A surveyed area in Arkansas typically had about two quakes a year, before the beginning of fracking-water disposal. The year water disposal began, the number rose to ten. The next year, to 54. After water injection was halted, the quakes tapered off. The *Science* authors observe the "strongly suggestive" correlation between water disposal and seismic activity: "The quakes began only after injection began, surged when the rate of injection surged, were limited to the vicinity of the wells, and trailed off after injection was stopped." The scientists' main conclusion is the adoption of the precautionary principle: "look before you leap ... Stopping injection has stopped significant earthquakes within days to a year. ... The new regulations in Ohio and Arkansas at least move in the direction of such a learn-as-you-go approach."

Fracknapping

You might wonder why the EPA has not limited or regulated fracking operations, in light of the combustible water, cancer-causing chemicals, and earthquake clusters. The EPA might well have adopted significant national policies on fracking by now, had the practice not been made exempt from the main national environmental laws in the Energy Policy Act of 2005, an offspring of Dick Cheney's secretive energy committee. The exemptions from the Clean Water Act, the Safe Drinking Water Act, the Clean Air Act, and the Superfund law drastically limit the agency's authority to act on fracking.

The drive to limit even EPA *research* into fracking is decades old. An extensive *New York Times* report, based on interviews with scientists and reviews of confidential files, found that "more than a quarter-century of efforts by some lawmakers and regulators to force the federal government to police the industry better have been thwarted, as EPA studies have been repeatedly narrowed in scope and important findings have been removed." When Congress first directed the EPA to investigate fracking in the 1980s, the *Times* reported, EPA scientists found that some fracking waste was "hazardous and should be tightly controlled." But the final report sent to Congress eliminated these conclusions. An agency scientist relates, "It was like science didn't matter. ... The industry was going to get what it wanted, and we were not supposed to stand in the way."

Similarly, when an EPA public-advisory letter to the state of New York called for a moratorium on drilling, the advice was stripped from the released version. A staff scientist said the redaction was due to "politics," but could as well have said "business power." More importantly, the first major EPA review of fracking found "little or no threat to drinking water." This was an eyebrow-raising claim, given that five of seven members of the peer review panel had current or former energy industry affiliations, a detail noted by agency whistle-blower Weston Wilson. Other studies have been narrowed in scope or colored by similar conflicts of interest. More recently, the agency announced that its study finding contamination of Wyoming groundwater will not be subjected to outside peer review, and that further work instead will be funded directly by industry. As the EPA is presently drafting a brand-new report on the subject, these past embarrassments should be kept in mind.

This brings up the problem of *regulatory capture*, where an industry to be monitored gains major influence over regulators' policies. As mentioned above, fracking is very loosely regulated by the states, which is always a favorite outcome for corporate America since the regulatory resources of state governments are far smaller and the regulators are even more easily dominated than those of the federal government. The industry-sponsored FracFocus website is the state-sanctioned chemical-information clearing house, and a masterpiece of smooth PR design, suggesting clear water and full transparency. But Bloomberg News reports that "more than 40 percent of wells fracked in eight major drilling states last year had been omitted from the voluntary site."

Other state reactions have varied. In 2010, the New York State legislature voted to ban fracking, but then-Governor Paterson vetoed the bill and instead issued a temporary moratorium on the practice, though fracking remains illegal in the New York City watershed. Finally, while the EPA's main study is still pending, the agency has taken some steps, as in 2012 when it required well operators to reduce methane gas emissions from wells and storage pits to limit air pollution. But even here the regulation wears kid gloves: The new moves do not cut into industry profits. In fact, capturing the "fugitive" methane, the agency estimates, will *save* the industry $11 to $19 million annually. Also, the regulation won't take effect until 2015.

Neoclassical Gas

Mainstream, or "neoclassical," economic theory considers itself to have solutions to these problems—solutions centered as always on "free markets." The idea is that if firms create chronic health problems or combustible tap water, market forces should drive up their costs, as landowners learn of these firms' practices and demand higher payment for drilling. But as seen above, even households that have already leased their land for gas development remain unaware of the identities and effects of the obscure synthetic chemicals to which they are exposed. This *informational asymmetry*—the firms know things the landowners don't—significantly attenuates the ability of landowners to make informed choices.

On the other hand, households that are located near a drill pad but uninvolved in licensing the drilling will experience the ill effects as externalities. Neoclassicals suggest these can be fixed through a better property-rights system, where surrounding individuals can sue drillers for injuring their health. But this solution runs up against another problem: proving cause-and-effect from a drilling pad to a particular individual's health problems is extremely difficult. The tobacco industry notoriously made this point in court for many years, arguing that it was impossible to prove if a man's lung cancer was caused by a four-pack-a-day cigarette habit, as opposed to, say, local auto exhaust. If cause-and-effect is hard to prove in court for cigarettes, doing so for air-delivered volatile organic compounds will be almost impossible.

This problem is aggravated by the use of corporate resources to influence research. The showcase example is a study produced by the University of Texas, "Fact-Based Regulation for Environmental Protection in Shale Gas Development." The study gave fracking a guardedly positive bill of health, finding no evidence of negative health impacts. The commercial media gave the study a good deal of favorable attention, until the revelation that the lead researcher, Dr. Charles G. Groat, formerly of USGS, sits on the board of the Plains Exploration & Production Company, a Houston-based energy firm heavily invested in gas development. His compensation from the board was several times his academic salary, and he also held 40,000 shares of its stock. An in-house review by the university was outspoken, saying "the term 'fact-based' would not apply" to the paper, which was "inappropriately selective ... such that they seemed to suggest that public concerns were without scientific basis and largely resulted from media bias." Groat retired from the university the day the review was released, but this practice has become increasingly common from industries under fire for environmental or public-health impacts. Bloomberg News flatly stated that "producers are taking a page from the tobacco industry playbook: funding research at established universities that arrives at conclusions that counter concerns raised by critics." This raises the ugly possibility of *science capture.*

No Frackin' Way

Not that Americans are taking it lying down. A diverse popular coalition successfully fought to block a Gulf Coast gas terminal that stood to inflict major damage on local wildlife. The *Oil & Gas Journal* reports on the "firestorm" of activism: "In an unlikely but massive undertaking, environmental activists, sports fishermen, local politicians, media groups, and other citizens formed a coalition known as the 'Gumbo Alliance' that united opposition to the technology." The Louisiana governor vetoed the project "under considerable public pressure." Elsewhere, local residents have taken action to keep fracking and its negative externalities out of their communities. New York State "fractivists" have won an impressive 55 municipal bans and 105 local moratoriums against fracking, to date. The state's Court of Appeals—New York's highest court—recently upheld the bans against an industry lawsuit. These activist successes are an early challenge to what the *Wall Street Journal* called the new "shale barons."

American job markets remain highly depressed and state budgets are strained. What we need, instead of dogged extraction of every particle of fossil fuels from the ground, is a public employment program geared toward the construction of a new sustainable energy system. This would be a far superior alternative to fracking—on grounds of health, ecology, and employment. It could also serve as a springboard for a broader questioning of the suitability of capitalism for the challenges of the 21st century. That kind of radical approach would see the glass of water as half full, not half on fire. ❑

Sources: Russel Gold, "Gas Boom Projected to Grow for Decades," *Wall Street Journal*, February 28, 2013; Tom Fowler, "US Oil Sector Notches Historic Annual Gusher," *Wall Street Journal*, January 19, 2013; Stephen Osborn, Avner Vengosh, Nathaniel Warner, and Robert Jackson, "Methane contamination of drinking water accompanying gas-well drilling and hydraulic fracturing," *Proceedings of the National Academy of the Sciences*, Vol. 108, No. 20, May 17, 2011; Kirk Johnson, "EPA Links Tainted Water in Wyoming to Hydraulic Fracturing for Natural Gas," *New York Times*, December 8, 2011; Tennille Tracy, "New EPA Findings Test Fracking Site," *Wall Street Journal*, October 11, 2012; Felicity Barringer, "Spread of Hydrofracking Could Strain Water Resources in West, Study Finds," *New York Times*, May 2, 2013; Russel Gold and Ana Campoy, "Oil's Growing Thirst for Water," *Wall Street Journal*, December 6, 2011; Ben Elgin, Benjamin Haas and Phil Kuntz, "Fracking Secrets by Thousands Keep US Clueless on Wells," *Bloomberg News*, November 30, 2012; Theo Colborn, Carol Kwiatkowski, Kim Schultz and Mary Bachran, "Natural Gas Operations form a Public Health Perspective," *Human and Ecological Risk Assessment: An International Journal*, Vol. 17, No. 5, September 20, 2011; Lisa McKenzie,

Roxana Witter, Lee Newman, John Adgate, "Human health risk assessment of air emissions from development of unconventional natural gas resources," *Science of the Total Environment*, Vol. 424, May 1 2012; Nadia Steinzor, Wilma Subra, and Lisa Sumi, "Investigating Links between Shale Gas Development and Health Impacts Through a Community Survey Project in Pennsylvania," *New Solutions*, Vol. 23, No. 1, 2013; Austin Holland, Oklahoma Geological Survey, "Examination of Possibly Induced Seismicity from Hydraulic Fracturing in the Eolga Field, Garvin County, Oklahoma, August 2011; Richard Kerr, "Learning How NOT to Make Your Own Earthquakes," *Science*, Vol. 335, No. 6075, March 23 2012; Zoe Corbyn, "Method predicts size of fracking earthquakes," *Nature* News, December 9, 2011; Ian Urbina, "Pressure Limits Efforts to Police Drilling for Gas," *New York Times*, March 3, 2011; Devlin Barrett and Ryan Dezember, "Regulators Back 'Fracking' in New York," *Wall Street Journal*, July 1, 2011; John Broder, "US Caps Emissions in Drilling for Fuel," *New York Times*, February 4, 2012; Norman Augustine, Rita Colwell, and James Duderstadt, "A Review of the Processes of Preparation and Distribution of the report 'Fact-Based Regulation for Environmental Protection in Shale Gas Development,'" University of Texas at Austin, November 30, 2012; Jim Efsthathiou, "Frackers Fund University Research That Proves Their Case," Bloomberg News, July 23, 2012; Daron Threet, "US offshore LNG terminals face technical, legal maze," *Oil & Gas Journal*, December 24, 2007; Ellen Cantarow, "New York's Zoning Ban Movement Fracks Big Gas," Truthout, May 9, 2013 (Truthout.org); Alyssa Abkowitz, "The New Texas Land Rush," *Wall Street Journal*, April 25, 2013; Daron Threet, "US offshore LNG terminals face technical, legal maze," *Oil & Gas Journal*, December 24, 2007.

Chapter 7

LABOR, UNIONS, AND WORKING CONDITIONS

Article 7.1

OUR TRIPLE JOBS PROBLEM

BY ALEJANDRO REUSS

September/October 2013

If you hear somebody talking about the U.S. "jobs problem," ask them which one they mean. Let's talk about three: First, even as unemployment has inched down, the economy has created barely enough jobs to match population growth. Second, this enormous labor-market "slack" has stifled workers' bargaining power and kept wages low. Third, even with a "tighter" labor market, workers would still be in a weak bargaining position due to the policies of the last thirty-some years, which have undermined unions, the welfare state, and labor-market regulation.

First, the Great Recession has left the United States with an enormous jobs hole. The silver lining of declining unemployment—down from 10% to about 7.5% over the last few years—surrounds a gigantic dark cloud: The employment-to-population ratio fell dramatically during the recession and has hardly budged since. That's because labor-force participation, the percentage of working-age individuals who are employed or looking for work, has plummeted. A stimulus too small to make up for the collapse in private spending and a premature turn toward deficit reduction have helped keep us in this jobs hole.

Next, high unemployment makes it hard for workers to bargain higher wages or better working conditions. Recoveries and booms bring lower unemployment and "tighter" labor markets, which increase workers' bargaining power and should make it easier for them to demand (and win) improvements in pay and conditions. This effect typically kicks in, however, only when the unemployment rate gets quite low—below 5%—and the lethargic employment growth during the last four years means we're a long way from there. With economic growth resuming but wages stagnant, corporate profits now account for a near-record percentage of total income. This helps explain why corporations have been content with policies allowing the crisis to drag on through years of lethargic "recovery."

Finally, the lack of high-quality jobs is no mere cyclical problem. It has been a central problem for three decades. Mainstream economists tend to emphasize the ostensibly inexorable forces of globalization and technological change, insinuating that the lack of good jobs is an unavoidable fact of life.

As economist Dean Baker of the Center for Economic and Policy Research (CEPR) notes, however, there's not much evidence that technological change is faster now than in earlier eras, nor particularly damaging to ordinary workers (as opposed to technical, professional, or managerial employees). Meanwhile, the current form of economic globalization is not some inevitable course of nature, but a result of the distribution of political power in our society. Elites designed laws and treaties to make capital more mobile across international borders—that is, to make it easier for companies to move (or threaten to move) operations to places where wages are lower and regulations weaker.

The current form of globalization, in turn, is only one of several changes undermining workers' bargaining power—along with government and employer attacks on labor unions, the weakening of the welfare state, and the rollback of labor regulations. These factors are missing from the mantra that workers should just resign themselves to the new reality, that the "good jobs" are gone and never coming back. But they're also missing from some well-meaning suggestions for getting those jobs back—whether a more favorable exchange rate, increased education and skills, or industrial policies to create new "blue collar" or "green collar" employment.

Whether a job is good or bad, for the most part, is not an inherent fact of industry or occupation. Manufacturing jobs became "good jobs"—in particular times and places—due to unionization, full-employment policies, labor-market regulations, etc. So-called good jobs in transportation and construction have not "gone" anywhere, but job quality in those sectors has declined due to deunionization, deregulation, and employers' increasing use of contingent labor.

Meanwhile, so-called "bad jobs" in hospitality, maintenance, and other service occupations are not uniformly bad. As Paul Osterman and Beth Shulman note in *Good Jobs America* (2011), food-service workers in Las Vegas, where unions are relatively strong, make about $2 more per hour than in largely non-union Orlando. Hotel room cleaners in Vegas, meanwhile, make about $4 more per hour than in Orlando.

There is nothing that makes food service an intrinsically bad job, any more than something makes factory work or trucking intrinsically good.

The fault, in other words, lies not in our jobs, but in our politics. ❑

Sources: Dean Baker, "Inequality: The Silly Tales Economists Like to Tell," Al Jazeera English, Oct. 30, 2012; Dean Baker, "Technology and Inequality: The Happy Myth," *The Guardian* Unlimited, July 16, 2012; Paul Osterman and Beth Shulman, *Good Jobs America: Making Work Better for Everyone* (Russell Sage Foundation, 2011).

Article 7.2

HOW HIGH COULD THE MINIMUM WAGE GO?

A 70% boost would help millions of workers, without killing jobs.

BY JEANNETTE WICKS-LIM
July/August 2012

The minimum wage needs a jolt—not just the usual fine-tuning—if it's ever going to serve as a living wage. Annual full-time earnings at today's $7.25 federal minimum wage are about $15,000 per year. This doesn't come anywhere near providing a decent living standard by any reasonable definition, for any household, least of all households with children. But among the seventeen states that either have active campaigns to raise their minimum wage or have raised them already this year, none have suggested raising the wage floor by more than 20%.

How high can the minimum wage go? As it turns out, a lot higher. Economists typically examine whether current minimum-wage laws hike pay rates up too high and cause employers to shed workers from their payrolls in response. But the current stockpile of economic research on minimum wages suggests that past increases have not caused any notable job losses. In other words, minimum wages in the United States have yet to be set too high. In fact, if we use past experience as a guide, businesses should be able to adjust to a jump in the minimum wage as great as 70%. That would push the federal minimum wage up to $12.30. In states with average living costs, full-time earnings at $12.30 per hour can cover the basic needs of the typical low-income working household (assuming both adults in two-adult households are employed).

Why is such a large increase possible? It's because minimum-wage hikes—particularly those in the 20-to-30% range adopted in the United States—impose very modest cost increases on businesses. This is true even for the low-wage, labor-intensive restaurant industry. And because these cost increases are so modest, affected businesses have a variety of options for adjusting to their higher labor costs that are less drastic than laying off workers.

Take, for example, the 31% rise in Arizona's state minimum wage in 2006, from $5.15 to $6.75. My colleague Robert Pollin and I have estimated that the average restaurant in Arizona could expect to see its costs rise between 1% and 2% of their sales revenue. What kind of adjustment would this restaurant need to make? A price hike of 1% or 2% would completely cover this cost increase. This would amount to raising the price of a $10.00 meal to $10.20.

To figure out what is the largest increase businesses can adjust to without laying off workers, we can take stock of what we know about how businesses have adjusted in the past and then figure out how much businesses can adjust along those lines.

Let's stick with the example of restaurants, since these businesses tend to experience the largest rise in costs. And let's start with a big increase in the minimum wage: 50%. If we add together all the raises mandated by such an increase in the minimum wage (assuming the same number of workers and hours worked), the raises employers would need to give workers earning wages above the minimum wage to maintain a stable wage hierarchy, and their higher payroll taxes, the total cost increase of a 50% minimum-wage hike would be 3.2% of restaurant sales.

The cost increase that these restaurants need to absorb, however, will actually be even smaller than 3.2% of their sales revenue. That's because when workers' wages rise, workers stay at their jobs for longer periods of time, saving businesses the money they would otherwise have spent on recruiting and training new workers. These savings range between 10% and 25% of the costs from raising the minimum wage. If the higher wage motivates workers to work harder, businesses would experience even more cost savings.

So what would happen if restaurants raised their prices to cover their minimum wage cost increases? One answer is that people may react to the higher prices by eating out less often and restaurant owners would lose business. With a large enough falloff in business, restaurants would have to cut back on their workforce. But it's unlikely that a price increase as small as 3% would stop people from eating out. Think about it: if a family is already willing to pay $40.00 to eat dinner out, it hardly seems likely that a price increase as small as $1.20 would to cause them to forgo all the benefits of eating out like getting together with family or friends and saving time in meal preparation, clean up, and grocery shopping.

Still, let's assume that a 3% price hike actually does influence people to eat out less. The key questions now are how much less and can restaurant owners make up their lost business activity? Economists have found that restaurant patrons do not react strongly to changes in menu prices (economists call this an "inelastic" demand). Estimates from industry research suggest that a price increase of 3% may reduce consumer demand by about 2%.

However, if these small price increases take place within a growing economy—even a slow-growing economy—restaurant owners will probably see basically no change in their sales. This is because as the economy expands and peoples' incomes rise, people eat out more. In an economy growing at a rate of 3% annually, which is slower than average for the U.S. economy, consumer demand for restaurant meals will typically rise by about 2.4%. This would boost sales more than enough to make up for any loss that restaurants may experience from a 3% price increase. In other words, consumers would still eat out more often even after a 50% minimum-wage hike.

After taking account of the ways that restaurants can adjust to the higher labor costs from a minimum wage hike, it turns out that the biggest minimum wage increase that restaurants can absorb while maintaining at least the same level of business activity is 70%. In 2004, Santa Fe, New Mexico, came close to this. Its citywide living-wage ordinance raised the wage floor by 65%—from $5.15 to $8.50. A city-commissioned report after it was put into effect found that "overall employment levels have been unaffected by the living wage ordinance."

However, even if the federal minimum rate were 70% higher, or $12.30, it would still fall short for two major groups of workers. First, one-worker families raising young children need generous income supports in addition to minimum wage earnings to help cover the high cost of raising children. Second, minimum-wage workers who live in expensive areas, such as New York City and Washington, D.C., require affordable housing programs.

A 70% minimum-wage hike is the biggest one-time increase that U.S. businesses can absorb without cutting jobs, but it's not the end of the story. In the future, the minimum wage can inch further upward. For example, it could rise in step with the expanding productive capacity of the U.S. economy, as it did in the 1950s and 1960s. A $12.30 minimum wage today rising each year with worker productivity would reach $17.00 in just over ten years (in 2011 dollars). This wage would be high enough so that a single parent with one child could support a minimally decent living standard. We would finally begin transforming the minimum wage into a living wage for all workers.

Policy discussions around the minimum wage need to move past the debate of whether or not it causes job loss. The evidence is clear: minimum wages, in the range of what's been adopted in the past, do not produce any significant job losses. Now it is time to focus on how we can use minimum wages to maximally support low-wage workers. Can we raise the minimum wage rate to a level we can call a living wage? By my reckoning, we can. ❏

Sources: Jeannette Wicks-Lim and Jeffrey Thompson, "Combining the Minimum Wage and Earned Income Tax Credit Policies to Guarantee a Decent Living Standard to All U.S. Workers" (Political Economy Research Institute, October 2010).

Article 7.3

BATTLING BUSINESS-AS-USUAL UNIONISM
Excerpt: How the Chicago Teachers Did It

BY BRIAN WALSH
May/June 2013

The September 2012 Chicago teachers' strike received a great deal of media attention. To most observers, the newly militant, revitalized Chicago Teachers' Union (CTU), led by fiery president Karen Lewis, seemed to have sprung up overnight. But the strong, confident organization, which battled neoliberal Democrat Rahm Emanuel's political establishment to a draw in Chicago's first teacher strike in 25 years, had its origins much earlier in the battle over the privatization of the city's public schools.

Teacher-activists had been meeting and working with community groups since 2001 to save neighborhood schools from closing. In 2008, angry about the school closures forced by Chicago's "Renaissance 2010" charter-school plans—and frustrated by their union leadership's reluctance to fight back—these teachers formed the Caucus of Rank and File Educators (CORE) in 2008. From there, CORE grew quickly. By 2010, dissatisfaction with top-down leadership, lack of member involvement, and lack of transparency led to a five-slate election for leadership of the CTU. After a May 2010 election and June run-off, candidates from CORE had unseated the incumbents.

The new leadership faced the problems typical of "neoliberal" education reform: teacher evaluations based on high-stakes standardized testing, the institution of merit pay, and management unwillingness to address the overall inequity of the educational system. CORE realized that, in order to succeed, the union would need to empower members to assume school-level contract enforcement and prepare for a pitched contract struggle. They also established partnerships with parents and others to oppose Chicago's neoliberal charter school program and fight for equitable educational opportunities for all the city's students. In other words, CTU's new leadership team recognized that member democracy and community coalitions were vital to preserve both the union and Chicago's public education system.

The union quickly established an internal organizing department to make the transition from a business-unionism model, focused on providing services to a passive membership, to an organizing model promoting member action. It instituted stewards' workshops to organize and train members to initiate activity in their workplaces and in their communities—both on union matters and on broader public issues. It expanded decision-making opportunities for members, such as committee service, in order to increase the number of members able to advocate for themselves and their union. Open, well-attended union meetings are critical to internal democracy and compel the leadership to remain transparent and true to the caucus' original vision. Although many of CORE's most active members now work full-time for the union, monthly union meetings continue to draw substantial numbers of caucus members.

Less than two years after its election, CORE faced a test of its leadership ability as negotiations began with a school district determined to cut costs by increasing class sizes, imposing a longer school day, replacing raises for experience and education with merit pay, and increasing teachers' health-care premiums. The union created a larger bargaining team, drawn from all grade levels, seniority ranges, job categories, and other CTU caucuses. Contract-action committees were organized at each of the city's more than 600 public schools. These committees were charged with keeping their members informed on bargaining issues, and with staying connected with other committees on any new developments. The union emphasized member education. Teachers produced a video responding to the anti-public school teacher propaganda of the 2010 documentary *Waiting for Superman*. CTU organized presentations on the neoliberal privatization agenda championed by Mayor Rahm Emanuel and Chicago public schools CEO Jean-Claude Brizard. (Brizard is a "graduate" of Eli Broad's leadership institute, which trains business people to run school districts with privatization as the goal.) The union held workshops and countless one-on-one conversations with members. These efforts helped teachers understand the larger situation and developed a cadre of activists-leaders ready to take "responsibility if a job action proved necessary," Debby Pope, a retired Chicago teacher working for CTU, told Labor Notes.

The results of CTU's internal organizing were evident by spring 2012, as the union concluded negotiations were going nowhere. Membership grew as agency-fee payers—teachers covered by the union contract, but who had chosen not to join the union and so paid a fee in place of dues—increasingly joined CTU. Throughout the spring, internal union "practice" votes showed overwhelming support for a strike. When schools began reopening in August, CTU conducted informational pickets, broken into groups of ten to support and keep each other

---

The Charter-School Organizing Dilemma

An important and potentially divisive issue facing the union was whether or not to try to organize charter-school teachers. According to CTU staff coordinator Jackson Potter, writing in *Labor Notes*, there are CORE members who "believe charters threaten public schools' very existence and [that] teachers there should be treated as scabs." Others, however, argue that unions need to organize the unorganized, wherever they work, and that these charter-school teachers could become valuable union members. In order to resolve these differences democratically, CORE held member study groups on charter schools, organized meetings at which members could discuss their differences, and ultimately fostered a decision by consensus. Members affirmed the formation, in 2008, of CTU's Charter Outreach Committee.

Since then, the Chicago Alliance of Charter Teachers and Staff (Chicago ACTS), a joint program of CTU, the Illinois Federation of Teachers, and the American Federation of Teachers (AFT), has been working to organize Chicago charter school teachers. As union staff coordinator Jackson Potter told the *New York Times*, "At some point we would like all the charter schools to be part of CTU." By April 2011, twelve of Chicago's 85 charter schools had been unionized through the efforts of the Chicago ACTS. In March 2013, the United Neighborhood Organization, one of Chicago's largest charter-school operators, agreed to remain neutral during an organizing campaign conducted by Chicago ACTS. While charter teachers in other cities have also organized, Chicago is the first city where the major education union has directed the effort, according to the AFT.

informed, and to acquaint members with what they would face during a strike. Jen Johnson, a history teacher at Lincoln Park High School, told *Labor Notes* that"even though [the prospect of][a strike was scary [teachers] weren't horrified by the idea; the teachers were organizationally, mentally and emotionally prepared." When the real strike vote was held in September, 90% of CTU's members authorized the leadership to call a strike if negotiations failed. Once the strike was called, Chicago writer and organizer Howard Ryan reported that red-shirted teacher picket lines were "plenty spirited." CTU's commitment to democracy continued even after an agreement was reached with the district—the strike lasted an additional two days for members to read, discuss, and debate the merits and drawbacks of the tentative agreement. When teachers did vote, they approved the contract with a nearly 80% majority.

While internal organizing and a commitment to democracy helped transform CTU into a dynamic member-run organization, the union also built connections with other community and labor organizations. As union president Karen Lewis wrote in a *Nation* article titled "Fight for the Whole Society," meeting with community stakeholders, especially members of other public-sector unions, is essential to "discuss mutual concerns ... to build bridges of mutual trust." CTU has convened a community board composed of the city's largest and strongest community organizations. The union hopes this board will help parents revamp Chicago's education governance, replacing the current mayoral-appointed school board with an elected one composed of parents, teachers, students, administrators, and other stakeholders. They also hope to replace the the "corporate-oriented schools 'CEO,'" according to the CTU's Jackson Potter, with a "superintendent with an education background."

Teachers' salaries and benefits played only a small part in CTU's decision to strike; negotiators had come very close to a compensation agreement before talks broke down. Rather, the conflict was over two opposing views of education. At the forefront of the struggle, CTU Vice President Jesse Sharkey told *Labor Notes*, were "pedagogical issues," like class size, curriculum, and support services inside schools to address the many needs of poverty-stricken students. The CTU focuses its solutions on getting resources into neighborhood schools—to provide the rich curriculum and social services that students need—as opposed to dismantling the schools in favor of charter schools or privatization, as neoliberal reformers advocate.

The union's research department produced a 45-page report, titled *The Schools Chicago's Children Deserve*, presenting a vision where every child, regardless of socioeconomic status, would receive a world-class education. CTU's commitment to schools and students won it widespread support, reversing the teachers-versus-parents narrative that neoliberal education-reform advocates had pushed. As a result, polls indicated strong public backing for the striking teachers. Parents and students walked the picket lines, held a vigil with community activists outside the mayor's home, and some even occupied a school. These and other actions, including a May 2012 rally and march with Stand Up Chicago, a militant union-sponsored organization, have been notable examples of union-community solidarity.

Where to Now?

The organized labor movement in the United States today, which has mostly become a pale bureaucratic shadow of the corporations it opposes, has been in a freefall for 30 years. The model of business unionism, in which union staff "service" members much like a law firm or insurance company, has proven to be a failure at protecting workers' rights; mostly, national unions function to preserve labor peace. However, union members, operating independently of the official union hierarchy, are fighting back. In order to do so, they've had to jettison the baggage of service unionism and restore democratic member control. Forming alliances with community and other organizations, these organized workers, such as the Chicago teachers, are models for the rest of the labor movement to emulate.

The key lessons—that internal, grassroots democracy and an expansive, accessible vision for society are essential for labor success—can be applied by non-union workers as well. In this time of austerity, when powerful corporate entities are imposing a cost-cutting, rights-shredding agenda, and labor and the working class have had little to celebrate, these women and men have shown how workers can successfully fight back. Indeed, their strategies and tactics might be the only way. ❑

Sources: Stanley Aronowitz, "One, Two, Many Madisons: The War on Public Sector Workers," *New Labor Forum*, June 2011; Steven Ashby, "Standing Up to Corporate School Agenda, Chicago Teachers Greenlight Strike," labornotes.org, Sept. 12, 2012; Jenny Brown, "In a Year of Politicians and Bad News, Surprising Stories of Resistance," *Labor Notes*, January 2013; Ellen David Friedman and Amelia Abromaitis, "Wisconsin Everywhere," *Labor Notes*, Feb. 21, 2011; Norine Gutekanst, "How Chicago Teachers Got Organized to Strike," *Labor Notes*, November 2012; Karen GJ Lewis,."Fight for the Whole Society," in "How Can Labor Be Saved?: A Forum," Josh Eidelson, ed., *The Nation*, March 4, 2013; Dan Mihalopoulos, "UNO charter schools allow teachers to join a union," *Chicago Sun-Times*, March 9, 2013; Theresa Moran, "Behind the Chicago Teachers Strike, labornotes.org, Sept. 10, 2012; Kyle Olson, "Crowd Laughs as Chicago Teachers Union President Talks about Killing the Rich," townhall.com, Jan. 8, 2013; Paul, "Chicago Teachers Hit Core Issues Before Union Elections," labornotes.org, May 20, 2010; Jackson Potter, "Reformers in Chicago Teachers Union Grapple with Leadership Challenges," labornotes.org, Jan. 13, 2011; Howard Ryan, "How Chicago Teachers Reached the Boiling Point," labornotes.org, Sept. 12, 2012; Elizabeth Schulte, "A Victory for Solidarity and Struggle," socialistworker.org, Sept. 19, 2012.; Rebecca Vevea, "Unions Move In at Chicago Charter Schools, and Resistance Is Swift," nytimes.com, April 7, 2011.

Article 7.4

WE'RE NOT LOVIN' IT

Low-wage workers fight to make bad jobs better.

BY NICOLE ASCHOFF
September/October 2013

There's a line in Johnny Paycheck's 1977 hit song that goes "I'd give the shirt right off my back, if I had the guts to say ... Take this job and shove it, I ain't working here no more." In the past year, fast-food, retail, and warehouse workers have shown they do have the guts—but instead of quitting, they're fighting back. From New York to California they're taking to the streets. They're fighting for a living wage, for respect from their bosses, and in some cases, for the right to form a union.

Back in June 2012, eight immigrant workers peeling crawfish under sweatshop conditions for C.J.'s Seafood (then a Walmart supplier) went on strike in Louisiana. They stayed out for weeks, demanding an end to forced labor, wage theft, and other unfair labor practices—and they won. Following up on the C.J.'s workers' successful action, Walmart warehouse workers in California and Illinois walked out in September, calling for improved workplace safety and a fair wage. A month later, Walmart associates walked out at 28 stores in twelve cities. The strikes marked the first time in history that Walmart retail workers had ever gone on strike, and were quickly followed by more strikes and demonstrations on Black Friday, the biggest shopping day of the year.

Walmart workers took a breather after the fall strikes, as they battled an NLRB lawsuit brought by the company and strategized their next action. But low-wage workers in other cities quickly picked up the baton. On November 29, hundreds of fast-food workers staged a one-day strike in New York City. The walkout marked the launch of Fast Food Forward, a new coalition of workers, unions, and community and civil-rights groups working to increase the wages of New York City fast-food workers. By April of this year, more workers were ready to join the fight. In a wave of strikes that would last through June, fast-food and retail workers in New York, Chicago, Seattle, Milwaukee, St. Louis, and Detroit walked off the job. Pickets popped up at KFC, Jimmy John's, Chipotle, Target, McDonald's, Burger King, Popeye's, Long John Silver's, Subway, Sears, Victoria's Secret, and dozens of other establishments. On August 29, a day after the fiftieth anniversary of the March on Washington, workers took to the streets again. Thousands of workers in nearly sixty cities participated in work stoppages, demanding $15 an hour, respect from management, safe working conditions, better hours, and the right to unionize.

What has sparked this upsurge? It's hard to say. Unions have been trying to gain a foothold in the low-wage service sector for decades—a task made more difficult by the declining bargaining power of unions like the United Food and Commercial Workers union (UFCW) in the face of grocery-industry restructuring. When unions were strong, their very presence pushed up wages and working conditions across the industry, and helped inspire workers hoping to organize a union, or move into existing union jobs in restaurants and supermarkets.

But those days are long gone.

Perhaps a major catalyst to the recent strikes is the nature of the "recovery" from the Great Recession. During the downturn, 78% of jobs lost were either mid-wage or high-wage jobs and, according to the Bureau of Labor Statistics (BLS), three out of five newly created jobs are part-time, low-wage jobs. A growing number of Americans is realizing that "good jobs" aren't coming back, and that for things to get better, they're going to have to fight to turn their McJobs into something better.

Myths about Retail and Fast-Food Jobs

Lousy jobs at fast-food joints and retail stores have been around for a long time. Sam Walton (of Walmart) and Ray Kroc (of McDonald's) designed their business models around underpaying their employees. But experts have always brushed off calls to improve these jobs, arguing that they were stepping-stones—summer jobs for teenagers; flexible, part-time jobs for moms; or extra-cash jobs for retirees. It didn't matter that the jobs paid low wages and offered little opportunity for advancement because they weren't designed to support a family or be a career.

But, as good jobs have steadily disappeared over the past three decades, these rationalizations are starting to sound pretty tired. A recent report by Catherine Ruetschlin at the think-tank Dēmos shows that more than 90% of retail workers are over the age of 20 and that, for the vast majority, this is their full-time, long-term occupation. Labor researchers Stephanie Luce and Naoki Fujita paint a similar picture in a study of New York City-area retail workers. According to their survey, the median age of retail workers in New York is 24 years and the average retail worker has been working in the industry for five years.

The Hamster Wheel of Low-Wage Work

Widespread coverage of the strikes suggests growing public concern over the sustainability of a McJobs economy. Dozens of newspapers, magazines, and blogs have covered the walkouts and the plight of low-wage workers, with many telling a similar story: After working for years, or even decades, at the minimum wage, workers have little to show for their efforts. They make poverty-level wages. They don't make enough money to pay their bills and provide for their families. They have to beg their bosses for more hours to put food on the table and make them eligible for healthcare, but they are often rebuffed or told that hours are contingent on working harder. Many workers try to improve their job prospects by combining work and school, but in most cases, their wages don't pay enough for tuition, so they drop out or just take one class at a time.

And many retail and fast-food workers describe horrible working conditions. They get burned by the fryers, assaulted by customers, and humiliated by their bosses. If they ask for sick days or time off to heal from injuries, or speak up about unsafe working conditions, their hours are cut, they get harassed by their supervisors, they get demerits, or they get fired. At the recent Left Forum conference, a Brooklyn KFC worker described a common scenario: While covering a late-night shift, her boss would call her from home, screaming at her to get off the clock because there were not enough customers to justify paying her. The worker would have to finish her shift without pay.

This scenario is not unique to KFC. A recent report put out by Fast Food Forward shows that, of the 500 fast-food workers surveyed, nearly 85% had experienced some form of wage theft by their employer. The report corroborates the findings of a major study conducted by the National Employment Law Project (NELP) in 2008. The NELP study demonstrated severe and widespread workplace violations in low-wage industries across the United States, ranging from minimum wage, overtime, and "off-the-clock" violations, employer retaliation and discrimination, and straight-up theft through tip-stealing, illegal payroll deductions, and pay-stub violations (see sidebar). Sophisticated workflow software exacerbates the problem. In recent years, companies like Microsoft have put out new software that enables managers to schedule workers down to the minute, calling them in for two-to-four-hour shifts once or twice a week, and telling them to be on call all other days.

Does It Have to Be This Way?

Big companies and business organizations like the National Restaurant Association and the National Retail Association are vocal in their opposition to wage increases. Spokespeople for Walmart and Target argue that low wages are necessary to keep prices low and provide jobs in the communities where they operate. In a recent op-ed for the *Washington Post*, Walmart general regional manager Alex Barron argued against legislation to increase the pay of workers at big-box stores in Washington, D.C., claiming higher wages would "result in fewer jobs, higher prices and fewer total retail options."

In fast food, the argument against increasing wages is slightly different. Companies like KFC (owned by Yum! Brands) and McDonald's are dominated by franchisees who rent their businesses from the parent corporation. These franchise owners claim that their margins are paper thin as a result of parent company demands, so they simply can't increase wages and stay in business. The Employment Policies Institute, a Washington, D.C., business lobbying group, reiterated this argument recently in a full-page scare ad published in *USA Today*. The ad warned workers that, if the $15 campaign was successful, owners would be forced to replace workers with "less-costly, automated alternatives like touch-screen ordering and payment devices."

A number of scholars have challenged these arguments, particularly Walmart's low-wages-for-low-prices ultimatum. University of Colorado-Denver management professor Wayne Cascio has shown, through a comparison of Walmart/Sam's Club and Costco, that low wages are not necessary for high profits and productivity. Costco employees average roughly $35,000 per year ($17 per hour), while Sam's Club workers average roughly $21,000 per year ($10 per hour) and Walmart workers earn an average of less than $9 an hour. Costco also provides its workers predictable, full-time work and health benefits. However, contrary to popular assumptions, Costco actually scores higher in relative financial and operating performance than Walmart. Its stores are more profitable and more productive, and its customers and employees are happier.

Costco is not exceptional. Zeynep Ton, of MIT's Sloan School of Management, has studied retail operations for a decade and argues that "the presumed tradeoff between investment in employees and low prices can be broken." "High-road" employers like Trader Joe's, Wegmans, and the Container Store have all found ways to make high profits and provide decent jobs. Catherine Ruetschlin's research shows that a modest wage increase—bumping up the average annual salary of Walmart or Target workers to $25,000—would barely make a dent in big retailers' bottom line, costing them the equivalent of about 1% of total sales. Even if a company like Walmart passed on half the cost of the increase to customers, the average customer would pay roughly $17 more per year, or about 15 cents per shopping visit. And, considering most low-wage workers spend nearly their entire paycheck on necessities, the industry would see a boost in sales ($4 billion to $5 billion more per year) to its own workers. Fast-food companies are highly profitable. McDonald's alone saw profits more than double between 2007 and 2011. They could easily send some of these profits downstream to franchise owners and workers.

So why do most big retailers and fast-food chains insist on a bad-jobs or "low road" model? There are a few reasons. MIT's Ton argues that labor costs are a large, controllable expense, and retailers generally view them as a "cost-driver" rather than a "sales-driver." Store-level managers are pressured by higher-ups to control labor costs as a percentage of weekly or monthly sales. And because store managers have no control over sales (or merchandise mix, store layout, prices, etc.) they respond to pressure from above by cutting employment or forcing workers to work off-the-clock when sales dip. Another factor is financialization—the increasing dominance of finance in the economy. Firms feel a lot of pressure from Wall Street to be a Walmart and not a Costco. As Gerald Davis has argued, the rise of finance and the dominance of "shareholder value" rhetoric have resulted in an emphasis on short-term profits that register in increased share prices and big CEO bonuses.

Perhaps the main reason why companies refuse to invest in creating good jobs is that they can. In this era of neoliberalism, there is little external pressure from unions, community groups, or the government forcing companies to create jobs that

Rampant Wage-Theft and Abuse

A 2008 study by the National Employment Law Project (NELP) sought to uncover the scope of exploitative and coercive managerial practices that violate workers' legal rights. As expected, the abuses were myriad. The most common one? Wage-theft. According to the NELP report:
- Over 25% of workers interviewed were regularly paid below the minimum wage.
- Nearly 20% did not receive proper compensation for overtime.
- Nearly 17% had not been paid for off-the-clock work in the previous week.

The managers responsible for workplace abuses exhibit a disregard for labor rights that does not stop at underpayment of wages. The NELP study found many workers still remain in harm's way:
- 12% of tipped workers had experienced tip-theft within the previous week.
- 20% of workers had withheld complaints of wage-theft, dangerous conditions, or similar violations from their employer for fear of retaliation.
- 50% of workers who had filed for workers' compensation faced illegal managerial intimidation in reaction their claim. Common tactics include: Denying the claim, calling immigration, or even firing the worker.   —Aaron Markiewitz

offer a predictable, full-time workweek paying decent wages and benefits. When ten Walmart butchers in Jacksonville, Tex., voted for a collective-bargaining agreement in 2000, the company simply negated their decision by eliminating delis from every one of its stores in the United States and switching to pre-packaged meat. Even companies with a positive image like Costco have dumped millions of dollars into fighting pro-worker legislation like the Employee Free Choice Act, preferring a paternalistic strategy over unionization.

The Alt-Labor Upsurge

The organizations behind the recent fast-food and retail actions, and even the demands of the strikers themselves, vary considerably. However, one unifying characteristic across the movement is the absence of traditional union-organizing strategies, pushing many observers to classify the movement as an alternative labor, or "alt-labor" movement. "Alt-labor" is shorthand for organizations and campaigns that eschew old-school, one-worksite, one-union strategies, in favor of less risky, and often more effective, community-based methods of organizing and outreach.

Alt-labor strategies are not actually new. Workers adopted them in the 1930s, and organizations like New Labor in New Brunswick, N.J., have been around for years, fighting against wage theft and unsafe workplaces. But as labor scholar Janice Fine notes, non-traditional labor organizations have become increasingly important during the past two decades. New organizations like Brooklyn's New York Communities for Change (out of the ashes of ACORN) have appeared on the scene and are registering real gains. NYCC worked as part of WASH New York, a hybrid labor/community group organizing *washeros* at Astoria Car Wash & Hi-Tek in Queens. The groundbreaking campaign resulted in the first collective-bargaining agreement for New York car-wash workers. NYCC is also behind Fast Food Forward, another hybrid group that is organizing fast-food workers in Brooklyn, using community support networks to help workers stand up for better wages, hours, and working conditions.

The wave of fast-food and retail strikes that spread from New York to St. Louis, Detroit, Seattle, and other cities in April was spearheaded by broad coalitions like Fast Food Forward. These coalitions are comprised of unions like the Service Employees International Union (SEIU), religious organizations, alt-labor groups like Jobs With Justice, community groups, and immigrant-rights groups. They also share common goals—Fast Food Forward, the St. Louis Organizing Committee, the Workers Organizing Committee of Chicago, and other coalitions in Milwaukee, Detroit, and Seattle are all calling for $15 an hour and the right to organize a union. And rather than organizing through one union, one store at a time, the coalitions are targeting the industry as a whole, staging one-day protests designed to inspire other workers and call attention to their struggle.

The Organization United for Respect at Walmart (OUR Walmart) is the grassroots organization behind the Walmart campaign. OUR Walmart gets much of its funding from UFCW and differs from the fast-food campaigns in that it is explicitly not seeking to form a union. Instead, OUR Walmart's goal is to build a worker-community support network that can pressure Walmart to improve its wages, hours, and working conditions without a collective-bargaining agreement. OUR Walmart has organized short (one-hour or one-day) simultaneous strikes that spotlight Walmart's abuses, while limiting the risk for workers involved. The strategy comes from decades of failing to crack Walmart using traditional organizing strategies.

Many labor scholars laud the actions of these coalitions, but don't see the alt-labor formations as a long-term solution. They argue that because the organizations are funded by external sources like unions, religious organizations, and grants, rather than by members, the organizations will eventually fade away after workers achieve initial successes and the public loses interest. Without a concerted, long-term strategy to unionize, workers will have no way to cement their gains, and will have to keep hitting the streets.

This may be the case, but for many workers, they've got nothing left to lose. There are so few good jobs out there that all strategies with the potential to make bad jobs better and increase wages need to be on the table. Fast-food and retail workers are showing they've got the guts to try something new, and if the past year is sign of things to come, one of these days we might finally have something to sing about on Labor Day. ❑

Sources: Catherine Ruetschlin, "Retail's Hidden Potential: How Raising Wages would Benefit Workers, the Industry and the Overall Economy," Dēmos, November 2012; Stephanie Luce and Naoki Fujita, "Discounted Jobs: How Retailers Sell Workers Short," Murphy Institute, City University of New York and Retail Action Project, 2012; Wayne F. Cascio, "Decency Means More than 'Always Low Prices': A Comparison of Costco to Walmart's Sam's Club," *Academy of Management Perspectives*, August 2006; Zeynep Ton, "Why Good Jobs are Good for Retailers," *Harvard Business Review*, January-February 2012; Gerald Davis, *Managed by the Markets: How Finance Re-Shaped America*, Oxford University Press, USA, 2009; Janice Fine, *Worker Centers: Organizing Communities at the Edge of the Dream*, ILR Press, 2006; Annette Bernhardt, et al., "Broken Laws, Unprotected Workers: Violations of Employment and Labor Laws in America's Cities," National Employment Law Project, 2008 (available at unprotectedworkers.org).

Article 7.5

AFTER HORROR, APOLOGETICS

Sweatshop apologists cover for intransigent U.S. retail giants.

BY JOHN MILLER
September/October 2013

> Bangladesh just isn't rich enough to support the sort of worker safety laws that we have ourselves. ...
>
> [S]horter working hours ... , safer workplaces, unemployment protections and the rest ... are the products of wealth. ...
>
> [A]ll of us who would like to see those conditions improve ... should be cheering on the export led growth of that Bangladeshi economy.
>
> —Tim Worstall, "Sadly, Bangladesh Simply Cannot Afford Rich World Safety And Working Standards," *Forbes*, April 28, 2013.

The April 24 collapse of the Rana Plaza building, just outside of Dhaka, Bangladesh's capital city, killed over 1,100 garment workers toiling in the country's growing export sector.

The horrors of the Rana Plaza disaster, the worst ever in the garment industry, sent shockwaves across the globe. In the United States, the largest single destination for clothes made in Bangladesh, newspaper editors called on retailers whose wares are made in the country's export factories to sign the legally binding fire-and-safety accord already negotiated by mostly European major retailers. Even some of the business press chimed in. The editors of *Bloomberg Businessweek* admonished global brand-name retailers that safe factories are "not only right but also smart." But just two U.S. retailers signed on, while most opted to sign a non-legally-binding ersatz accord.

The business press, however, also turned their pages over to sweatshop defenders, contrarians who refuse to let the catastrophic loss of life in Bangladesh's export factories shake their faith in neoliberal globalization. Tim Worstall, a fellow at London's free-market Adam Smith Institute, told *Forbes* readers that "Bangladesh simply cannot afford rich world safety and working standards." Economist Benjamin Powell, meanwhile, took the argument that sweatshops "improve the lives of their workers and boost growth" out for a spin on the *Forbes* op-ed pages.

The sweatshop defenders are twisting Bangladesh workers' need for more and better jobs into a case for low wages and bad working conditions. Their misleading arguments, moreover, are no excuse for major U.S. retailers to refuse to sign onto the European-initiated safety agreement, a truly positive development in the fight against sweatshops.

More Jobs, Not More Sweatshops

Bangladesh is "dirt poor," as Worstall puts it. The country is on the United Nations' list of 46 Least Developed Countries. Its gross domestic product (GDP) per capita, the most common measure of economic development, is about one-fiftieth that of the United States.

The garment industry is the leading sector of the Bangladeshi economy, responsible for some 80% of total exports by value. Bangladesh's garment exports tripled between 2005 and 2010, boosting the nation's growth rate. By 2011, Bangladesh was the third-largest exporter of clothes in the world, after China and Italy.

On top of that, the garment industry has provided much-needed jobs. Bangladesh has about 5,000 garment factories that employ 3.6 million workers, the vast majority of them women. Wages for women in the garment industry were 13.7% higher than wages for women with similar years of education and experience in other industries in Bangladesh, according to a 2012 study. And the most common alternative employments for women, such as domestic service and agriculture labor, pay far less than factory jobs.

Still, none of that is a good reason to endorse sweatshops.

While Bangladesh's garment industry boosted economic growth and added to employment, neither its horrific working conditions nor its dismally low wages improved without government intervention.

Rana Plaza was a deathtrap. But it was only the latest tragedy to have struck Bangladeshi workers sewing garments for major U.S. and European retailers. Less than five months earlier, a devastating fire at Tazreen Fashions, a garment factory not far from Rana Plaza, killed 117 workers. In addition to the 1,129 workers killed at Rana Plaza, more than 600 garment workers have died in factory fires in Bangladesh since 2005, according to *Fatal Fashion*, a 2013 report published by the Centre for Research on Multinational Corporations (SOMO). From 2000 to 2010, wages in the garment industry remained flat, according to a survey conducted by War on Want, a British nonprofit. Even after the minimum wage in the garment industry nearly doubled in 2010, itself part of the fight against sweatshop conditions, wages remained among the lowest in the world. A seamstress in Bangladesh earns less than $50 a month, versus $100 in Vietnam and $235 in China, according to World Bank data. The bottom line, as *Businessweek* puts it, is that "Bangladesh's $18 billion garment industry relies on super-low wages and women desperate for work."

This does not mean that trying to improve these conditions is a futile undertaking. Safer working conditions and higher wages are unlikely to stand in the way of investment in Bangladesh's garment industry and job creation.

Factory costs, including wages, make up only a small portion of the overall cost of most garments. Leading Bangladesh garment makers told *Businessweek* that their total factory costs for a $22 pair of jeans was just 90 cents. That's just 4% of the price paid by consumers. On the other hand, a 2009 study of the sales in a major New York retail store found that the company could use "social labeling" to charge up to 20% more and still expect sales revenues to rise. In other words, doubling the wages paid to Bangladeshi garment workers and at the same time improving working conditions would not have to diminish retailer revenues.

Nor does improving worker safety have to be that expensive. The Worker Rights Consortium, an independent labor-rights monitoring group, estimates that it would cost an average of $600,000 to elevate each of Bangladesh's 5,000 factories to Western safety standards, for a total of $3 billion. If the $3 billion were spread over five years, it would add an average of less than 10 cents to the price paid by retail companies for each of the 7 billion garments that Bangladesh sells each year to Western brands.

How to Stop Sweatshop Abuse

For sweatshop apologists like Worstall and Powell, yet more export-led growth is the key to improving working and safety conditions in Bangladesh. "Economic development, rather than legal mandates," Powell argues, "drives safety improvements." Along the same lines, Worstall claims that rapid economic growth and increasing wealth are what improved working conditions in the United States a century ago, and that those same forces, if given a chance, will do the same in Bangladesh.

But their arguments distort the historical record and misrepresent the role of economic development in bringing about social improvement. Working conditions have not improved because of market-led forces alone, but due to economic growth combined with the very kind of social action that sweatshops defenders find objectionable.

U.S. economic history makes that much clear. It was the 1911 Triangle Shirtwaist fire, which cost 146 garment workers their lives, along with the hardships of the Great Depression, that inspired the unionization of garment workers and led to the imposition of government regulations to improve workplace safety. Those reforms, combined with the post-World War II economic boom, nearly eliminated U.S. sweatshops.

Since then, declining economic opportunity, severe cutbacks in inspectors, and declining union representation have paved the way for the return of sweatshops to the United States. This trend further confirms that economic development, by itself, will not eliminate inhuman working conditions.

In contrast, a combination of forces that could eliminate sweatshops is forming in Bangladesh today. Despite the government's record of repressing labor protest and detaining labor leaders, the horror of the Rana Plaza collapse has sparked massive protests and calls for unionization in Bangladesh. In reaction, the government has amended its labor laws to remove some of the obstacles to workers forming unions, although formidible obstacles remain (including the requirement that at least 30% of the workers at an entire company—not at a single workplace as in the United States—be members of a union before the government will grant recognition).

Meanwhile, 80 mostly European retail chains that sell Bangladesh-made garments have signed the legally binding Accord on Fire and Building Safety in Bangladesh. For the first time, apparel manufacturers and retailers will be held accountable for the conditions in the factories that make their clothes. This "joint liability" aspect, a long-held goal of labor-rights advocates, is precisely what makes this international accord so important.

Negotiated with worker-safety groups and labor unions, the five-year accord sets up a governing board with equal numbers of labor and retail representatives, and a chair chosen by the International Labor Organization (ILO). An independent inspector will conduct audits of factory hazards and make the results public. Corrective actions recommended by the inspector will be mandatory and retailers will be forbidden from doing business with noncompliant facilities. Each retailer will contribute to the cost of implementing the accord based on how much they produce in Bangladesh, up to a maximum of $2.5 million over five years to pay for administering the safety plan and pick up the tab for factory repairs and renovations. The accord subjects disputes between retailers and union representatives to arbitration, with decisions enforceable by a court of law in the retailer's home country.

The signatories include Swedish retailer Hennes and Mauritz, which has more of its clothes made in Bangladesh than any other company; Benetton Group S.p.A., the Italian retailer whose order forms were famously found in the rubble of the collapsed Rana Plaza factory; and Canada's Loblow Companies, whose Joe Fresh clothing was also found at Rana Plaza. Together, their clothes are made in over 1,000 of Bangladesh's 5,000 factories.

However, only two U.S. companies, Abercrombie & Fitch and PVH (parent of Tommy Hilfiger and Calvin Klein), have signed the accord. Walmart, The Gap, J.C. Penney, Sears, and the rest of the major U.S. retailers doing business in Bangladesh have refused. The industry trade group, the National Retail Federation, objected to the accord's "one-size-fits-all approach" and its "legally questionable binding arbitration provision" that could bring disputes to court in the highly litigious United States. Several of those retailers cobbled together an alternative agreement signed so far by 17 mostly U.S. retailers.

But their "company-developed and company-controlled" plan, as a coalition of labor-rights groups described it, falls well short of the European-initiated plan. It is not legally binding and lacks labor organization representatives. Moreover, while retailers contribute to the implementation of their safety plan, they will face no binding commitment to pay for improving conditions. An AFL-CIO spokesperson put it most succinctly: "This is a matter of life or death. Quite simply, non-binding is just not good enough." ❑

Sources: Benjamin Powell, "Sweatshops in Bangladesh Improve the Lives of Their Workers, and Boost Growth," *Forbes*, May 2, 2013; Centre for Research on Multinational Corporations (SOMO) and Clean Clothes Campaign, *Fatal Fashion*, March 2013; International Labor Rights Forum, "Accord on Fire and Building and Safety in Bangladesh," May 13, 2012; Michael Hiscox and Nicholas Smyth, "Is There Consumer Demand for Improved Labor Standards: Evidence from Field Experiments in Social Labeling," Department of Government, Harvard University, 2012; Rachel Heath and Mushfiq Mubarak, "Does Demand or Supply Constrain Investments in Education? Evidence from Garment Sector Jobs in Bangladesh," Aug. 15, 2012; Rubana Huq, "The Economics of a $6.75 Shirt," *Wall Street Journal*, May 16, 2003; "Halfhearted Labor Reform in Bangladesh," *New York Times*, July 17, 2013; International Labour Organization, "A Handbook on the Bangladesh Labour Act, 2006"; Renee Dudley, "Bangladesh Fire Safety to Cost Retailers $3 Billion, Group Says," *Bloomberg Businessweek*, Dec. 10, 2012; Mehul Srivastava and Arun Deynath, "Bangladesh's Paradox for Poor Women Workers," *Bloomberg Businessweek*, May 9, 2013; Mehul Srivastava and Sarah Shannon, "Ninety Cents Buys Safety on $22 Jeans in Bangladesh," *Bloomberg Businessweek*, June 6, 2013; "Bloomberg View: How to Fix Bangladesh's Factories," *Bloomberg Businessweek*, May 2, 2013; Steven Greenhouse and Stephanie Clifford, "U.S. Retailers Offer Plan For Safety at Factories," *New York Times*, July 10, 2013; Alliance for Bangladesh Worker Safety, "Alliance of Leading Retailers in North America Join Forces in Comprehensive, Five-Year Commitment to Improve Factory Safety Conditions For Workers in Bangladesh," press release, July 10, 2013.

Article 7.6

THE WAGES OF GENDER

BY GERALD FRIEDMAN
September/October 2013

Fifty years ago, in June 1963, President John F. Kennedy signed the Equal Pay Act, forbidding what he called the "unconscionable practice of paying female employees less wages than male employees for the same job." While acknowledging that "much remains to be done to achieve full equality of economic opportunity," he pronounced the law a "significant step forward."

Women have made much progress since then because of anti-discrimination legislation and the work of millions of activists to open occupations previously closed to women. The gap between men's and women's wages has narrowed significantly, and women have gained access to a broad range of professional and managerial occupations. With these economic gains, the balance of power between the genders and within families has changed because women can support themselves and their families even without a husband.

A great deal, however, still remains to be done. Women still earn less than men for reasons tied to gender—including outright discrimination in many occupations as well as the continued expectation that women will bear the primary responsibility for childcare and other household responsibilities. The great progress made in reducing gender disparities over the past decades shows the importance of maintaining political and social movements to eliminate remaining gender inequities.

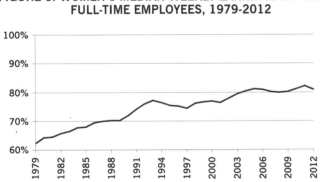

FIGURE 1: WOMEN'S MEDIAN WEEKLY EARNINGS VS. MEN'S, FULL-TIME EMPLOYEES, 1979-2012

The median weekly wage for women employed full time is 81% of the figure for men. While this is a significant shortfall, it is also a significant improvement over the 1979 figure of 62%. While there has been progress in most years, improvement may have slowed. The ratio of women's earnings to men's increased by nearly eight percentage points in the 1980s, five points in the 1990s, and only four points since 2000.

FIGURE 2: WOMEN'S MEDIAN WEEKLY EARNINGS VS. MEN'S, BY AGE GROUP AND YEAR

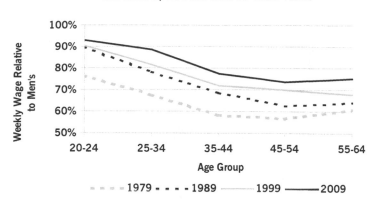

This graph shows median earnings for women compared to men, across different age groups, in 1979, 1989, 1999, and 2009. At least in part because of gender discrimination and the unequal burdens of family care work, women's wages grow more slowly with age than do those of men (reflected in the downward slope of each curve). This pattern has persisted even while women's wages have increased relative to men's for all age groups (reflected in the curve's consistent rise from one decade to the next).

FIGURE 3: PERCENTAGE CHANGE IN INFLATION-ADJUSTED MEDIAN WEEKLY EARNINGS, BY GENDER AND EDUCATION, 1979-2011

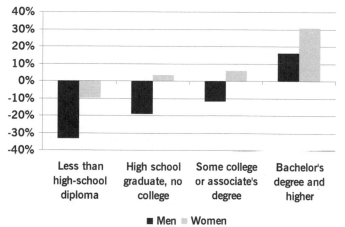

Rising relative earnings for women reflect both the entry of women into higher-paid occupations and rising earnings for women relative to men within occupations. Women's wages have risen relative to men's for all levels of education. For less-educated workers, however, much of the narrowing of the gender wage gap has come because women's wages have fallen less than men's have. Only among college graduates has the gender gap narrowed because wages have risen for both women and men, but have risen faster for women.

FIGURE 4: WOMEN'S MEDIAN WEEKLY EARNINGS VS. MEN'S, BY POSITION IN FEMALE AND MALE INCOME RANKINGS

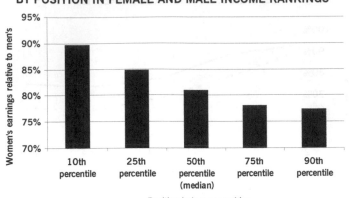

The gender pay gap is greater for higher-income workers. At low-paying jobs, women earn almost as much as men. (Women who are low in the female income ranking make almost 90% as much as men who are low in the male income ranking.) At higher income levels, however, women's pay lags further behind men's. This reflects the continuing exclusion of women from many of the highest-paid occupations and the top positions within occupations—the so-called "glass ceiling."

FIGURE 5: PERCENTAGE OF MARRIED WOMEN WHO EARN MORE THAN THEIR HUSBANDS, 1947-2011

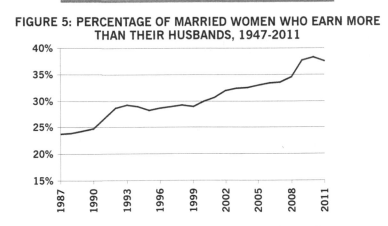

Women earn more than their husbands in a growing share of opposite-sex marriages. This increase is due not only to rising relative wages for women but also to an increase in the proportion of married women working outside the home. In addition, there has been a decline, especially since the beginning of the Great Recession, in the share of married men working outside the home—due both to higher male unemployment and more men dropping out of the labor force altogether. ❏

Sources: Bureau of Labor Statistics (BLS), Weekly and hourly earnings data from the Current Population Survey; BLS, "Highlights of Women's Earnings in 2011," October 2012; BLS, 1988–2012 Annual Social and Economic Supplements to the Current Population Survey (CPS).

Chapter 8

POVERTY AND WEALTH

Article 8.1

THE 99%, THE 1%, AND CLASS STRUGGLE

BY ALEJANDRO REUSS
November/December 2011

Between 1979 and 2007, the income share of the top 1% of U.S. households (by income rank) more than doubled, to over 17% of total U.S. income. Meanwhile, the income share of the bottom 80% dropped from 57% to 48% of total income. "We are the 99%," the rallying cry of the Occupy Wall Street movement, does a good job at calling attention to the dramatic increase of incomes for those at the very top—and the stagnation of incomes for the majority.

This way of looking at income distribution, however, does not explicitly focus on the different *sources* of people's incomes. Most people get nearly all of their incomes—wages and salaries, as well as employment benefits—by working for someone else. A few people, on the other hand, get much of their income not from work but from ownership of property—profits from a business, dividends from stock, interest income from bonds, rents on land or structures, and so on. People with large property incomes

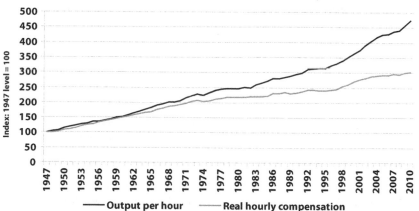

GROWING GAP BETWEEN PRODUCTIVITY AND PAY, 1947-2010

Index: 1947 level = 100

——— Output per hour   ——— Real hourly compensation

Source: Bureau of Labor Statistics, Real Hourly Compensation, Private Business Sector, Series ID number: PRS84006153; Bureau of Labor Statistics, Output Per Hour, Private Business Sector, Series ID number: PRS84006093.

may also draw large salaries or bonuses, especially from managerial jobs. Executive pay, though treated in official government statistics as labor income, derives from control over business firms and really should be counted as property income.

Over the last forty years, the distribution of income in the United States has tilted in favor of capitalists (including business owners, stock- and bond-holders, and corporate executives) and against workers. Between the 1940s and 1960s, U.S. workers' hourly output ("average labor productivity") and workers' real hourly compensation both grew at about 3% per year, so the distribution of income between workers and capitalists changed relatively little. (If the size of a pie doubles and the size of your slice also doubles, your share of the pie does not change.) Since the 1970s, productivity has kept growing at over 2% per year. Average hourly compensation, however, has stagnated—growing only about 1% per year (see figure below). As the gap between what workers produce and what they get paid has increased, workers' share of total income has fallen, and capitalists' share has increased. Since income from property is overwhelmingly concentrated at the top of the income scale, this has helped fuel the rising income share of "the 1%."

The spectacular rise in some types of income—like bank profits or executive compensation—has provoked widespread outrage. Lower financial profits or CEO pay, however, will not reverse the trend toward greater inequality if the result is only to swell, say, profits for nonfinancial corporations or dividends for wealthy shareholders. Focusing too much on one or another kind of property income distracts from the fact that the overall property-income share has been growing at workers' expense.

Workers and employers—whether they like it or not, recognize it or not, prepare for it or not—are locked in a class struggle. Employers in the United States and other countries, over the last few decades, have recognized that they were in a war and prepared for it. They have been fighting and winning. Workers will only regain what they have lost if they can rebuild their collective fighting strength. In the era of globalized capitalism, this means not only building up labor movements in individual countries, but also creating practical solidarity between workers around the world.

A labor resurgence could end workers' decades-long losing streak at the hands of employers and help reverse the tide of rising inequality. Ultimately, though, this struggle should be about more than just getting a better deal. It should be—and can be—about the possibility of building a new kind of society. The monstrous inequalities of capitalism are plain to see. The need for an appealing alternative—a vision of a cooperative, democratic, and egalitarian way of life—is equally stark. ❑

Sources: Bureau of Labor Statistics, Real Hourly Compensation, Private Business Sector, Series ID number: PRS84006153; Bureau of Labor Statistics, Output Per Hour, Private Business Sector, Series ID number: PRS84006093; Congressional Budget Office, Trends in the Distribution of Household Income Between 1979 and 2007 (October 2011) (www.cbo.gov); James Heintz, "Unpacking the U.S. Labor Share," *Capitalism on Trial: A Conference in Honor of Thomas A. Weisskopf,* Political Economy Research Institute, University of Massachusetts-Amherst (September 2011).

Article 8.2

NO THANKS TO THE SUPER-RICH
We don't owe them gratitude for their "superior productivity."

BY ALEJANDRO REUSS
January/February 2012

"Look at the industries that have dramatically improved over the past several decades, and you'll see a pattern: certain super-productive individuals have led the way. These individuals invariably fall under the 1% of income earners-- often the 1% of the 1%. ...

"In no other country are high achievers as free to have a vision, to act on it, to reap the rewards, and to accumulate and reinvest capital--even when they are unpopular, even when 'the 99%' disagree or are resentful or envious.

"So, at a time when the 1% are the easy scapegoats, it's fitting this Thanksgiving to take a moment to thank the 1%--and to be grateful that our country rewards success. And as we approach the new year, let's resolve to keep it that way."

—Alex Epstein, "Let's Give Thanks for the One Percent,"
FoxNews.com, November 23, 2011

Leave it to Fox News to publish an opinion piece, on the eve of Thanksgiving, titled "Let's Give Thanks for the One Percent." Author Alex Epstein, a former fellow of the Ayn Rand Institute, argues that most of "the 1%" (the Occupy Wall Street movement's designation of the richest 1% of the population) "earn their success—through superior productivity that benefits us all."

Is it true that the United States "fosters and rewards productivity like no other," as Epstein argues? Is greater inequality the price we pay for greater economic dynamism? As a first cut, let's compare Gross Domestic Product (GDP) per capita in different high-income countries. Here, the United States ranks second among large industrial countries (excluding small, oil-rich countries, city-states, etc.) behind only Norway. In 2010, Norway's GDP per capita was nearly $56,000, compared to just under $47,000 for the United States. This difference was not a one-year anomaly—Norway's GDP per capita has exceeded that of the United States for over twenty years. One doubts that Epstein would see Nordic social democracy as the kind of society—in which "high achievers [are] free to have a vision, to act on it, to reap the rewards, and to accumulate and reinvest capital"—that fosters high productivity. Yet the GDP figures suggest that it does just that.

Still, second place is not bad. The United States does outpace most of Western Europe on GDP per capita. So maybe Norway is an anomaly, and the more general picture is that the United States and its incentives to "high achievers" vastly outperform Western European "socialism" in fostering productivity. Here, we need to look at a more refined measure, GDP per hour worked, in place of GDP per capita. Average work hours per year vary dramatically among different countries. Workers in many Western European countries enjoy a shorter work week and much longer vacations than workers in the United States. Employed U.S. workers work an average of over 1700 hours per year. Their counterparts in France, Germany, the Netherlands, and Norway, in contrast, average just over 1400 hours. These differences in hours worked explain much of the variation in GDP per capita among these high-income countries. Shifting from GDP per capita to GDP per hour worked, we find that the United States (at about $59/hour) still ranks second to Norway (about $74/hour). The big difference in the rankings, however, is that the gap between the United States and several Western European countries all but disappears. Ireland, The Netherlands, Belgium, and France (yes, France!) all boast figures of over $57/hour, belying the idea that the United States "fosters … productivity like no other" country (see Figure 1 below).

The idea that greater inequality fosters greater productivity is a widely held article of faith in the United States, and not only among conservatives. Even liberals may accept the idea that there is a tradeoff between equality and productivity, though they may see some loss in productivity as a price worth paying for greater equality. In fact, some countries may enjoy high labor productivity *because of*, not despite, their higher degree of economic equality (both in terms of the distribution of private incomes and the provision of public services). Near-universal access to education and health care, for example, helps people develop greater productive capabilities. Greater overall economic security (including an extensive social safety net and full-employment policies) can make it easier for people to take risks and attempt new ventures. Maybe these are some of the reasons that greater equality in many Western European countries is compatible with such high material standards of living.

While the United States does little better (or, in one case, worse) than five different Western European countries on productivity, we are clearly number one when it comes

FIGURE 1: GDP PER HOUR WORKED, HIGH-INCOME COUNTRIES

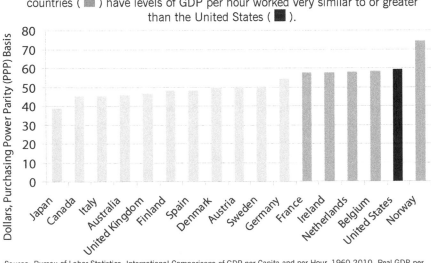

Which is the country that "fosters productivity like no other"? Five European countries (▨) have levels of GDP per hour worked very similar to or greater than the United States (■).

Source: Bureau of Labor Statistics, International Comparisons of GDP per Capita and per Hour, 1960-2010, Real GDP per hour worked, by country, 1960-2010, Table 3a. Converted to U.S. dollars using 2010 PPPs (2010 dollars).

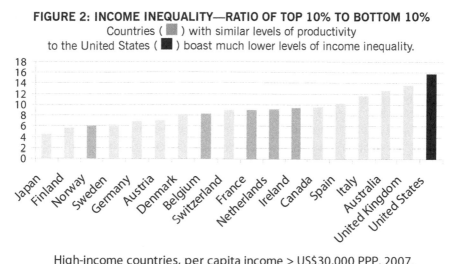

FIGURE 2: INCOME INEQUALITY—RATIO OF TOP 10% TO BOTTOM 10%
Countries (■) with similar levels of productivity
to the United States (■) boast much lower levels of income inequality.

High-income countries, per capita income > US$30,000 PPP, 2007.

Source: United Nations Development Programme (UNDP), Human Development Report 2009, Table M: Economy and inequality, Share of income or expenditure, Richest 10%, Poorest 10%, p. 195 (hdr.undp.org/en/media/HDR_2009_EN_Complete.pdf).

to income inequality. One way to measure income inequality is to compare the share of total income going to the top 10% of the population, by income ranking, to the share going to the bottom 10%. (Using other measures does not change the basic story.) In the United States, the top 10% receives nearly 16 times as much income as the bottom 10%. In the four countries with GDP per hour very similar to the United States'—Belgium, France, Ireland, and Holland—this ratio is less than ten to one. These countries are all in the middle of the pack, in terms of income inequality, among high-income industrial economies. Norway, the country with the highest GDP per hour, has a ratio of just six to one. By this measure, it boasts the third-lowest level of income inequality among these high-income countries (see Figure 2).

Average labor productivity in the U.S. economy, measured by output per hour in the private business sector, has nearly doubled over the last thirty years. Part of the increase is explained by an increase in the education and skills of U.S. workers; part, by the fact that they are working with more and better tools. Most of the increase in income inequality in the United States is not due to an increasing gap in incomes between highly educated (and supposedly more productive) workers and less-educated workers. It is due, rather, to an increase in incomes from property (profits, rent, dividends, interest, capital gains, etc.) at the expense of incomes from labor, and to an increase in the incomes of top corporate executives (which derive from corporate control, and should be classified as part of property income).

That one person's income is higher than another's does not prove that the former is more productive than the latter. If a particular person or group's income is rising, this does not prove that they are being "rewarded" for their increasing productivity. Gains in productivity, like those in the United States in recent decades, must go to someone or other. It is the way that these gains have been split up among different groups that explains the United States' high and rising income inequality—and that has less to do with changes in the relative productivity of different people than shifts in the balance of power between owners and workers.

That does call for a response from the majority, but it's not "thank you." ❑

Sources: Alex Epstein, "Let's Give Thanks for the One Percent," FoxNews. com, November 23, 2011; Bureau of Labor Statistics, International Comparisons of GDP per Capita and per Hour, 1960-2010, Real GDP per hour worked, by country, 1960-2010, Table 3a. Converted to U.S. dollars using 2010 PPPs (2010 dollars), (bls.gov); Bureau of Labor Statistics, Output Per Hour, Private Business Sector, Series ID number: PRS84006093 (bls.gov); United Nations Development Programme, *Human Development Report 2009*, Table M: Economy and inequality, Share of income or expenditure, Richest 10%, Poorest 10%, p. 195 (undp.org).

Article 8.3

THE GREAT RECESSION IN BLACK WEALTH

BY JEANNETTE WICKS-LIM

January/February 2012

The Great Recession produced the largest setback in racial wealth equality in the United States over the last 25 years. In 2009 the average white household's wealth was 20 times that of the average black household, nearly double that in previous years, according to a 2011 report by the Pew Research Center.

Driving this surge in inequality is a devastating drop in black wealth. The typical black household in 2009 was left with less wealth than at any time since 1984 after correcting for inflation.

It's important to remember wealth's special role—different from income—in supporting a household's economic well-being. Income pays for everyday expenses—groceries, clothes, and gas. A family's wealth, or net worth, includes all the assets they've built up over time (e.g., savings account, retirement fund, home, car) minus any money they owe (e.g., school loans, credit card debt, mortgage). Access to such wealth determines whether a layoff or medical crisis creates a bump in the road, or pushes a household off a financial cliff. Wealth can also provide families with financial stepping-stones to advance up the economic ladder—such as money for college tuition, or a down payment on a house.

Racial wealth inequality in the United States has always been severe. In 2004, for example, the typical black household had just $1 in net worth for every $11 of a typical white household. This is because families slowly accumulate wealth over their lifetime and across generations. Wealth, consequently, ties the economic fortunes of today's households to the explicitly racist economic institutions in America's past—especially those that existed during key phases of wealth redistribution. For example, the Homesteading Act of 1862 directed the large-scale transfer of government-owned land nearly exclusively to white households. Also starting in the 1930s, the Federal Housing Authority made a major push to subsidize home mortgages—for primarily white neighborhoods. On top of that, Jim Crow Laws—in effect until the mid-1960s—and racial violence severely curtailed efforts by the black community to start their own businesses to generate their own wealth.

The housing market crisis and the Great Recession made racial wealth inequality yet worse for two reasons. First, the wealth of blacks is more concentrated in their

MEDIAN HOUSEHOLD NET WORTH (2009 DOLLARS)

	1984	1988	1991	1993	1995	2004	2009
White	$76,951	$75,403	$68,203	$67,327	$68,520	$111,313	$92,000
Black	$6,679	$7,263	$7,071	$6,503	$9,885	$9,823	$4,900
Ratio of White to Black	12	10	10	10	7	11	19

Source: Taylor et al., *Twenty-to-One: Wealth Gaps to Rise to Record High Between Whites, Blacks and Hispanics*, Pew Research Center.

homes than the wealth of their white counterparts. Homes of black families make up 59% of their net worth compared to 44% among white families. White households typically hold more of other types of assets like stocks and IRA accounts. So when the housing crisis hit, driving down the value of homes and pushing up foreclosure rates, black households lost a much greater share of their wealth than did white households.

Second, mortgage brokers and lenders marketed subprime mortgages specifically to black households. Subprime mortgages are high-interest loans that are supposed to increase access to home financing for risky borrowers—those with a shaky credit history or low income. But these high-cost loans were disproportionately peddled to black households, even to those that could qualify for conventional loans. One study estimated that in 2007 nearly double the share of upper-income black households (54%) had high-cost mortgages compared to low-income white households (28%).

Subprime mortgages drain away wealth through high fees and interest payments. Worse, predatory lending practices disguise the high-cost of these loans with initially low payments. Payments then shoot up, often leading to default and foreclosure, wiping out a family's home equity wealth. In 2006, Mike Calhoun, president of the Center for Responsible Lending, predicted that the surge of subprime lending within the black community would "...likely be the largest loss of African-American wealth that we have ever seen, wiping out a generation of home wealth building." It was a prescient prediction.

To reverse the rise in racial wealth inequality, we need policies that specifically build wealth among black households, such as the "baby bonds" program proposed by economists William Darity of Duke University and Darrick Hamilton of The New School. Baby bonds would be federally managed, interest-bearing trusts given to the newborns of asset-poor families, and could be as large as $50,000 to $60,000 for the most asset-poor. By using a wealth means-test, this program would disproportionately benefit black communities, while avoiding the controversy of a reparations policy. When recipients reach age 18, they could use the funds for a house down payment, tuition, or to start a business. This program would cost about $60 billion per year, which could easily be covered by letting the Bush-era tax cuts expire for the top 1% of income earners. ❏

Sources: Amaad Rivera, Brenda Cotto-Escalera, Anisha Desai, Jeannette Huezo, and Dedrick Muhammad, *Foreclosed: State of the Dream 2008*, United for a Fair Economy, 2008; Citizens for Tax Justice, "The Bush Tax Cuts Cost Two and a Half Times as Much as the House Democrats' Health Care Proposal," CTJ Policy Brief, September 9, 2009; Darrick Hamilton and William Darity, Jr., "Can 'Baby Bonds' Eliminate the Racial Wealth Gap in Putative Post-Racial America?" *Review of Black Political Economy*, 2010; Paul Taylor, Rakesh Kochhar, Richard Fry, Gabriel Velasco, and Seth Motel, *Twenty-to-One: Wealth Gaps to Rise to Record High Between Whites, Blacks and Hispanics*, Washington DC: Pew Research Center, 2011.

Article 8.4

UNDERCOUNTING THE POOR
The U.S.'s New, But Only Marginally Improved, Poverty Measure

BY JEANNETTE WICKS-LIM
May/June 2013

In 1995, a blue-ribbon panel of poverty experts selected by the National Academy of the Sciences (NAS) told us that the "current U.S. measure of poverty is demonstrably flawed judged by today's knowledge; it needs to be replaced." Critics have long pointed out shortcomings including the failure to adequately account for the effects of "safety net" programs and insensitivity to differences in the cost of living between different places.

The Census Bureau, the federal agency charged with publishing the official poverty numbers, has yet to replace the poverty line. However, in the last couple years it has published an alternative, the Supplemental Poverty Measure (SPM). The SPM is the product of over two decades of work to fix problems in the federal poverty line (FPL).

This new measure takes us one step forward, two steps back. On the one hand, it has some genuine improvements: The new measure makes clearer how the social safety net protects people from economic destitution. It adds basic living costs missing from the old measure. On the other hand, it does little to address the most important criticism of the poverty line: it is just too damned low. The fact that the poverty line has only now been subject to revision—50 years after the release of the first official poverty statistic—likely means that the SPM has effectively entrenched this major weakness of the official measure for another 50 years.

The 2011 official poverty rate is 15.1%. The new poverty measure presented—and missed by a wide margin—the opportunity to bring into public view how widespread the problem of poverty is for American families. If what we mean by poverty is the inability to meet one's basic needs a more reasonable poverty line would tell us that 34% of Americans—more than one in three—are poor.

What's in a Number?

The unemployment rate illustrates the power of official statistics. In the depths of the Great Recession, a new official statistic—the rate of underemployment, counting people working part time who want full-time work and those who have just given up on looking for work—became part of every conversation about the economy. One in six workers (17%) counted as underemployed in December 2009, a much higher number than the 9.6% unemployment rate. The public had not been confronted with an employment shortage that large in recent memory; it made political leaders stand up and pay attention.

The supplemental poverty measure had the potential to do the same: a more reasonable poverty line—the bottom line level of income a household needs to avoid poverty—would uncover how endemic the problem of economic deprivation is here in the United States. That could shake up policymakers and get them to prioritize anti-poverty policies in their political agendas. Just as important, a more accurate count of the poor would acknowledge the experience of those struggling mightily to put food on the table or to keep the lights on. No one wants to be treated like "just a number," but not being counted at all is surely worse.

With a couple of years of data now available, the SPM has begun to enter into anti-poverty policy debates. Now is a good time to take a closer look at what this measure is all about.

The supplemental measure makes three major improvements to the official poverty line: It accounts for differences in the cost of living between different regions. It changes the way it calculates the standard of living necessary to avoid poverty. And it accounts more fully for benefits from safety net programs.

Different Poverty Lines for Cost-of-Living Differences

Everyone knows that $10,000 in a small city like Utica, New York, can stretch a lot farther than in New York City. In Utica, the typical monthly cost of rent for a two-bedroom apartment, including utilities, was about $650 during 2008-2011. The figure for New York City? Nearly double that at $1,100. Despite this, the official poverty line has been the same regardless of geographic location.The supplemental poverty measure adjusts the poverty income threshold by differences in housing costs in metropolitan and rural areas in each state—a step entirely missing in the old measure.

We can see how these adjustments make a real difference by simply comparing the official poverty and SPM rates by region. In 2011, according to the official poverty line, the Northeast had the lowest poverty rate (13.2%), the South had the highest (16.1%), and the Midwest and the West fell in between (14.1% and 15.9%, respectively). With cost-of-living differences factored in, the regions shuffled ranks. The SPM poverty rates of the Northeast and South look a lot more alike (15.0% and 16.0%, respectively). The Midwest's cheaper living expenses pushed its SPM rate to the lowest among the four regions (12.8%). The West, on the other hand, had an SPM rate of 20.0%, making it the highest-poverty region.

Updating Today's Living Costs

Obviously, household expenses have changed a lot over the last half-century. The original formula used to construct the official poverty line used a straightforward rule-of-thumb calculation: minimal food expenses time three. It's been well-documented since then that food makes up a much smaller proportion of households' budgets, something closer to one-fifth, as new living expenses have been added (e.g., childcare, as women entered the paid workforce in droves) and the costs of other expenses ballooned (e.g., transportation and medical care).

The new poverty measure takes these other critical expenses into account by doing the following. First, the SPM income threshold tallies up necessary spending on food, clothing, shelter and utilities. The other necessary expenses like work-related child care and medical bills are deducted from a household's resources to meet the SPM income threshold. A household is then called poor if its resources fall below the threshold.

These non-discretionary expenses clearly take a real bite out of family budgets. For example, the "costs of working" cause the SPM poverty rate to rise to nearly doubles that of the official poverty rate among full-time year-round workers from less than 3% to over 5%.

Bringing the Social Safety Net into Focus

Today's largest national anti-poverty programs operate in the blind spot of the official poverty line. These include programs like the Supplemental Nutrition Assistance Program (SNAP) and the Earned Income Tax credit (EITC). The supplemental measure does us a major service by showing in no uncertain terms how our current social safety net protects people from economic destitution.

The reason for this is that the official poverty measure only counts cash income and pre-tax cash benefits (e.g., Social Security, Unemployment Insurance, and Temporary Assistance to Needy Families (TANF)) towards a household's resources to get over the poverty line. The supplemental poverty measure, on the other hand, adds to a household's resources near-cash government subsidies—programs that help families cover their expenditures on food (e.g. SNAP and the National School Lunch program), shelter (housing assistance from HUD), and utilities (Low Income Home Energy Assistance Program (LIHEAP))— as well as after-tax income subsidies (e.g., EITC). This update is long overdue, since the 1996 Personal Responsibility and Work Opportunity Reconciliation Act (a.k.a., the Welfare Reform Act) largely replaced the traditional cash assistance program AFDC with after-tax and in-kind assistance.

Here are some figures for 2011 that illustrate the impact of each of twelve different economic assistance programs. Social Security, refundable tax credits (largely EITC but also the Child Tax Credit (CTC)), and SNAP benefits do the most to reduce poverty. In the absence of Social Security, the supplemental poverty rate would be 8.3 percentage points higher, shooting up from 16.1% to over 23.8%. Without refundable tax credits, the supplemental poverty rate would rise 2.8 percentage points, up to nearly 19%, with much of the difference being in child poverty. Finally, SNAP benefits prevent poverty across households from rising 1.5 percentage points.

The SPM gives us the statistical ruler by which to measure the impact of the major anti-poverty programs of the day. This is crucial information for current political feuds about falling over fiscal cliffs and hitting debt ceilings.

A Meager Supplement

Unfortunately, the new poverty measure adds all these important details to a fundamentally flawed picture of poverty.

In November 2012, the Census Bureau published, for only the second time, a national poverty rate based on the Supplemental Poverty Measure: it stood at 16.1% (for 2011), just one percentage point higher than the official poverty rate of 15.1%.

Why such a small difference? The fundamental problem is that the supplementary poverty measure, in defining the poverty line, builds from basically the same level of extreme economic deprivation as the old measure.

The Federal Poverty Line vs. the Supplemental Poverty Measure

The new supplemental measure (SPM) modestly bumps up the federal poverty line (FPL). Let's start with the published measures of the two thresholds. When you compare these, for a family of four (two adults, two children) the SPM is only 11% more than the official poverty line: $22,800 versus $25,200. But this isn't an apples-to-apples comparison. The official income poverty threshold is supposed to represent the income a family needs to cover all the expenses they have to support a minimal standard of living. The SPM income threshold on the other hand represents only the income a family needs to cover necessary food, clothing, shelter, and utility expenses (FCSU). "Nondiscretionary spending"—money spent on things like work-related expenses (transportation, childcare, and taxes) don't get counted in the income threshold. Instead, the SPM deducts these from what they call the "economic resources" a household has to cover their FCSU expenses. This way of accounting for such work-related expenses has the effect of making the SPM threshold look lower than it is actually is relative to the official poverty line. In order to make an apples-to-apples comparison, we have to adjust the SPM income threshold upward so that it includes the income needed to cover "nondiscretionary spending" the way the official poverty line does. This adds about 20% to the SPM income threshold, so that the supplementary poverty measure actually stands about 30% higher than the FPL.

In an apples-to-apples comparison (see sidebar, above), the new supplemental measure effectively represents a poverty line roughly 30% higher than the official poverty income threshold for a family of four. For 2011, the official four-person poverty line was $22,800, an adjusted SPM income threshold—one that can be directly compared to the FPL—is about $30,500.

Unfortunately, the NAS panel of poverty experts appears to have taken an arbitrarily conservative approach to setting poverty income threshold.

Reasonably enough, NAS panel uses as their starting point how much households spend on the four essential items: food, clothing, shelter, and utilities. A self-proclaimed "judgment call," they choose what they call a "reasonable range" of expenditures to mark poverty. What's odd is that their judgment leans back toward the official poverty line—the measure they referred to as "demonstrably flawed."

To justify this amount they show how their spending levels fall within the range of two other "expert budgets" (i.e., poverty income thresholds) in the poverty research. What they do not explain is why, among the ten alternative income thresholds they review in detail, they focus on two of the lower ones. In fact, one of these two income thresholds they describe as an "outlier at the low end." The range of the ten thresholds actually spans between 9% and 53% more than the official poverty line; their recommended range for the threshold falls between 14% and 33% above the official poverty line.

Regardless of the NAS panel's intention, the Inter-agency Technical Working group (ITWG) tasked with the job of producing the new poverty measure adopted the middle point of this "reasonable range" to establish the initial threshold for the revised poverty line.

This conflicts with what we know about the level of economic deprivation that households experience in the range of the federal poverty line. In a 1999 book *Hardship in America*, researchers Heather Boushey, Chauna Brocht, Bethney Gunderson, and Jared Bernstein examined the rates and levels of

---

What Is a "Conservative Updating"?

The National Academy of Sciences panel states that their recommended range "falls within but toward the lower end of the estimated range of other thresholds. Thus it represents a conservative updating in real terms of the current threshold, consistent with our recommendation." This statement seems to confuse two different goals: periodically updating the poverty threshold—whatever its initial value may be—in a conservative way (avoiding large year-to-year changes) versus improving the initial value of the poverty threshold that is to be updated. Here, they seem to suggest that they want to be conservative on both fronts—the updating technique as well as the method for establishing the initial threshold, but provide no justification for the latter. Given this "conservative" ideal, it seems that the fact that the new poverty rate looks much like the old one is baked into its development.

---

economic hardship among officially poor households (with incomes less than the poverty line), near-poor households (with incomes between the poverty line and twice the poverty line), and not poor households (with incomes more than twice the poverty line).

As expected, they found high rates of economic distress among households classified as "officially poor." For example, in 1996, 29% of poor households experienced one or more "critical" hardships such as missing meals, not getting necessary medical care, and having their utilities disconnected. Near-poor households experienced these types of economic crises only a little less frequently (25%). Only when households achieved incomes above twice the poverty line did the incidence of these economic problems fall substantially—down to 11%. (Unfortunately, the survey data on which the study was based have been discontinued, so more up-to-date figures are unavailable.) This pattern repeats for "serious" hardships that include being worried about having enough food, using the ER for health care due to lack of alternatives, and falling behind on housing payments. So if what we mean by poverty is the inability to meet one's basic needs, then twice the poverty line—rather than the SPM's 1.3 times—appears to be an excellent marker.

Let's consider what the implied new poverty income threshold of $30,500 feels like for a family of four. (This, by the way, is about what a household would take in with two full-time minimum-wage jobs.)

This annual figure comes out to $585 per week. Consider a family living in a relatively low-cost area like rural Sandusky, Michigan. Based on the basic-family-budget details provided by the Economic Policy Institute, such a family typically needs to spend about $175 on food (this assumes they have a nearby grocery store, a stove at home, and the time to cook all their meals) and another $165 on rent for a two-bedroom apartment each week. This eats up 60% of their budget, leaving only about $245 to cover all other expenses. If they need child-care to work ($180), then this plus the taxes they have to pay on their earnings ($60) pretty much wipes out the rest. In other words, they have nothing left for such basic needs as telephone service, clothes, personal care products like soap and toilet paper, school supplies, out of pocket medical expenses, and transportation they may need to get to work. Would getting above this income threshold seem like escaping poverty to you?

For many federal subsidy programs this doesn't seem like escaping poverty either. That's why major anti-poverty programs like that National School Lunch program, Low Income Home Energy Assistance Program (LIHEAP), State Children's Health Insurance Program (SCHIP) step in to help families with incomes up to twice the poverty line.

If the supplementary poverty measure tackled the fundamental problem of a much-too-low poverty line then it would likely draw an income threshold closer to 200% of the official poverty line (or for an apples-to-apples comparison, about 150% of the SPM income threshold). This would shift the landscape of poverty statistics and produce a poverty rate of an astounding one in three Americans.

Now What?

The Census Bureau's supplemental measure doesn't do what the underemployment rate did for the unemployment rate—that is, fill in the gap between the headline number and how many of us are actually falling through the cracks.

The poverty line does a poor job of telling us how many Americans are struggling to meet their basic needs. For those of us who fall into the "not poor" category but get struck with panic from time to time that we may not be able to make ends meet—with one bad medical emergency, one unexpected car repair, one unforeseen cutback in work hours—it makes us wonder, if we're not poor or even near poor, why are we struggling so much? The official statistics betray this experience. The fact is that so many Americans are struggling because many more of us are poor or near-poor than the official statistics lead us to believe.

The official poverty line has only been changed—supplemented, that is— once since its establishment in 1963. What can we do to turn this potentially once-in-a-century reform into something more meaningful? One possibility: we should simply rename the supplemental poverty rates as the severe poverty rate. Households with economic resources below 150% of the new poverty line then can be counted as "poor." By doing so, politicians and government officials would start to recognize what Americans have been struggling with: one-third of us are poor. ❏

Sources: Kathleen Short, "The Research Supplemental Poverty Measure: 2011," Current Population Report, U.S. Bureau of the Census, November 2012 (census.gov); Constance F. Citro and Robert T. Michael (eds.), *Measuring Poverty: A New Approach*, Washington D.C.: National Academy Press, 1995; Trudi Renwick, "Geographic Adjustments of Supplemental Poverty Measure Thresholds: Using the American Community Survey Five-Year Data on Housing Costs," U.S. Bureau of the Census, January 2011 (census.gov).

Article 8.5

THE RISE OF THE GLOBAL BILLIONAIRES

BY ROBIN BROAD AND JOHN CAVANAGH
October 2013

With the help of *Forbes* magazine, we and colleagues at the Institute for Policy Studies have been tracking the world's billionaires and rising inequality the world over for several decades. Just as a drop of water gives us a clue into the chemical composition of the sea, these billionaires offer fascinating clues into the changing face of global power and inequality.

After our initial gawking at the extravagance of this year's list of 1,426, we looked closer. This list reveals the major power shift in the world today: the decline of the West and the rise of the rest. Gone are the days when U.S. billionaires accounted for over 40% of the list, with Western Europe and Japan making up most of the rest. Today, the Asia-Pacific region hosts 386 billionaires, 20 more than all of Europe and Russia combined.

In 2013, of the nine countries that are home to over 30 billionaires each, only three are traditional "developed" countries: the United States, Germany, and the United Kingdom.

Next in line after the United States, with its 442 billionaires today? China, with 122 billionaires (up from zero billionaires in 1995), and third place goes to Russia with 110. China's billionaires have made money from every possible source. Consider the country's richest man, Zong Qinghou, who made his $11.6 billion through his ownership of the country's largest beverage maker. Russia's lengthy billionaire list is led by men who reaped billions from the country's vast oil, gas, and mineral wealth with devastating consequences to the environment.

Germany is fourth on the list with 58 billionaires, followed by India (55), Brazil (46), Turkey (43), Hong Kong (39), and the United Kingdom (38). Yes, Turkey has more billionaires than any other country in Europe save Germany.

Moving beyond these top nine countries, Taiwan has more billionaires than France. Indonesia has more billionaires than Italy or Spain. South Korea now has more billionaires than Japan or Australia.

This surging list of billionaires is tribute to the growing inequality in almost all nations on earth. The richest man in the world, for example, is Carlos Slim of Mexico—with a net worth of $73 billion, comparable to a whopping 6.2% of Mexico's GDP. The world's third richest person is Spain's retail king, Amancio Ortega, who has accumulated a net worth of $57 billion in a country where over a quarter of the people are now unemployed.

U.S. billionaires still dominate. The United States' 442 billionaires represent 31% of the total number. Bill Gates and Warren Buffett remain number two and four, and are household names given the combination of their wealth, their philanthropy, and their use of their power and influence to convince other billionaires to increase their own charitable giving.

But, also among the 12 U.S. billionaires in the top 20 richest people in the world are members of two families who have used their vast wealth and concomitant power to corrupt our politics. Charles and David Koch stand at number six and seven in the world; they have drawn on a chunk of their combined $68 billion to fund not only candidates of the far right but also political campaigns against environmental and other regulation. So too do four Waltons stand among the top 20; their combined wealth of $107.3 billion has skyrocketed thanks to Walmart's growing profits as the company pressures cities and states to oppose raising wages to livable levels.

How have the numbers changed over the years? Let's travel back to 1995, a time of surging wealth amidst the deregulation under the Clinton administration in the United States, and the widespread pressure around the world to deregulate, liberalize, and privatize markets.

In 1995, *Forbes* tallied 376 billionaires in the world. Of these, 129 (or 34%) were from the United States. The fact that the number of U.S. billionaires rose to 442 over the next 18 years while the percentage of U.S. billionaires fell only from 34% to 31% of the global total is testimony to how the deregulatory and tax-cutting atmosphere in the United States under Clinton and Bush proved so favorable to the super-rich.

Notable over these past 18 years is that the so-called developed world has been eclipsed by the so-called developing world. In 1995, the billionaire powerhouses were the United States (129), Germany (47), and Japan (35). These three countries were home to 56% of the world's billionaires. No other country came close, with France, Hong Kong, and Thailand tied in fourth place, with twelve billionaires each. Russia and China didn't have a single billionaire in 1995, although for Russia, Forbes admitted that financial disclosure in that country in the years after the Berlin Wall fell was sketchy. And, in 1995, Brazil had only eight billionaires and India only two.

Today, these four countries (Russia, China, Brazil, and India) host 333 of the world's 1,426 billionaires—23% of the total. And Japan's total number of billionaires has actually fallen in the 18 years, from 35 to 22.

The figures offer a dramatic snapshot of the relative decline of the United States, Europe, and Japan in less than two decades and the stunning rise of Brazil, Russia, India, and China, as well as the rest of Asia. And, they remind us that countries where income was relatively equal twenty years ago, like China and Russia, have rushed into the ranks of the unequal.

Across the globe, the rapid rise of billionaires in dozens of countries (again, with Japan as the notable exception) is testimony to how the deregulatory climate of these past two decades sped the rise of the super-rich, while corporations kept workers' wages essentially flat.

Suffice it to say: More equal and more healthy societies require a vastly different approach to public policy. As Sam Pizzigati has chronicled in *The Rich Don't Always Win*, fair taxes created a vast middle class in the United States between the 1940s-1960s. Such fair tax policies are needed today the world over if the gap between the super-haves and the have-nots is to be narrowed rather than widened. ❏

Sources: "The World's Billionaires," *Forbes*, March 25, 2013 (forbes.com); "Bill Gates Again at No. 1 on Forbes Wealthiest List," *Los Angeles Times*, October 2, 1995 (latimes.com); World/ Global Inequality, Inequality.org (inequality.org); "Change Walmart, Change America," Jobs with Justice (jwj.org); Mexico GDP, Trading Economics (tradingeconomics.com); "Spanish Jobless Rate Dips to 25.98% as Recession Ends," Yahoo News, October 24, 2013 (news.yahoo.com); Robin Broad and John Cavanaugh, "A Tax System for the 99%," Yes! magazine blog, April 17, 2013; Koch Cash (website), International Forum on Globalization (kochcash.org), Sam Pizzigati, *The Rich Don't Always Win: The Forgotten Triumph over Plutocracy that Created the American Middle Class, 1900–1970* (Seven Stories Press, 2012).

Chapter 9

THE GLOBAL ECONOMY

Article 9.1

FAMINE MYTHS

Five Misunderstandings Related to the 2011 Hunger Crisis in the Horn of Africa

BY WILLIAM G. MOSELEY

March/April 2012

The 2011 famine in the horn of Africa was one of the worst in recent decades in terms of loss of life and human suffering. While the UN has yet to release an official death toll, the British government estimates that between 50,000 and 100,000 people died, most of them children, between April and September of 2011. While Kenya, Ethiopia, and Djibouti were all badly affected, the famine hit hardest in certain (mainly southern) areas of Somalia. This was the worst humanitarian disaster to strike the country since 1991-1992, with roughly a third of the Somali population displaced for some period of time.

Despite the scholarly and policy community's tremendous advances in understanding famine over the past 40 years, and increasingly sophisticated famine early-warning systems, much of this knowledge and information was seemingly ignored or forgotten in 2011. While the famine had been forecasted nearly nine months in advance, the global community failed to prepare for, and react in a timely manner to, this event. The famine was officially declared in early July of 2011 by the United Nations and recently (February 3, 2012) stated to be officially over. Despite the official end of the famine, 31% of the population (or 2.3 million people) in southern Somalia remains in crisis. Across the region, 9.5 million people continue to need assistance. Millions of Somalis remain in refugee camps in Ethiopia and Kenya.

The famine reached its height in the period from July to September, 2011, with approximately 13 million people at risk of starvation. While this was a regional problem, it was was most acute in southern Somalia because aid to this region was much delayed. Figure 1 provides a picture of food insecurity in the region in the November-December 2011 period (a few months after the peak of the crisis).

The 2011 famine received relatively little attention in the U.S. media and much of the coverage that did occur was biased, ahistorical, or perpetuated long-held misunderstandings about the nature and causes of famine. This article addresses "famine myths"—five key misunderstandings related to the famine in the Horn of Africa.

Myth #1: Drought was the cause of the famine.

While drought certainly contributed to the crisis in the Horn of Africa, there were more fundamental causes at play. Drought is not a new environmental condition for much of Africa, but a recurring one. The Horn of Africa has long experienced erratic rainfall. While climate change may be exacerbating rainfall variability, traditional livelihoods in the region are adapted to deal with situations where rainfall is not dependable.

The dominant livelihood in the Horn of Africa has long been herding, which is well adapted to the semi-arid conditions of the region. Herders traditionally ranged widely across the landscape in search of better pasture, focusing on different areas depending on meteorological conditions.

The approach worked because, unlike fenced in pastures in America, it was incredibly flexible and well adapted to variable rainfall conditions. As farming expanded, including large-scale commercial farms in some instances, the routes of herders became more concentrated, more vulnerable to drought, and more detrimental to the landscape.

FIGURE 1: FOOD INSECURITY IN THE HORN OF AFRICA REGION, NOVEMBER-DECEMBER 2011.

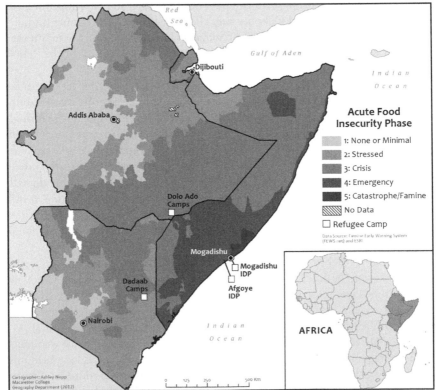

Based on data and assessment by FEWS-Net (a USAID-sponsored program).

Cartography by Ashley Nepp, Macalester College.

Agricultural livelihoods also evolved in problematic ways. In anticipation of poor rainfall years, farming households and communities historically stored surplus crop production in granaries. Sadly this traditional strategy for mitigating the risk of drought was undermined from the colonial period moving forward as households were encouraged (if not coerced by taxation) to grow cash crops for the market and store less excess grain for bad years. This increasing market orientation was also encouraged by development banks, such as the World Bank, International Monetary Fund, and African Development Bank.

The moral of the story is that famine is not a natural consequence of drought (just as death from exposure is not the inherent result of a cold winter), but it is the structure of human society which often determines who is affected and to what degree.

Myth #2: Overpopulation was the cause of the famine.

With nearly 13 million people at risk of starvation last fall in a region whose population doubled in the previous 24 years, one might assume that these two factors were causally related in the Horn of Africa. Ever since the British political economist Thomas Malthus wrote "An Essay on the Principle of Population" in 1798, we have been concerned that human population growth will outstrip available food supply. While the crisis in Somalia, Ethiopia and Kenya appeared to be perfect proof of the Malthusian scenario, we must be careful not to make overly simplistic assumptions.

Land Grabs In Africa

Long term leases of African land for export-oriented food production, or "land grabs," have been on the rise in the past decade. Rather than simply buying food and commodity crops from African farmers, foreign entities increasingly take control of ownership and management of farms on African soil. This trend stems from at least two factors. First, increasingly high global food prices are a problem for many Asian and Middle Eastern countries that depend on food imports. As such, foreign governments and sovereign wealth funds may engage in long-term leases of African land in order to supply their own populations with affordable food. Secondly, high global food prices are also seen as an opportunity for some Western investors who lease African land to produce crops and commodities for profitable global markets.

In the Horn of Africa, Ethiopia (which has historically been one of the world's largest recipients of humanitarian food aid) has made a series of long-term land leases to foreign entities. The World Bank estimates that at least 35 million hectares of land have been leased to 36 different countries, including China, Pakistan, India and Saudi Arabia. Supporters of these leases argue that they provide employment to local people and disseminate modern agricultural approaches. Critics counter that these leases undermine food sovereignty, or people's ability to feed themselves via environmentally sustainable technologies that they control.

For starters, the semi-arid zones in the Horn of Africa are relatively lightly populated compared to other regions of the world. For example, the population density of Somalia is about 13 persons per sq. kilometer, whereas that of the U.S. state of Oklahoma is 21.1. The western half of Oklahoma is also semi-arid, suffered from a serious drought in 2011, and was the poster child for the 1930s Dust Bowl. Furthermore, if we take into account differing levels of consumption, with the average American consuming at least 28 times as much as the average Somali in a normal year, then Oklahoma's population density of 21.1 persons per sq. kilometer equates to that of 591 Somalis.

Despite the fact that Oklahoma's per capita impact on the landscape is over 45 times that of Somalia (when accounting for population density and consumption levels), we don't talk about overpopulation in Oklahoma. This is because, in spite of the drought and the collapse of agriculture, there was no famine in Oklahoma. In contrast, the presence of famine in the Horn of Africa led many to assume that too many people was a key part of the problem.

Why is it that many assume that population growth is the driver of famine? For starters, perhaps we assume that reducing the birthrate, and thereby reducing the number of mouths to feed, is one of the easiest ways to prevent hunger. This is actually a difficult calculation for most families in rural Africa. It's true that many families desire access to modern contraceptives, and filling this unmet need is important. However, for many others, children are crucial sources of farm labor or important wage earners who help sustain the family. Children also act as the old-age social security system for their parents. For these families, having fewer children is not an easy decision. Families in this region will have fewer children when it makes economic sense to do so. As we have seen over time and throughout the world, the average family size shrinks when economies develop and expectations for offspring change.

Second, many tend to focus on the additional resources required to nourish each new person, and often forget the productive capacity of these individuals. Throughout Africa, some of the most productive farmland is in those regions with the highest population densities. In Machakos, Kenya, for example, agricultural production and environmental conservation improved as population densities increased. Furthermore, we have seen agricultural production collapse in some areas where population declined (often due to outmigration) because there was insufficient labor to maintain intensive agricultural production.

Third, we must not forget that much of the region's agricultural production is not consumed locally. From the colonial era moving forward, farmers and herders have been encouraged to become more commercially oriented, producing crops and livestock for the market rather than home consumption. This might have been a reasonable strategy if the prices for exports from the Horn of Africa were high (which they rarely have been) and the cost of food imports low. Also, large land leases (or "land grabs") to foreign governments and corporations in Ethiopia (and to a lesser extent in Kenya and Somalia) have further exacerbated this problem. These farms, designed solely for export production, effectively subsidize the food security of other regions of the world (most notably the Middle East and Asia) at the expense of populations in the Horn of Africa.

Myth #3: Increasing food production through advanced techniques will resolve food insecurity over the long run.

As Sub-Saharan Africa has grappled with high food prices in some regions and famine in others, many experts argue that increasing food production through a program of hybrid seeds and chemical inputs (a so-called "New Green Revolution") is the way to go.

While outsiders benefit from this New Green Revolution strategy (by selling inputs or purchasing surplus crops), it is not clear if the same is true for small farmers and poor households in Sub-Saharan Africa. For most food insecure households on the continent, there are at least two problems with this strategy. First, such an approach to farming is energy intensive because most fertilizers and pesticides are petroleum based. Inducing poor farmers to adopt energy-intensive farming methods is short sighted, if not unethical, if experts know that global energy prices are likely to rise. Second, irrespective of energy prices, the New Green Revolution approach requires farmers to purchase seeds and inputs, which means that it will be inaccessible to the poorest of the poor, i.e., those who are the most likely to suffer from periods of hunger.

If not the New Green Revolution approach, then what? Many forms of bio-intensive agriculture are, in fact, highly productive and much more efficient than those of industrial agriculture. For example, crops grown in intelligent combinations allow one plant to fix nitrogen for another rather than relying solely on increasingly expensive, fossil fuel-based inorganic fertilizers for these plant nutrients. Mixed cropping strategies are also less vulnerable to insect damage and require little to no pesticide use for a reasonable harvest. These techniques have existed for centuries in the African context and could be greatly enhanced by supporting collaboration among local people, African research institutes, and foreign scientists.

Myth #4: U.S. foreign policy in the Horn of Africa was unrelated to the crisis.

Many Americans assume that U.S. foreign policy bears no blame for the food crisis in the Horn and, more specifically, Somalia. This is simply untrue. The weakness of the Somali state was and is related to U.S. policy, which interfered in Somali affairs based on Cold War politics (the case in the 1970s and 80s) or the War on Terror (the case in the 2000s).

During the Cold War, Somalia was a pawn in a U.S.-Soviet chess match in the geopolitically significant Horn of Africa region. In 1974, the U.S. ally Emperor Haile Selassie of Ethiopia was deposed in a revolution. He was eventually replaced by Mengistu Haile Mariam, a socialist. In response, the leader of Ethiopia's bitter rival Somalia, Siad Barre, switched from being pro-Soviet to pro-Western. Somalia was the only country in Africa to switch Cold War allegiances under the same government. The U.S. supported Siad Barre until 1989 (shortly before his demise in 1991). By doing this, the United States played a key role in supporting a long-running dictator and undermined democratic governance.

More recently, the Union of Islamic Courts (UIC) came to power in 2006. The UIC defeated the warlords, restored peace to Mogadishu for the first time in 15 years, and brought most of southern Somalia under its orbit. The United States and its Ethiopian ally claimed that these Islamists were terrorists and a threat to the region. In contrast, the vast majority of Somalis supported the UIC and pleaded with the international community to engage them peacefully. Unfortunately, this peace did not last. The U.S.-supported Ethiopian invasion of Somalia begun in December 2006 and displaced more than a million people and killed close to 15,000 civilians. Those displaced then became a part of last summer and fall's famine victims.

The power vacuum created by the displacement of the more moderate UIC also led to the rise of its more radical military wing, al-Shabaab. Al-Shabaab emerged to engage the Transitional Federal Government (TFG), which was put in place by the international community and composed of the most moderate elements of the UIC (which were more favorable to the United States). The TFG was weak, corrupt, and ineffective, controlling little more than the capital Mogadishu, if that. A low-grade civil war emerged between these two groups in southern Somalia. Indeed, as we repeatedly heard in the media last year, it was al-Shabaab that restricted access to southern Somalia for several months leading up to the crisis and greatly exacerbated the situation in this sub-region. Unfortunately, the history of factors which gave rise to al-Shabaab was never adequately explained to the U.S. public. Until July 2011, the U.S. government forbade American charities from operating in areas controlled by al-Shabaab—which delayed relief efforts in these areas.

Myth #5: An austere response may be best in the long run.

Efforts to raise funds to address the famine in the Horn of Africa were well below those for previous (and recent) humanitarian crises. Why was this? Part of it likely had to do with the economic malaise in the U.S. and Europe. Many Americans suggested that we could not afford to help in this crisis because we had to pay off our own debt. This stinginess may, in part, be related to a general misunderstanding about how much of the U.S. budget goes to foreign assistance. Many Americans assume we spend over 25% of our budget on such assistance when it is actually less than one percent.

Furthermore, contemporary public discourse in America has become more inward-looking and isolationist than in the past. As a result, many Americans have difficulty relating to people beyond their borders. Sadly, it is now much easier to separate ourselves from them, to discount our common humanity, and to essentially suppose that it's okay if they starve. This last point brings us back to Thomas Malthus, who was writing against the poor laws in England in the late 18th century. The poor laws were somewhat analogous to contemporary welfare programs and Malthus argued (rather problematically) that they encouraged the poor to have more children. His essential argument was that starvation is acceptable because it is a natural check to over-population. In other words, support for the poor will only exacerbate the situation. We see this in the way that some conservative commentators reacted to last year's famine.

The reality was that a delayed response to the famine only made the situation worse. Of course, the worst-case scenario is death, but short of death, many households were forced to sell off all of their assets (cattle, farming implements, etc.) in order to survive. This sets up a very difficult recovery scenario because livelihoods are so severely compromised. We know from best practices among famine researchers and relief agencies in that you not only to detect a potential famine early, but to intervene before livelihoods are devastated. This means that households will recover more quickly and be more resilient in the face of future perturbations.

Preventing Famines

While the official famine in the horn of Africa region is over, 9.5 million people continue to need assistance and millions of Somalis remain in refugee camps in Ethiopia and Kenya. While this region of the world will always be drought prone, it needn't be famine prone. The solution lies in rebuilding the Somali state and fostering more robust rural livelihoods in Somalia, western Ethiopia and northern Kenya. The former will likely mean giving the Somali people the space they need to rebuild their own democratic institutions (and not making them needless pawns in the War on Terror). The latter will entail a new approach to agriculture that emphasizes food sovereignty, or locally appropriate food production technologies that are accessible to the poorest of the poor, as well as systems of grain storage at the local level that anticipate bad rainfall years. Finally, the international community should discourage wealthy, yet food-insufficient, countries from preying on poorer countries in Sub Saharan African countries through the practice of land grabs. ❏

Sources: Alex de Waal, *Famine That Kills: Darfur, Sudan*, Oxford University Press, 2005; William G. Moseley, "Why They're Starving: The man-made roots of famine in the Horn of Africa," *The Washington Post*. July 29, 2011; William G. Moseley and B. Ikubolajeh Logan, "Food Security," in B. Wisner, C. Toulmin and R. Chitiga (eds)., *Toward a New Map of Africa*, Earthscan Publications, 2005; Abdi I. Samatar, "Genocidal Politics and the Somali Famine," Aljazeera English, July 30, 2011; Amartya Sen, *Poverty and Famines*, Oxford/Clarendon, 1981; Michael Watts and Hans Bohle, "The space of vulnerability: the causal structure of hunger and famine," *Progress in Human Geography*, 1993.

Article 9.2

IS CHINA'S CURRENCY MANIPULATION HURTING THE U.S.?

BY ARTHUR MacEWAN
November/December 2010

> Dear Dr. Dollar:
> Is it true that China has been harming the U.S. economy by keeping its currency "undervalued"? Shouldn't the U.S. government do something about this situation?   —*Jenny Boyd, Edmond, W.Va.*

The Chinese government, operating through the Chinese central bank, does keep its currency unit—the yuan—cheap relative to the dollar. This means that goods imported *from* China cost less (in terms of dollars) than they would otherwise, while U.S. exports *to* China cost more (in terms of yuan). So we in the United States buy a lot of Chinese-made goods and the Chinese don't buy much from us. In the 2007 to 2009 period, the United States purchased $253 billion more in goods annually from China than it sold to China.

This looks bad for U.S workers. For example, when money gets spent in the United States, much of it is spent on Chinese-made goods, and fewer jobs are then created in the United States. So the Chinese government's currency policy is at least partly to blame for our employment woes. Reacting to this situation, many people are calling for the U.S. government to do something to get the Chinese government to change its policy.

But things are not so simple.

First of all, there is an additional reason for the low cost of Chinese goods—low Chinese wages. The Chinese government's policy of repressing labor probably accounts for the low cost of Chinese goods at least as much as does its currency policy. Moreover, there is a lot more going on in the global economy. Both currency problems and job losses involve much more than Chinese government actions—though China provides a convenient target for ire.

And the currency story itself is complex. In order to keep the value of its currency low relative to the dollar, the Chinese government increases the supply of yuan, uses these yuan to buy dollars, then uses the dollars to buy U.S. securities, largely government bonds but also private securities. In early 2009, China held $764 billion in U.S. Treasury securities, making it the largest foreign holder of U.S. government debt. By buying U.S. government bonds, the Chinese have been financing the federal deficit. More generally, by supplying funds to the United States, the Chinese government has been keeping interest rates low in this country.

If the Chinese were to act differently, allowing the value of their currency to rise relative to the dollar, both the cost of capital and the prices of the many goods imported from China would rise. The rising cost of capital would probably not be a serious problem, as the Federal Reserve could take counteraction to keep interest rates low. So, an increase in the value of the yuan would net the United States some jobs, but also raise some prices for U.S. consumers.

It is pretty clear that right now what the United States needs is jobs. Moreover, low-cost Chinese goods have contributed to the declining role of manufacturing in the United States, a phenomenon that both weakens important segments of organized labor and threatens to inhibit technological progress, which has often been centered in manufacturing or based on applications in manufacturing (e.g., robotics).

So why doesn't the U.S. government place more pressure on China to raise the value of the yuan? Part of the reason may lie in concern about losing Chinese financing of the U.S. federal deficit. For several years the two governments have been co-dependent: The U.S. government gets financing for its deficits, and the Chinese government gains by maintaining an undervalued currency. Not an easy relationship to change.

Probably more important, however, many large and politically powerful U.S.-based firms depend directly on the low-cost goods imported from China. Wal-mart and Target, as any shopper knows, are filled with Chinese-made goods. Then there are the less visible products from China, including a power device that goes into the Microsoft Xbox, computer keyboards for Dell, and many other goods for many other U.S. corporations. If the yuan's value rose and these firms had to pay more dollars to buy these items, they could probably not pass all the increase on to consumers and their profits would suffer.

Still, in spite of the interests of these firms, the U.S. government may take some action, either by pressing harder for China to let the value of the yuan rise relative to the dollar or by placing some restrictions on imports from China. But don't expect too big a change. ❏

Article 9.3

BRAZIL'S BIG PUSH

With a leading government role in industrialization, "neo-developmentalism" represents a sharp break from neoliberalism.

BY JAMES M. CYPHER
March/April 2013

As the undertow of the great financial crash of 2008 sank Brazil's economy in 2009, the Brazilian government quickly responded with a massive, jobcreating public-spending program, while facilitating the expansion of consumer credit. Even as the economies of other Latin American nations slowed or declined, Brazil's economy shot ahead, growing at an astonishing 7.5% rate in 2010. Hopes that this miraculous recovery signaled a new era were soon disappointed, as growth slid to less than 3% in 2011 and only about 1% in 2012.

Since Luiz Inácio Lula da Silva's election as president of Brazil in 2002, the Brazilian government has emphasized, above all, "growth with redistribution," including higher minimum wages, pensions for the elderly, and a massive anti-poverty program (Bolsa Família). Under Lula, as da Silva is universally known, and his successor, Dilma Rousseff, also of Brazil's Workers' Party, this approach has reduced income inequality and raised over 30 million people above the poverty line. The economic strategy has also increased demand for goods produced in Brazil, creating virtuous circles of increased production, growing employment, and rising wages.

The role of government, however, goes well beyond Keynesian-style policies to promote growth in aggregate demand, full employment, and income redistribution; in fact, it is centered in the sphere of production (on supply rather than demand). In contrast to other South American nations that have enjoyed economic growth since 2002, Brazil's "neo-developmentalist" approach has emphasized the role of the government in promoting the country's industrial competitiveness, spearheaded by an active industrial policy and the construction of a national innovation system. Industrial policy entails an activist government and an agile cadre of state functionaries, ideally working constructively with the private sector to identify and incubate new, growth-leading economic sectors. Today, such a policy requires national capabilities for scientific research and product-and-process innovation in the favored sectors.

Developmentalist ideas—emphasizing national industrialization, a growing internal market powered by wage gains for the working class and emerging middle class, and often a key role for stateowned enterprises in filling the gaps left by a diffident business class—swept Latin America's policymaking elite back in the 1930s. The results were startling: Annual (inflation-adjusted) per-capita economic growth from 1940-80 doubled the level achieved in the 1900-39 period (2.7% vs. 1.3%), and was more than four times greater than that achieved in the neoliberal period, 1980-2000, for the six economically largest nations (Argentina, Brazil, Chile, Colombia, Mexico, and Venezuela). Despite the social gains arising from developmentalist policies, neoliberal economics largely supplanted developmentalism during the 1970s and 1980s. (Neoliberal ideas were notoriously championed by the Latin American economists, trained at the University of Chicago, who became known as the "Chicago boys.") In the 1970s, U.S.-supported military dictatorships overthrew developmentalist regimes in several Southern Cone countries (Argentina, Chile and Uruguay), elevated Chicago-boys-style economists to positions of power, and imposed neoliberal policies. During the 1980s, such policies were pushed on still more countries by the debt crisis and the structural-adjustment programs favored by the International Monetary Fund.

Brazil's current "neo-developmentalist" approach harkens back to the earlier developmentalist approach in various important ways: The state is leading the accumulation project through prodigious catch-up efforts directed at bottlenecks and "choke points" of the Brazilian infrastructure, including railroads, highways, water management, ports, electricity and energy. What is new is the placement of social justice issues on a par with the big-push efforts promoting industrialization and infrastructure. Neo-developmentalism is pushing to even out the distribution of income through large increases in the minimum wage and several comprehensive social programs that protect the poor and the aged (including badly needed support for housing and sanitation), while beginning to target educational reform that will have a dramatic effect on underprivileged youth. Many of the industrialization/ infrastructure issues that engrossed the developmentalists remain a central focus of public policy, but now efforts to strengthen the industrial base are complemented by socially driven programs that have the effect of increasing domestic demand and broadening the social base of this demand—hence the idea of inclusive growth. Finally, there has been a concerted public-sector effort to foster innovative capacity through expanded national funding for science and engineering.

The Key Role of Petroleum

As Brazil's efforts to implement this neo-developmentalist strategy unfolded, it made major discoveries of offshore oil. This has led to a policy reorientation designed to use petroleum as a major pillar of the industrial strategy. In addition to achieving long-sought energy independence, Brazil anticipates capturing multiple benefits from this effort, including becoming the world leader in "ultra-deep" offshore drilling technologies. Including these offshore efforts, Petrobras, the state-owned oil company, has over 700 projects underway. The government—particularly through the national development bank (Banco Nacional de Desenvolvimento Econômico e Social, or BNDES)—would, once again, play a catalytic role in directing long-term public investment flows to state-owned and public-private enterprises, promoting technological innovation in offshore drilling and production. Since 2007, Brazil has made a massive commitment to developing the oil reserves, a long- term effort with an estimated price tag of $1 trillion. While BNDES is deeply involved, its reach extends far beyond just the petroleum sector. Its annual lending to Brazil's federal, state, and municipal governments (for long-term infrastructure projects) and to state-owned and private Brazilian firms is roughly four times as much as the World Bank's.

Following the insights of Albert Hirschman, an important early developmentalist who acted as an economic advisor to Latin American governments in the 1950s, the state-led effort in the oil sector is designed to exploit forward and backward "linkage" effects, promoting growth in other, related industries. As Hirschman emphasized, investments in one important area can lead to a broad range of mutually supporting economic activities driving the creation of new skills, massive new employment opportunities, improved productivity, and higher wages. Success opens a path for the expansion of education and social programs. In the oil industry today, backward linkages include the vast web of potential suppliers for specialty steel, motors, pumps, ships, drilling platforms, and tools of every size and description. Providing these inputs will stimulate a sweeping revitalization and deepening of the machine-tool sector. Forward linkages constitute the range of activities that spin off from petroleum extraction, producing goods such as fertilizers, plastics, refined petroleum products, and synthetic fibers. The importance of such linkages is well understood by neo-developmentalists, particularly President Rousseff, who was molded by her extensive developmentalist training in economics at two excellent Brazilian public universities.

The state will enable Petrobras to make $224 billion in capital investments during 2011-2015. One result of these massive outlays is that, by 2014, Brazil will have two new petroleum refineries under operation (in the states of Pernambuco and Rio de Janiero), enabling the country to meet its burgeoning need for refined petroleum products. These investments will thereby close a major developmental bottleneck— where Brazil had exported crude while importing high-value-added refined products. Prior to the major oil discoveries, state support and promotion had helped Brazil develop a viable and efficient ethanol industry, a large-scale, innovative strategy to overcome its petroleum resource gap. The current thrust into petroleum is partially based in the developmental legacy of the ethanol industry.

One aspect of Brazil's neo-developmentalist strategy for the oil industry is the ambitious goal of reserving the "supply chain" for Brazilian companies. Unlike Venezuela's efficient national oil company PDVSA—which strives to promote the "democratization of oil resources" by channeling a major portion of its surplus to social programs—Brazil intends to promote national technological capabilities by building a national supplier base. The objective is to have as much as 95% local content in portions of the supply chain by 2017. By mid-2012, Petrobras was already buying nearly 70% of its equipment from Brazilian producers. This approach is designed to internalize, as much as possible, the various positive spinoffs of this massive initiative. Taking into account direct exploration, drilling, and production, transportation and refining, and production of machinery and other inputs, it will encompass an estimated 25% of Brazil's entire economy by 2020. As this industry expands, it will create learning opportunities for both production employees and managers. The development of new homegrown technological capacities, meanwhile, will create increasing returns in a broad range of associated industrial activities, such as shipbuilding, steel fabrication, and machine tools and machinery production.

Macroeconomic Trials and Tribulations

Development economics is concerned with locating and realizing a long-term, sustainable, structural transformation of an entire economy. Struggling nations cannot often find the policy space for longterm commitments. In Brazil's case, the major oil discoveries in 2006 were followed by the snowballing effects of the financial panic and global recession. By late 2012, the aftershocks were still convulsing much of Europe, with devastating unemployment levels pushed ever higher by backfiring Chicago-boys-style austerity programs.

Quick, adroit, and massive recession-fighting policies held Brazil's GDP decline in 2009 to less than 1%. As noted earlier, these policies reached their full impact in 2010, allowing the economy to grow dramatically. In part, this was possible because Brazil's dependence on world trade is relatively light—exports were only about 10% of GDP in 2011. (This meant that Brazil was not dragged down by the collapse in export demand, as many other developing countries were.) Furthermore, an increasing portion of Brazil's exports—nearly 20% in late 2012, compared to only 1% in 2000—are sent to China, on which the Great Recession of 2008-2010 scarcely had an impact.

Nonetheless, the fallout from the financial turbulence of the high-income "core" economies has had an impact on Brazil. First, scarred by repeated bouts of hyperinflation, rising above 1,000% per year in 1988-1994, the Brazilian central bank maintained an unnecessarily tight money policy, restricting economic growth. Second, since 2003, a stronger currency (which makes a country's exports more expensive and imports cheaper) has caused imports to boom. During the worst of the current crisis, Brazil had the world's most overvalued currency. Third, households rapidly took on new debt and now repayment problems are rising, making it harder for consumer demand to drive economic growth.

Until recently, Brazil's central bank—functioning independently of the elected government— operated under a monetarist director dedicated solely to defeating phantom inflationary pressures. (Monetarists have been historically known for their single-minded focus on maintaining very low inflation, as opposed to achieving full employment.) Working against the neo-developmentalist strategy, he set interest rates at the highest level in the world. This policy both tended to slow down the economy and to encourage financialization, the diversion of funds away from productive investment and toward speculation and other purely financial activities. Meanwhile, the U.S. Federal Reserve (the "Fed") pushed interest rates nearly down to zero and created massive waves of liquidity, from late 2008 through 2012. With Brazilian interests rates high and U.S. rates low, hot money (financial investments seeking a big, fast return) sloshed into Brazil. One result was to push up Brazil's exchange rate. Another was to expose Brazil to the risk that the hot funds would quickly exit— creating financial instability and macroeconomic turmoil that could detain, if not derail, Brazil's neo-developmentalist strategy. (See Armagan Gezici, "The Return of Capital Controls," *Dollars & Sense*, January/February 2013.)

Vitally important for the future, investment has been falling as a share of GDP since 2010. In spite of an 83% rise in net foreign direct investment—to a record $68 billion in 2011—total investment (public + private + transnational) was only 18% of GDP in 2012. As foreign money has flowed in, a record number of Brazilian firms— 679 from 2010 through 2012—have been bought out by transnational corporations, fanning fears of denationalization. Transnationals were a major reason for Brazil's negative overall current-account balance, because they returned a record $85 billion of profits reaped from their Brazil operations to their home-office locations in

2011. The high exchange rate (strong real) has meant Brazil's manufacturing exports are very expensive, while foreign made, especially Chinese, imports are a bargain. During these years imports of goods and (especially) services soared, with volume growth averaging 15% per year, opening up a rising current-account deficit from 2008 onward, equal to 2.4% of GDP in 2012. (The main component of the current account is the trade balance.) As a result, Brazil has been deindustrializing, contrary to the developmentalist vision.

Only in 2011, when President Rousseff brought in a pragmatic non-monetarist, Alexandre Tombini, to run the central bank, was the "hard money" policy abandoned. The interest rate was cut ten times in a row, to about 7%. By Brazilian standards this is "cheap money," but it remains to be seen whether the everhesitant business strata can pivot from trading financial assets to actually building industrial capacity. Since then, the bank has also devised policies to push down the exchange rate, which has declined from about $0.65 to the real to less than $0.50 to the real in late 2012. This depreciation of the currency will help boost Brazil's exports, but most importantly will reduce imports of consumer goods and give Brazil's broad national manufacturing an opportunity to recover from the import surge.

While a lower exchange rate is important, the new policy to reduce interest rates is much more critical. In 2010-2011, central-bank inflation-adjusted interest rates hovered around 6%. But the new leadership at the central bank—acting in concert for the first time with the state's neo-developmentalist efforts—had forced the interest rate down to only 1.8% by September 2012. The central bank is no longer consistently choking off the forward momentum of the economy and encouraging the diversion of productive investment into the financial sphere. The declines in the exchange rate and interest rates, plus a new surge in government investment, are beginning to reverse over two consecutive years of a consistently declining growth rate. Between September 2011 and September 2012, industrial production grew by over 3%, while the real median household income of the employed increased by more than 4%.

The "Big Push"

Until recently, Brazil had been unable to confront three major barriers: 1) The monetarist doctrine of tight-money and high-interest loans, as practiced by the central bank from 2003 to 2011, 2) a dysfunctional educational system that left Brazilians bereft of adequate knowledge and skills, and 3) a decrepit infrastructure that could not meet the growing demand for transportation, electricity, port facilities, and railways. In addition to reversing the monetarist central-bank policy, the Brazilian government has also taken important steps to address the latter two barriers in the past year.

In what may be the first major step to address the deficiencies in the educational system, President Rousseff announced the "Law of Social Quotas" in August 2012. The law's objective is to change the composition of the student body in the federal university system. By 2016, half the students will enter from the public school system—where poor and working-class students are concentrated. A new admissions policy also aims to change the universities' racial composition, targeting a six-fold increase in enrollment of Afro-Brazilians.

President Rousseff's approach to the pressing issue of infrastructure expansion, meanwhile, is a departure from previous neo-developmentalist initiatives. A February 2012 decision to auction off the operation of three major airports to private companies was followed in August by the major policy innovation of using public-private partnerships to address the infrastructure problem. Under public-private partnerships, firms will commit to invest $66 billion to build over 4,500 miles of new toll roads and over 6,000 miles of railways, supplementing the more than 1% of GDP the federal government allocated to infrastructure in 2011. In addition, further auctions of licenses to form public-private partnerships in port facilities and airports were announced in late 2012 and early 2013. Public-private consortiums in Brazil are not just veiled forms of privatization, as they tend to be in the United States. The state retains broad decision-making powers, including setting relatively low profit rates for the private companies.

According to Robert Devlin and Graciela Moguillansky, who have undertaken a comprehensive study of public-private partnerships in several nations (including Korea, Malaysia, and Singapore), success requires three crucial elements: First, there must be a long-term strategic vision that is shared by society at large. Second, there must be an "understanding" between the public and private sectors—regarding how problems are defined and how they are resolved— that is seen as legitimate by public opinion. Third, state capacity must be sufficient to implement the strategy and to avoid "capture" by the private sector. Brazil's state capacity is considerable— best represented by BNDES and Petrobras—and improving as a result of President Rousseff's relentless efforts to raise professional standards and reduce corruption in the public sector. But, in the case of this infrastructure initiative, the hesitant business sector has answered with resistance and pleas for higher returns (which mean higher user fees) and longer concession contracts than the government had planned. A lack of public-private consensus has slowed this program. At the broader societal level, if sports facilities for the 2014 World Cup and the 2016 Summer Olympics are viewed as crowding out crucial social needs— needs constantly highlighted by the progressive administrations in power since 2002—clashes over policy could escalate. Brazil has broken into new territory with this latest initiative, which will test the strength of the Brazilian state.

Another element of the new strategy will be to lower electricity rates to private firms by 28% in 2013. Meanwhile, in late 2012 railroad freight rates dropped by 25-30%, depending on the nature of the cargo. These measures are designed to lower the so-called "Brazil cost," which, due to infrastructure bottlenecks, has kept the price of producing in Brazil quite high. For example, logistics costs currently absorb 12-15% of GDP, nearly three times the level of the German economy. Thus, policy is shifting from a "demand focus"—transfers to the poor, higher minimum wages, full-employment policies, etc.—to a "supply focus" designed to both promote necessary long-term investment and massively lower costs of production.

Brazil's outsized effort to implement a viable industrial policy and pursue a neo-developmentalist strategy is reminiscent of former Brazilian President Juscelino Kubitschek's massive, and largely successful, drive to accelerate the country's economic growth in the late 1950s and early 1960s. Kubitschek's motto was "fifty years in five." As political scientist Kathryn Sikkink argues, the "Brazilian industrialists saw themselves as protagonists and leaders of the process of industrialization." The interests of the state and the industrialists converged, with the state playing the crucial coordinator role. The always-in-a-hurry Kubitschek set and met ambitious developmental targets in 30 areas, focusing on five key sectors: energy, transportation, agriculture, basic (or "heavy") industries, and technical training. Lacking Kubitschek's high-wire talent to mobilize disparate factions, successor João Goulart was toppled by a U.S.-backed and -funded military coup in 1964, as he sought to address taboo issues such as land reform and the role of (mostly U.S.-based) multinational corporations. Developmentalism continued under nationalist military rule until the neoliberal 1980s, but without any regard for an inclusive social agenda.

Led ably by Lula and Rousseff, Brazil is once again conjuring memories of the Kubitschek era, while breaking the mold in Latin America. ❑

Sources: Pablo Astorga, Ame R. Bergés, and Valpy FitzGerald, "The Standard of Living in Latin America During the Twentieth Century," QEH Working Paper Series—QEHWPS103, Latin American Centre, St. Antony's College, Oxford, 2003; Jeb Blount, "Brazil's onceenvied Energy Matrix a Victim of 'Hubris,'" *Reuters Business and Financial News*, Jan. 7, 2013; Raymond Colitt and Matthew Malinowski, "Brazil to Reduce Power Costs, Pressure Banks to Foster Growth," *Bloomberg News*, Sept. 6, 2012; Robert Devlin and Graciela Moguillansky, "Aliazas público-privadas como estrategias nacionales de desarrollo a largo plazo," *RevistaCepal*, Vol. 97, April 2009; Economic Commission for Latin America and the Caribbean, Economic Survey of Latin American and the Caribbean, 2012; Economic Commission for Latin America and the Caribbean, Macroeconomic Report on Latin America and the Caribbean, June 2012; "Briefing: Brazil's oil boom, filling up the future," *The Economist*, Nov. 5, 2011; "The lore of ore," *The Economist*, Oct. 13, 2012; "Brazilian Banks: No more free lunch," *The Economist*, Oct. 20, 2012; "Brazil's economy: Facing Headwinds, Dilma changes course," *The Economist*, Aug. 18, 2012; Albert Hirschman, "A Generalized Linkage Approach to Development, with Special Reference to Staples," *Economic Development and Cultural Change*, Vol. 25, 1977; Joe Leahy, "Brazil's burgeoning appetite for construction," *The Globe and Mail*, Aug. 28, 2012; Carlos Lopes, "Em 2011, foram desnacionalizadas 206 empresas," *Informa CUT*, Jan. 21, 2013; Lecio Morais and Alfredo Saad-Filho, "Da economia política à política econômica: o novo-desenvolvimentismo e o governo Lula," in *Revista de Economia Política*, Vol. 31, No. 4 Oct.-Dec. 2011; PDVSA, "What is Endogenous Development" (pdvsa.com); Simon Romero, "Brazil enacts affirmative action law for universities," *New York Times*, Aug. 31, 2012; Paul Rosenstein-Rodan, "The Theory of the 'Big Push,'" in Gerald Meier, ed., *Leading Issues in Economic Development*, 3rd ed., 1976; Kathryn Sikkink, Ideas and Institutions: Developmentalism in Brazil and Argentina, 1991; World Trade Organization, "Country Profile: Brazil," Sept. 2012.

Article 9.4

THE RETURN OF CAPITAL CONTROLS

BY ARMAGAN GEZICI
January/February 2013

In the wake of the global financial crisis, low interest rates and slow growth in advanced economies have led to a massive influx of capital into so-called emerging markets, where interest rates and growth have been higher. International investors, seeking higher returns, have moved their funds away from advanced economies into emerging-market securities like stocks, bonds, and mutual funds. The governments of many developing countries, as a result, have become increasingly concerned about the effects of these capital inflows—including stronger currencies, asset-price bubbles, and even inflation. In March 2012, Brazil's president Dilma Rousseff accused developed nations of unleashing a "monetary tsunami," which is undermining the competitiveness of emerging economies like her own. These concerns have motivated many countries to introduce measures to cope with cross-border capital flows.

Starting in late 2009, for example, Brazil began to implement "capital controls"—including a tax on capital inflows and other measures—to keep its currency (the real) from growing stronger against the dollar. Several Asian countries, including South Korea, Taiwan, and Thailand, have also implemented controls of various kinds on capital inflows. Suddenly, it appears, capital controls are back.

Whatever Happened to Capital Controls?

The debate about controls on international capital flows goes back to the World War II era. During the Bretton Woods negotiations (1944) establishing the international monetary order for the postwar period, Britain's chief negotiator, John Maynard Keynes, and his U.S. counterpart, Harry Dexter White, agreed that a distinction should be made between "speculative" capital and "productive" capital. Both believed that speculative (or "hot money") capital flows should be subject to controls. Keynes went further, arguing that "control of capital movements, both inward and outward, should be a permanent feature of the post-war system." For much of the postwar period, controls such as restrictions on the types of assets banks could hold and limits on capital outflows (used even by the United States between 1963 and 1973) were, indeed, implemented by many capitalist countries. Beginning in the 1980s, however, international financial institutions like the International Monetary Fund (IMF), many Western governments, and private high finance began to oppose capital controls. The U. S. government and the IMF became staunch advocates of "capital-account liberalization" (that is, the deregulation of international capital flows) during this period.

The recent crisis resulted in widespread recognition, around the world, that deregulated financial activity can result in major economic disruptions. In most of the world's largest economies, possible measures to re-regulate finance on the national level came back on the political agenda. Cross-border finance, however, was largely left out of the discussion, as if it did not require any regulation. Conventional discussions of this issue have also involved a peculiar twist in terminology: financial regulations are typically called "regulations" when purely domestic, yet when they involve cross-border flows, they carry the more ominous-sounding label of "controls"—as if to emphasize the undesirable nature of these regulations from a free-market perspective.

Why Capital Controls?

The essential problem with international capital flows is that they are "pro-cyclical"— that is, they amplify the patterns of the business cycle. Capital tends to flow in when economies are expanding, promoting "overheating" and inflation, and tends to flow out during downturns, exacerbating the decline in output and rise in unemployment. They also narrow the ability of governments to respond to cyclical economic problems. The economic literature on capital flows cites five fears that drive countries to adopt capital controls:

Fear of appreciation: Massive and rapid capital inflows may cause the country's currency to become stronger (increase in value relative to other currencies), making its exports more expensive and damaging its international competitiveness.

Fear of "hot money": Short-term speculative capital inflows may cause financial instability and increase the fragility of the domestic financial system. The short-term nature of these flows leads to a "maturity mismatch" between domestic financial institutions' assets and liabilities. In effect, they have borrowed short-term while lending long-term. As the sudden reversal of hot money occurs at the whim of international investor sentiments, a domestic banking crisis is likely to follow.

Fear of large inflows that can disrupt the financial system, even if they are not all "hot money": Large inflows of foreign capital may feed asset bubbles, such as unsustainable increases in stock or real-estate prices or unsustainable booms in consumer credit.

Fear of loss of monetary autonomy: It is not possible for a country to achieve (simultaneously) full international capital mobility, monetary-policy autonomy, and exchange-rate stability. (This is known as the "trilemma" of international macroeconomics.) If a country does not control international capital flows, inflows can cause exchange-rate appreciation. The government can counteract this by increasing the money supply, but then its monetary policy is not independent. To avoid exchange-rate appreciation and sustain an independent monetary policy, a country should give up full capital mobility.

Fear of capital flight: In the event of a crisis, "herding" behavior by international investors may expose a country to the risk of sharp reversals in capital flows (with capital leaving just as quickly as it came).

What Happened During the Crisis?

Between 2002 and 2007, there were massive flows of capital into emerging markets with high growth rates and relatively developed financial systems. This surge in capital inflows was interrupted after the collapse of the U.S. investment house Lehman Brothers in September 2008, which led global capital to flee to the "safety" of the U.S. market, wreaking havoc in emerging markets. (See figure.) While there was no comparable financial crisis in these economies, more than half of them experienced negative growth in 2009. Countries with already-large trade deficits were among the hardest hit, as they were highly dependent on capital inflows.

Between 2008 and 2011, however, the governments of the industrialized countries lowered interest rates in an attempt to stimulate production and employment. Capital again began to flow into emerging markets, attracted by higher interest rates and growth. The "carry trade" was a key mechanism that triggered these flows. In the carry trade, investors borrow money in one country at a low interest rate and invest it in another country at a higher rate. This strategy allows investors not only to exploit the differences in interest rates, but also take advantage of exchange-rate movements. If the currency of the country with higher interest rates becomes stronger, over time, relative to the currency of the country with lower interest rates, investors stand to make even larger profits.

By late 2008, government policymakers in emerging economies had become alarmed about the problems these inflows could cause—currency appreciation, asset bubbles, inflation, and the sudden turn toward large outflows. From March 2009 to March 2010, Brazil saw the value of the real go up by 30% against the dollar, due at least in part to the carry trade. Under normal circumstances, the conventional macroeconomic tool to stem asset bubbles or inflation would have been an increase in interest rates. By increasing interest rates, monetary authorities would have curbed the appetite to borrow and reduced the amount of money available for spending in the economy. With less spending, the economy would slow down and inflation would decline. However, because of the carry trade, such a policy could actually fuel further inflows and therefore exacerbate these problems. For example, in 2009, interest rates were around 12% in Brazil and less than 1% in the United States; if Brazil had raised interest rates in an attempt to curb asset bubbles and inflation, it could actually have attracted even higher capital inflows.

The Brazilian government was the most vocal critic of these capital flows at the G-20's 2010 summit in Seoul. The Brazilian finance minister declared the surge in capital flows, the subsequent exchange-rate appreciations, and the various policy responses by emerging countries to be the beginning of a "currency war." In late 2009, the Brazilian government imposed a 2% tax on various forms of capital inflows. In October 2010, it twice increased the tax rate, first to 4% and then to 6%. In January 2011, Brazil introduced new reserve requirements on capital inflows (see sidebar) to curb the appreciation of the real against the dollar.

In 2009, nations across Asia also began to deploy controls, having seen large appreciations of their currencies. Between the end of 2008 and early 2010, South Korea's currency (the won) appreciated by over 30% against the dollar. Starting in July 2010, South Korean banks faced new restrictions on their international currency holdings. The South Korean government also tried to steer investment away from speculation by permitting bank loans in foreign currencies only for the purchase of raw materials, for foreign direct investment, and for repayment of debts. Meanwhile, in November 2009, the government of Taiwan

NET PORTFOLIO INVESTMENT—EQUITY, THREE DEVELOPING REGIONS

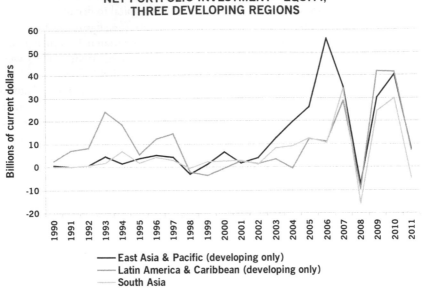

Source: World Bank, Data, Portfolio equity, net inflows (BoP, current US$), (data.worldbank.org)

banned foreign investment funds from investing in certificates of deposit with domestic banks, a move aimed at preventing foreign investors from betting on currency appreciation. At the end of 2010, it also placed restrictions on banks' holdings of foreign currencies. In 2010, Thailand introduced a 15% tax on interest income and capital gains earned by foreign investors. Meanwhile, Indonesia placed limits on short-term external borrowing and introduced a one-month minimum holding period for foreign investors purchasing some types of government-issued securities.

It is still too early to draw final conclusions about the effectiveness of these controls. A study by Kevin Gallagher of the Global Development and Environment Institute (GDAE) provides a preliminary assessment for the cases of Brazil, Taiwan, and South Korea. All three were trying to create a space for independent monetary policy and stem the appreciation of their currencies by placing restrictions on capital mobility. Interest rates between the United States and each of these nations have become less correlated. (A strong correlation between interest rates may indicate that, when the U.S. Fed lowers interest rates, causing capital flows to these other countries, the latter are forced to respond with lower interest rates of their own to stem the appreciation of the currency. That is, they lack monetary independence.) So these findings suggest that the controls have, to some extent, allowed a more autonomous monetary policy.

In the cases of Brazil and Taiwan, there is some evidence that controls have been associated with a slower rate of currency appreciation. But in the case of South Korea, currency appreciation has continued and the rate of appreciation has actually increased since controls were initiated. This difference can be explained by the structural differences across these countries, as well as the different types of controls used. South Korea's strong export performance is an important factor putting upward pressure on the value of its currency. (Demand for a country's exports is one factor determining the demand for its currency, since that country's companies usually require payment in the national currency.) Moreover, unlike Brazil and Taiwan, South Korean authorities did not use any of the "price-based controls" (see sidebar) that would have automatically placed additional costs on international investors seeking to enter Korean markets. These differences in effectiveness can shed some light on what kinds of capital controls might work in different countries, given their unique conditions.

How to Impose Capital Controls?

The particular form of capital controls that a government imposes depends on its policy goals. If its main goal is to slow down capital inflows, the types of regulations that it can choose from include:

- Unremunerated reserve requirements: A certain percentage of new capital inflows must be kept on reserve in the country's central bank. "Unremunerated" in this context refers to the fact that no interest would be earned on these funds.
- Taxes on new inflows.
- Limits or taxes on how much domestic banks and other financial institutions can owe in foreign currencies.
- Restrictions on currency mismatches: Borrowing and lending activities of domestic banks or firms should be denominated in the same currency. For example, only firms with foreign-exchange revenues from exports can borrow in foreign currencies.
- Limitations on borrowing abroad: For example, such borrowing may be allowed only for foreign investment and trade activities, or only for firms with positive net revenues in a foreign currency (as from exports).
- Mandatory government approvals for some or all international capital transactions.
- Minimum stay requirements: Foreign investors might be required to stay in the domestic economy for at least a certain length of time.

On the other hand, different measures are available to a country that wants to focus on preventing or slowing down outflows of capital, including:

- Mandatory government approval for domestic residents to invest abroad or hold bank accounts in a foreign currency.
- Requirements for domestic residents to report on foreign investments and transactions done with foreign bank accounts.
- Limits on sectors in which foreign individuals and companies can invest.
- Restrictions on amounts of principal or capital income that foreign investors can send abroad.
- Limits on how much non-residents can borrow in the domestic market.
- Taxes on capital outflows.

In addition to the distinction between controls imposed on outflows or inflows, measures are usually categorized as "price-based" or "quantity-based," depending on the mechanism through which they impact capital flows. Minimum stay requirements, for example, are one kind of quantity-based control. Taxes on inflows or on outflows are one kind of price-based control.

The IMF and Capital Controls

Not long after developing-country governments began implementing capital controls, official views about controls began to shift. Since 2010, the IMF has produced a series of official papers on capital-account liberalization, on capital inflows and outflows, and on the multilateral aspects of regulating international capital flows. In November 2012, it released a comprehensive "institutional view" on when and how nations should deploy capital-account regulations. The same institution that pushed for the global deregulation of cross-border finance in the 1990s now says that capital-account liberalization is more of a long-run goal, and is not for every country at all times. The IMF now accepts that capital controls—which it has renamed "capital-flow management measures"—are permissible for inflows, on a temporary basis, en route to liberalization; regulations on capital outflows, meanwhile, are permissible only during or just after financial crises.

While more flexible than its previous stances, the new IMF position still insists on the eventual deregulation of global financial flows and emphasizes that controls should only be temporary. Behind this insistence lies the institution's ideological commitment to free markets, as well as the influence of finance capital and Wall Street interests on the institution's decision making. As the experience of developing economies in the recent crisis bears out, rather than being treated as temporary measures, capital controls should be adopted as permanent tools that can be used counter-cyclically—to smooth out economic booms and busts. As described earlier, international capital flows are strongly pro-cyclical. By regulating inflows during a boom, a government can manage booms better, while avoiding exchange-rate problems or additional inflationary pressures. By restricting outflows during a downturn, it can mitigate capital flight, which has the potential of triggering financial crisis, and create some room for expansionary monetary policy.

The IMF guidelines, in addition, give scant attention to policy-design issues related to capital controls. A great deal of international experience shows that controls can lose their effectiveness over time, as foreign investors learn to evade regulation through the use of financial derivatives and other securities. Nations such as Brazil and South Korea have increasingly "fine-tuned" their regulations in an attempt to keep ahead of investors' ability to circumvent them.

The IMF also fails to acknowledge that capital flows should be regulated at "both ends." The industrialized nations are usually the source of international capital flows, but generally ignore the negative spillover effects on other countries. So far, the entire burden of regulation has fallen on the recipients of inflows, mostly developing countries.

Where to Now?

As industrialized nations aim to recover from the crisis, they hope that credit and capital will stay "at home." Meanwhile, the developing world has little interest in having to receive capital inflows. This creates an obvious alignment of interests. Industrialized nations could adjust their tax codes and deploy other types of regulation to keep capital in their countries, as emerging markets deploy capital controls to reduce the level and change the composition of capital flows that may destabilize their economies.

One important obstacle to such coordination is the prohibition, in many trade and investment treaties, on regulation of cross-border finance. For example, in Asia, where capital controls are most prevalent, the Association of South East Asian Nations (ASEAN) requires member countries to eliminate most controls by 2015, with relatively narrow exceptions. Trade and investment agreements with the United States, such as the North American Free Trade Agreement (NAFTA) and the Dominican Republic-Central America Free Trade Agreement (CAFTA-DR), provide the least flexibility. Since the 2003 U.S.-Chile Free Trade Agreement, every U.S. trade or investment agreement has required the free flow of capital (in both directions) between the United States and its trading partners, without exception.

In January 2011, some 250 economists from across the globe called on the United States to recognize that the consensus on capital controls has shifted and to permit nations the flexibility to deploy controls to prevent and mitigate crises. The appeal was rebuffed by prominent U.S. business associations and the U.S. government. Treasury Secretary Timothy Geithner declared that U.S. policy would remain unchanged: "In general, we believe that those risks are best managed through a mix of fiscal and monetary policy measures, exchange rate adjustment, and carefully designed non-discriminatory prudential measures, such as bank reserve or capital requirements and limitations on exposure to exchange rate risk." In other words, he suggested the use of mainly conventional domestic macroeconomic policies and some domestic financial regulation, but excluded controls on international flows.

With the exception of speculators who profit from volatility in the markets, all nations and actors within them would benefit from the financial stability that an international system of financial regulation could help provide. After the opening of capital markets in developing economies, in varying degrees, we have seen extreme volatility of international capital flows. This volatility has been exacerbated by the monetary policies of advanced economies: over the past 30 years expansionary monetary policy in advanced economies has led to capital flows to emerging-market economies, while contractionary policies have produced the reversal of capital flows and, in turn, helped set off the crises of the 1980s and 1990s. The stability provided by an international system of capital controls would not only allow emerging economies to preserve their own growth and stability but also improve the effectiveness of policies in advanced economies.

Some financial interests, however, would have to bear the costs. Capital controls would either make financial transactions more costly, reducing profit margins, or not allow financial companies to take advantage of certain investment opportunities, again reducing potential profits to investors. These "losers" from a capital-controls regime are highly concentrated and very powerful politically. The "winners," in terms of the general public, are comparatively scattered and weaker politically. Despite the optimism that briefly emerged, especially in policy circles, about a future with more effective regulation of international capital flows, these political realities may be the biggest obstacles for 21st-century capital controls. ❑

Sources: Kevin Gallagher, "Regaining Control? Capital Controls and the Global Financial Crisis," Political Economy Research Institute, Working Paper 250, 2011; Stephany Griffith-Jones and Kevin P. Gallagher, "Curbing Hot Money Flows to Protect the Real Economy," *Economic and Political Weekly*, January 15, 2011, Vol. XLVI, No 3; Ilene Grabel, "Not Your Grandfather's IMF: Global Crisis, Productive Incoherence, and Developmental Policy Space," Political Economy Research Institute, Working Paper 214, 2010; International Monetary Fund, The Liberalization And Management Of Capital Flows: An Institutional View, Washington, D.C., 2011.

Article 9.5

THE "TRADE DEAL" SCAM

BY DEAN BAKER
June 2013

As part of its overall economic strategy the Obama administration is rushing full speed ahead with two major trade deals. On the one hand it has the Trans-Pacific Partnership, which includes Japan and Australia and several other countries in East Asia and Latin America. On the other side there is an effort to craft a U.S.-EU trade agreement.

There are two key facts people should know about these proposed trade deals. First, they are mostly not about trade. Second, they are not intended to boost the economy in a way that will help most of us. In fact, it is reasonable to say that these deals will likely be bad news for most people in the United States. Most of the people living in our partner countries are likely to be losers too.

On the first point, traditional trade issues, like the reduction of import tariffs and quotas, are a relatively small part of both deals. This is the case because these barriers have already been sharply reduced or even eliminated over the past three decades.

As a result, with a few notable exceptions, there is little room for further reductions in these sorts of barriers. Instead, both deals focus on other issues, some of which may reasonably be considered barriers to trade, but many of which are matters of regulation that would ordinarily be left to national, regional, or even local levels of government to set for themselves. One purpose of locking regulatory rules into a trade deal is to push an agenda that favors certain interests (e.g., the large corporations who are at the center of the negotiating process) over the rest of society.

Both of these deals are likely to include restrictions on the sorts of health, safety, and environmental regulation that can be imposed by the countries that are parties to the agreements. While many of the regulations that are currently in place in these areas are far from perfect, there is not an obvious case for having them decided at the international level.

Suppose a country or region decides that the health risks posed by a particular pesticide are too great and therefore bans its use. If the risks are in fact small, then those imposing the ban will be the primary ones who suffer, presumably in the form of less productive agriculture and higher food prices. Is it necessary to have an international agreement to prevent this sort of "mistake"?

As a practical matter, the evidence on such issues will often be ambiguous. For example, does fracking pose a health hazard to the surrounding communities? These agreements could end up taking control of the decision as to whether or not to allow fracking away from the communities who would be most affected.

In addition to limiting local control in many areas these trade deals will almost certainly include provisions that make for stronger and longer copyright and patent protection, especially on prescription drugs. The latter is coming at the urging of the U.S. pharmaceutical industry, which has been a central player in all the trade agreements negotiated over the last quarter century. This is likely to mean much higher drug prices for our trading partners.

This is of course the opposite of free trade. Instead of reducing barriers, the drug companies want to increase them, banning competitors from selling the same drugs. The difference in prices can be quite large. Generic drugs, with few exceptions, are cheap to produce. When drugs sell for hundreds or thousands of dollars per prescription it is because patent monopolies allow them to be sold for high prices.

If these trade deals result in much higher drug prices for our trading partners, the concern should not just be a moral one about people being unable to afford drugs. The more money people in Vietnam or Malaysia have to pay Pfizer and Merck for their drugs, the less money they will have to spend on other exports from the United States. This means that everyone from manufacturing workers to workers in the tourist sector can expect to see fewer job opportunities because of the copyright and patent protection rules imposed through these trade deals.

To see this point, imagine someone operating a fruit stand in a farmers' market. If the person in the next stall selling meat has a clever way to short-change customers, then his scam will come at least partly at the expense of the fruit stand. The reason is that many potential fruit stand customers will have their wallets drained at the meat stand and won't have any money left to buy fruit.

The drug companies' efforts to get increased patent protection, along with the computer and entertainment industries efforts to get stronger copyright protection, will have the same effect. Insofar as they can force other countries to pay them more in royalties and licensing fees or directly for their products, these countries will have less money to spend on other goods and services produced in the United States. In other words, the short-change artist in the next stall is not our friend and neither are the pharmaceutical, computer, or entertainment industries.

However, these industries all have friends in the Obama administration. As a result, these trade deals are likely to give them the protections they want. The public may not have the power to stop the high-powered lobbyists from getting their way on these trade pacts, but it should at least know what is going on. These trade deals are about pulling more money out of their pockets in order to make the rich even richer. ❑

Chapter 10

RESISTANCE AND ALTERNATIVES

Article 10.1

SAVING ENERGY CREATES JOBS

BY HEIDI GARRETT-PELTIER
May/June 2009

Improving energy efficiency—using less energy to do the same amount of work—saves money and cuts pollution. But today, the other benefit of investing in energy efficiency may be the best draw: saving energy creates jobs.

Let's look at energy use in residential and commercial buildings. In the United States, buildings account for 40% of all energy use and are responsible for 38% of U.S. carbon emissions. Homes and other buildings lose energy through wasted heat, air-conditioning, and electricity. Following Jimmy Carter's suddenly fashionable example, we can turn down the thermostat in the winter and put on a sweater. We can unplug appliances that aren't used and save "phantom" power.

Beyond these personal changes, though, lie massive opportunities for systematic energy efficiency gains. These include insulating buildings, replacing old windows, and updating appliances and lighting. All of these generate new economic opportunities—read, jobs—in construction, manufacturing, and other sectors.

For instance, retrofitting existing homes, offices, and schools to reduce heating- and cooling-related energy waste (also known as weatherization) creates jobs of many kinds. Recent media attention has spotlighted "green jobs" programs that are hiring construction workers to add insulation, replace windows, and install more efficient heating systems. Perhaps less visible, retrofitting buildings also creates jobs for the engineers who design the new windows and furnaces, the factory workers who build them, and the office workers who make the appointments and handle the bookkeeping.

In fact, retrofitting creates more than twice as many jobs per dollar spent than oil or coal production, according to a detailed study that my colleagues and I at the Political Economy Research Institute conducted in 2008. For each $1 million spent, retrofitting creates about 19 jobs while spending on coal creates nine jobs and oil only six. Retrofitting also creates more jobs per dollar spent than personal consumption on typical items such as food, clothing, and electronics. Personal consumption does better than fossil fuels, but not as well as retrofitting, generating about 15 jobs per $1 million spent.

Why does retrofitting create more jobs? First, retrofitting is more labor-intensive than fossil-fuel production, meaning that more of each dollar spent goes to labor and less to machinery and equipment. Retrofitting also has higher domestic content than either fossil fuels or consumer goods; in other words, more of the supplies used to retrofit buildings are produced in the United States. In fact, about 95% of spending on retrofits stays in the domestic economy, versus only 80% of spending on oil (including refining and other related activities). Since more of its inputs are produced in the United States, retrofitting employs more U.S. workers. And this raises its multiplier effect: when those workers spend their earnings, each retrofitting dollar leads to yet more demand for goods and services.

To be fair, not all energy efficiency improvements will create jobs. When a more energy-efficient appliance or window design is widely adopted, the manufacturing worker who produced a less efficient good yesterday is simply producing a more efficient good today, with no net increase in employment. On the other hand, many retrofitting activities are pure job creators. Insulating attics and caulking leaky windows are activities that necessitate new workers—not just a shift from producing one good to another. With the collapse of the housing bubble and the huge rise in construction industry unemployment, retrofitting is an activity that could put tens of thousands of people back to work.

The Obama administration's stimulus package contains a wide variety of energy efficiency incentives, from 30% rebates for home insulation and for installing efficient windows, to rebates for builders of energy-efficient new homes and commercial buildings. These provisions will drive energy-saving improvements, accelerating the transition to a low-carbon economy while also creating jobs. ❏

Sources: U.S. Department of Energy, EERE Building Technologies Program; Robert Pollin, Heidi Garrett-Peltier, James Heintz, and Helen Scharber, "Green Recovery," Political Economy Research Institute, September 2008.

Article 10.2

CO-OP ECONOMICS
What can economics teach us about the challenges and potential of cooperation?

BY NANCY FOLBRE
September/October 2013

I teach economics, a discipline largely inhabited by people skeptical of human potential for cooperation. But I live in a small New England town and work in a university environment that are, for the most part, cooperative. If I eat lunch on campus, I buy it from a student-managed, democratically run business that offers the tastiest, healthiest, cheapest provisions available. If I need to buy bread or milk on the way home, I pull into the Leverett Village Co-op. If my car needs attention, it goes to a worker-owned business, Pelham Auto, where I know both service managers by name. My money sits at the Five College Federal Credit Union, where it earns more interest and gains me better service than I've ever gotten at any other bank.

About four years ago, I began to weave economic theory more closely into my everyday life. The threads began coming together when Adam Trott and Michael Johnson, two members of the local Valley Alliance of Worker Cooperatives, reached out to tell me about their efforts to promote locally owned and democratically managed firms.

Although we lived in the same community, they found me as a result of a short post I wrote for the *New York Times*' "Economix" blog, describing a collaborative agreement between the United Steel Workers and the largest worker-owned business in the world, Mondragón Corporation. It seemed ironic, but also encouraging, that we first connected online, and that it might be possible to go from the global to the local and then back again.

Even in our cooperative-rich area of Western Massachusetts, Adam and Michael explained, most potential worker/owners knew virtually nothing about the principles involved (beyond liking the general idea). Why couldn't a public university provide better education and training for students potentially interested in starting up or joining a worker-owned business? Of course it could, and should. We decided to try to make that happen.

In a collaborative process that involved interested faculty and graduate students, as well as representatives from the Valley Alliance, we developed a new upper-division economics course and designed a Certificate Program for Applied Economic Research on Cooperative Enterprises centered on a summer research internship with a local cooperative.

Here, I want to share some of the ideas and opinions I've formed in the process of developing this program, which we believe could be a good model for other colleges and universities.

History Matters

Most people, including most college students, seem to think that cooperatives are a counter-cultural leftover from the 1960s, a niche phenomenon confined to hip neighborhoods and college towns. The economic history of the United States is typically portrayed as the steady march of corporate capitalism, trampling all other institutional forms. Many on the right see it as a march of progress; many on the left, as a march of doom.

Ironically, the traditional left preoccupation with corporate capitalism may simply feed the beast—overstating its hegemonic role, as though it can't be contained until the revolution comes. J.K. Gibson-Graham makes this point persuasively in *The End of Capitalism (As We Knew It)*: What we call "capitalism" involves many different creatures. Families, communities, non-profit organizations, and the state actually account for a larger share of economic activity—broadly defined—than capitalist firms.

Though standard economics texts hardly mention them, consumer cooperatives and worker-owned businesses have shaped our history. Their influence, however, has been uneven, greater in some industries and regions than others.

Marxist scholars have often associated cooperatives with the so-called "utopian socialists"—whom they have traditionally considered well-meaning but misguided. Efforts to establish alternative businesses have often been labeled a form of co-optation less politically virtuous than trade-union organizing or socialist political parties. Yet cooperative efforts have typically been closely linked to and complementary with larger anti-corporate organizing efforts. In a fascinating article entitled "Toward an Organizationally Diverse American Capitalism? Cooperative, Mutual, and Local, State-Owned Enterprise," sociologist Mark Schnaiberg traces the history of cooperative marketing efforts in the grain and dairy industries, originally dominated by large monopsonies that used their market power to pay farmers as little as possible. (A monopsony is a single buyer that dominates a market, just as a monopoly is a single seller.) When farmers successfully started up cooperatives, other members of the community also became more likely to organize on their own behalf.

Even when cooperative enterprises represent only a small proportion of market transactions in a local community, they often exercise a disproportionate influence, disciplining capitalist enterprises or pioneering innovations that are later adopted by them. Local food cooperatives were the first to begin marketing organic and local produce, and large supermarket chains gradually followed suit. Local credit unions have made it harder for large banking institutions to charge excessive fees. Worker-owned businesses have pulled the small-business community in a more progressive direction, serving as a counterweight to large, footloose firms.

By demonstrating the viability of businesses aimed to serve larger social goals, cooperatives have altered our economic ecology.

Culture Matters

As an economist, I was trained to emphasize the difference between for-profit and non-profit firms. But that difference may be less significant than the moral and cultural values central to the definition of cooperative enterprises.

Consumer cooperatives seek to provide high-quality products at minimal cost. Worker-owned businesses need to generate profits both to pay themselves and to finance investment. Both, however, are committed to seven "cooperative principles" (see box, p. 211) that include democracy and concern for community.

In this respect, cooperative enterprises can be seen as a subset of efforts to develop a solidarity economy, which also includes non-profit businesses and community organizations. They are also closely aligned with "buy local" efforts that urge consumers to shop in locally owned stores and build a local supply chain (for instance, by patronizing restaurants utilizing locally grown products).

Not that it's always clear how "concern for community" should be defined. Almost by their very nature as small, decentralized businesses, co-ops prioritize those with whom they are most likely to come into contact. But local solidarity is not automatically consistent with broader forms of solidarity. In fact, it risks a kind of parochialism that could lead to happy little enclaves embedded in a larger economy built on hierarchy and exploitation.

On the other hand, co-op culture can promote values that may lead people toward other forms of positive engagement, with the goal of steadily expanding the cooperative reach and linking many kinds of progressive efforts together. Co-op ventures also offer people the opportunity to build something new, rather than merely trying to tear down something old.

The Seven Cooperative Principles

Cooperatives around the world generally operate according to the same core principles and values, adopted by the International Co-operative Alliance (www.ica.coop) in 1995. Cooperatives trace the roots of these principles to the first modern cooperative, founded in Rochdale, England, in 1844.

1. Voluntary and Open Membership: Cooperatives are voluntary organizations, open to all people able to use its services and willing to accept the responsibilities of membership, without gender, social, racial, political or religious discrimination.
2. Democratic Member Control: Cooperatives are democratic organizations controlled by their members—those who buy the goods or use the services of the cooperative—who actively participate in setting policies and making decisions.
3. Members' Economic Participation: Members contribute equally to, and democratically control, the capital of the cooperative. This benefits members in proportion to the business they conduct with the cooperative rather than on the capital invested.
4. Autonomy and Independence: Cooperatives are autonomous, self-help organizations controlled by their members. If the co-op enters into agreements with other organizations or raises capital from external sources, it is done so based on terms that ensure democratic control by the members and maintains the cooperative's autonomy.
5. Education, Training and Information: Cooperatives provide education and training for members, elected representatives, managers and employees so they can contribute effectively to the development of their cooperative. Members also inform the general public about the nature and benefits of cooperatives.
6. Cooperation among Cooperatives: Cooperatives serve their members most effectively and strengthen the cooperative movement by working together through local, national, regional and international structures.
7. Concern for Community: While focusing on member needs, cooperatives work for the sustainable development of communities through policies and programs accepted by the members.

From the National Cooperative Business Association, International Year of Cooperatives (usa2012.coop).

The commitment to democratic decision-making distinguishes worker-owned businesses from other institutional forms that aim to enlarge economic goals (such as the new "social benefit" corporate charters) or to help incentivize workers (such as profit-sharing or employee-stock-ownership plans). This commitment reflects a cultural value—as well as a political principle. Other shared values encouraging respect and concern for others may help lubricate the democratic process by making collective decision-making less contentious.

Democratic values and skills may grow stronger in communities where they are consistently exercised, explaining why some regions of the world seem to foster more cooperative enterprises than others. The famous Mondragón cooperatives grew up in the Basque area of northern Spain, among people who felt embattled and impoverished by their minority status and strengthened by their progressive Catholic traditions. Many small cooperatives have prospered in northern Italy, an area with a long history of labor radicalism and a strong Communist Party. In Canada, the province of Quebec has successfully encouraged the cooperative provision of social services under the banner of the "social economy."

In the United States, cooperatives have often helped improve living standards in African-American communities, from a cooperative shipyard in 1860s Baltimore, to a co-op buying club in Depression-era Gary, Ind., to the Common Ground Collective in post-Katrina New Orleans. As Jessica Gordon-Nembhard and Ajowa Nzinga point out (see *Dollars & Sense*, July/August 2006), a common history of economic exclusion and hardship can foster cooperation.

Public policies have also played a role in developing these epicenters of cooperative development. But culture is surely one of the factors shaping the political alignments that generate such policies.

Efficiency Matters

Economists often overstate the value of efficiency, or define it in excessively narrow terms. But that doesn't mean it's not important. Efficiency is an important arbiter of success in competition and, in the world we live in, co-operators need to compete. Since competition between firms is, to some extent a "team sport," successful cooperation among team members can prove advantageous.

Democratically managed firms may be more efficient than others, even from the relatively narrow perspective of costs and benefits. The British economist John Stuart Mill made this argument in the mid-19th century, pointing out that workers who were also owners would be likely to work harder and smarter than those merely paid an hourly wage.

This issue never received much attention from early-twentieth-century Marxists convinced of the virtues of central planning. However, it came to the fore with Yugoslavian experiments in worker self-management in the mid-20th century and has since had a big impact on progressive economic thinking—in part because it helps frame a critique of both the traditional family firm and the modern corporation.

A long-standing favorite of neoclassical economists is an argument, developed by economists Armen Alchian and Harold Demsetz, that workers will have a tendency to shirk on the job unless they are overseen by an owner who can capture any profits (or "residual") left over after the workers are paid. This gives the "residual claimant" an incentive to crack the whip and make them work as hard as possible. Ownership in most modern corporations is highly fragmented, but owners presumably hire managers—from the chief executive officer or CEO down to supervisors and foremen—to fulfill this disciplinary role.

Radical economist Samuel Bowles effectively rebuts this argument, pointing out that it is difficult and costly to monitor effort. Workers seeking to resist capitalist exploitation may be especially likely to shirk unless managers can find a way to either secure their loyalty or threaten them with costly job loss.

Unfortunately, worker ownership alone doesn't necessarily solve this incentive problem. Workers either have to be really good at monitoring one another's efforts (so that no one can free ride without being sanctioned), or they have to feel such strong solidarity toward one another that no one even tries to free ride. (The latter is preferable, since it's often hard for a collective to fire someone who is slacking off.)

Other tensions among owner-workers can arise. For instance, young owner-workers have a stronger incentive to reinvest firm profits to increase their future earnings than older owner-workers, who would prefer to retain more earnings and/or fund their pensions. The success of a worker-owned enterprise depends on the ability of worker-owners to anticipate and creatively respond to such conflicts of interest. But the process of doing so—negotiating and resolving differences of opinion—can itself be quite costly, in two ways.

First, democratic decision-making can be quite time-consuming, especially if based on rules of consensus. Worker-owned firms generally treat time in meetings as part of their paid work, and the time they devote to it can cut down on directly productive activities.

Second, democratic decision-making can prove emotionally costly, as when good friends disagree about important matters and find it difficult to accommodate one another. On the other hand, conflict avoidance—such as a desire not to discipline a fellow worker who is also a friend—can also lower efficiency. This problem can be described as a "second order" free-rider problem—that is, a reluctance to openly point to or discourage free riding.

Representative democracy and delegation to a manager can help minimize these problems, but also at some cost. Majority rule can alienate the minority, and unstable factions can lead to lack of continuity in decision-making.

Worker-owned firms will be more likely to prosper if they cultivate an awareness of decision-making problems and develop the institutional structures and skills necessary to over-come them.

Here comes the Catch-22. Neither our educational system nor most employers do much to help people develop democratic management skills, so there's a big start-up problem. If we could just create more opportunities for people to develop and practice such skills, worker-owned businesses could enjoy more success.

Efficiency gains can also come at the macro level. Worker-owned businesses that get off the ground tend to be more stable than other small businesses, in part because workers have an incentive to hang in over the long haul, even if revenue slumps. This can buffer the effects of recession on the economy as a whole.

Most importantly, worker-owned businesses depend more on positive incentives than on the threat of job loss. Unlike employer-owned businesses, they don't rely on the labor discipline imposed by a high unemployment rate. And consistently high unemployment rates are among the most inefficient features of our current economic system.

Collaboration Matters

For all the reasons given above, the cooperative movement may need to reach a certain critical mass before it can really take off. More collaboration among cooperatives—and between cooperatives and other institutions such as public universities—could make a big difference.

Relatively few worker-owned businesses are started up in a given year, leading some to speculate that they are inherently less expansionary than capitalist firms (for the simple reason that worker-owners care about more than the rate of return on their capital investment). They also care about the quality of their work life and their place in the community. Some of the decision-making problems described above, moreover, may be more easily solved in small firms where everyone knows everyone else. Expansion can lead to complications.

However, collaboration and expansion could help worker-owned businesses in several ways. First, it could help them gain access to more and better financing. By definition, worker-owned firms can't sell equity shares in their business (because all owners must be workers). They can develop other forms of self-financing, including bonds that can be especially attractive to socially responsible investors. But they can also develop ways of pooling resources and helping to finance one another. Each firm belonging to the Valley Alliance of Worker Coops sets aside a percentage of its profits to promote local cooperative development. One can even imagine a kind of franchise model in which one firm could spin off smaller firms, which could become financially independent, but remain closely allied.

Second, vertical networking along the supply chain could increase efficiency and the ability to compete with large conglomerate capitalist enterprises. International networking among cooperatives holds particular promise, because it advances a larger fair-trade agenda, and also helps escape parochialism. Many examples of this kind of networking exist, such as the People's Market at UMass-Amherst buying only cooperatively produced coffee and actively seeking other cooperatively produced goods and services.

Third, more networking could help develop the distinctive managerial and decision-making skills described above. Indeed, the more worker-owners gain experience in different types of firms, the richer the skills they bring to the task of democratic management. And the more visible worker-owners become, the more young people are likely to become attracted to new prospects for more socially meaningful and economically rewarding work.

Finally, the more worker-owned businesses and other cooperative enterprises expand, the easier it becomes to build political coalitions and implement policies that promote their efforts. These synergies help explain how regional economies in the Basque area of Spain, northern Italy, and the Canadian province of Quebec have evolved.

A worker-owned business is what economists call a "microeconomic structure." But its ultimate success may depend on its ability to change the macroeconomic structure, which can, in turn, improve its microeconomic efficiency. Even a small cooperative firm can help a community enhance its standard of living and quality of life. More importantly, however, it can provide a catalyst for social and political changes that not only bring more and more worker-owned businesses into being, but also enable them to compete more effectively with capital-owned firms.

That's why worker-owned businesses fit the description of what the 20th-century Italian theorist and revolutionary Antonio Gramsci called a "non-reformist reform" and what sociologist Erik Olin Wright terms a "real utopia." Take another look at those seven cooperative principles. They offer a pretty good guide to running not just a business, but a whole society. ❏

Sources: J.K. Gibson-Graham, *The End of Capitalism (As We Knew It)* (University of Minnesota Press, 2006); Mark Schnaiberg, "Toward an Organizationally Diverse American Capitalism? Cooperative, Mutual, and Local, State-Owned Enterprise," *Seattle University Law Review*, Vol. 34, No. 4 (2011); Jessica Gordon-Nembhard and Ajowa Nzinga, "African-American Economic Solidarity," *Dollars & Sense*, July/August 2006; Erik Olin Wright, *Envisioning Real Utopias* (Verso, 2010).

Article 10.3

PICKET, FIGHT, AND WIN
Solidarity networks scale down to defend tenants and workers.

BY SETH GRANDE
November/December 2013

Late this past July, a small group of activists from around the United States and Canada converged in Seattle for the first ever International Solidarity Network Conference, spending the weekend discussing organizing skills and listening to presentations from groups as far away as Hamilton, Ontario. On Sunday afternoon the attendees piled into cars and headed to the Tressa Apartment complex in the north Seattle neighborhood of Shoreline to do what solidarity networks do best: picket, fight, and win.

The apartment complex, owned by the national real-estate group FPI Management, had kept hundreds of dollars of a former tenant's security deposit, despite telling him that only sixty to seventy dollars would be deducted for general cleaning. The tenant and his family had considered taking the company to small claims court, until they heard about the Seattle Solidarity Network, or SeaSol for short. After consulting with SeaSol organizers, the family decided they would rather resolve their grievances through direct action. Together with activists from the network, they spoke with other Tressa residents and hung posters around their neighborhood urging potential tenants not to rent there. Following weeks of community outreach—and shortly after a spirited, attention-grabbing picket, the tenant received a check from FPI Management for the remainder of the security deposit.

This fight is just one example of a new model of worker and tenant organizing that has begun to emerge in recent years in the United States, Canada, and elsewhere. Solidarity networks are volunteer mutual support groups that organize around specific cases using collective, direct action tactics. Decisions within the group are made on a directly democratic basis at weekly meetings, with no elected officers. There are no specialized professional organizers, and groups don't have any regular funding sources outside of small individual donations. "We believe it's more advantageous to build power in the long run if we can structure ourselves in a way where we don't need paid staff, we don't need lawyers," Andrew, a SeaSol organizer who asked to be identified only by his first name, told *Dollars & Sense*. "All we need is to continue organizing regular people to solve these problems ourselves."

So far, the strategy seems to be paying off. Since a small group of activists in Seattle started organizing according to the solidarity network model in late 2007, SeaSol has taken on over forty different cases, winning the vast majority and getting back thousands of dollars in withheld wages and security deposits for dozens of workers and tenants. Such a high rate of success has inspired other groups, not only here but also around the world. The Seattle Solidarity Network's website lists contact information for over forty other solidarity networks, including groups as far away as Glasgow, Scotland, and Brisbane, Australia. "I think a lot of [activists] are frustrated with feeling like we're losing all the time," Andrew continues, explaining one appeal of the solidarity-network model and its smaller scale. "I think it's attractive to people in that they can see that here is something where we can use our skills, our energy, our organizing power to tangibly improve someone's life in a way that will also hopefully help us build a broader movement."

The general decline of union membership over the past decades, along with a shift towards a service-oriented economy, has also created a vacuum that solidarity networks aim to fill. Take, for example, the a small college town and former steel and manufacturing center of Huntington, West Virginia, a union stronghold until the 1970s when deindustrialization hit the region. "[Unions] just don't have a very heavy presence here anymore," Dan, an organizer with Huntington's Jewel City Solidarity Network told Dollars & Sense.

For their part, unions have been scrambling to adapt. At the AFL-CIO's quadrennial conference this past September in Los Angeles, six different resolutions were passed aimed at broadening the base of the labor movement. Some unions have began funding smaller, direct-action-oriented organizing efforts: OURWalmart, which organized protests and employee walkouts at Walmarts in 15 cities across the United States this September, and the SEIU-backed Fight For 15 campaign, which this August mobilized fast food workers in around 60 U.S. cities for a one day walk out.

But the decentralized character of most service-sector workplaces still poses serious challenges for organizing efforts, and some activists feel that big unions' efforts at broadening their base still fall short. "A lot of them don't deal with housing issues or see the connection between those issues and workplace issues," Dan told Dollars & Sense. "While labor seems to nationally be coming around to organizing service industry folks, or folks in more marginal employment, here [in Huntington] they haven't quite caught onto that yet. There doesn't seem to be much interest on their part."

Many workers at the kinds of small workplaces that solidarity networks target are desperate for a way to engage in collective action. A 2008 report by researchers at the University of Illinois at Chicago, UCLA, and the National Employment Law Project found that "workers at businesses with less than 100 employees were at greater risk of experiencing [workplace] violations than those at larger businesses."

For organizers like Andrew, this situation presents a gap that solidarity networks can help fill. "Here's a situation where we can actually, using only our own power and imagination, collectively really change something [and] win tangible victories, even if it's for scraps. Its something where we can actually have more power than a given boss or landlord and make them do what we want them to do." Frederick Douglass famously wrote, "Power concedes nothing without a demand. It never did and it never will." SeaSol and other solidarity networks are rediscovering this and pressing demands, one boss (or landlord) at a time. ❑

Article 10.4

GREECE AND THE CRISIS OF EUROPE: WHICH WAY OUT?

BY MARJOLEIN van der VEEN
May/June 2013

The Greek economy has crashed, and now lies broken on the ground. The causes of the crisis are pretty well understood, but there hasn't been enough attention to the different possible ways out. Our flight crew has shown us only one emergency exit—one that is broken and just making things worse. But there is more than one way out of the crisis, not just the austerity being pushed by the so-called "Troika" (International Monetary Fund (IMF), European Commission, and European Central Bank (ECB)). We need to look around a bit more, since—as they say on every flight—the nearest exit may not be right in front of us. Can an alternative catch hold? And, if so, will it be Keynesian or socialist?

The origins of the crisis are manifold: trade imbalances between Germany and Greece, the previous Greek government's secret debts (hidden with the connivance of Wall Street banks), the 2007 global economic crisis, and the flawed construction of the eurozone (see sidebar). As Greece's economic crisis has continued to deepen, it has created a social disaster: Drastic declines in public health, a rise in suicides, surging child hunger, a massive exodus of young adults, an intensification of exploitation (longer work hours and more work days per week), and the rise of the far right and its attacks on immigrants and the LGBT community. Each new austerity package brokered between the Greek government and the Troika stipulates still more government spending cuts, tax increases, or "economic reforms"—privatization, increases in the retirement age, layoffs of public-sector workers, and wage cuts for those who remain.

While there are numerous possible paths out of the crisis, the neoliberal orthodoxy has maintained that Greece had no choice but to accept austerity. The country was broke, argued the Troika officials, economists, and commentators, and this tough medicine would ultimately help the Greek economy to grow again. As Mark Weisbrot of the Center for Economic and Policy Research (CEPR) put it, "[T]he EU authorities have opted to punish Greece—for various reasons, including the creditors' own interests in punishment, their ideology, imaginary fears of inflation, and to prevent other countries from also demanding a 'growth option.'" By focusing on neoliberal solutions, the mainstream press controls the contours of the debate. Keynesian remedies that break with the punishment paradigm are rarely discussed, let alone socialist proposals. These may well gain more attention, however, as the crisis drags on without end.

Neoliberal Solutions

Despite the fact that 30 years of neoliberalism resulted in the worst economic crisis since the Great Depression, neoliberals are undaunted and have remained intent on dishing out more of the same medicine. What they offered Greece were bailouts

---

Causes of Greece's Deepening Crisis

Trade imbalances. Germany's wage restraint policies and high productivity made German exports more competitive (cheaper), resulting in trade surpluses for Germany and deficits for Greece. Germany then used its surplus funds to invest in Greece and other southern European countries. As German banks shoveled out loans, Greek real estate boomed, inflation rose, their exports became less competitive, and the wealthy siphoned money abroad.

Hidden debt. To enter the eurozone in 2001, Greece's budget deficit was supposed to be below the threshold (3% of GDP) set by the Maastricht Treaty. In 2009 the newly elected Panhellenic Socialist Movement (PASOK) government discovered that the outgoing government had been hiding its deficits from the European authorities, with the help of credit default swaps sold to it by Goldman Sachs during 2002-06. The country was actually facing a deficit of 12% of GDP, thanks to extravagant military spending and tax cuts for (and tax evasion by) the rich.

Global crisis. When the 2007 global economic crisis struck, Greece was perhaps the hardest-hit country. Investments soured, banks collapsed, and loans could not be repaid. Debt-financed household consumption could no longer be sustained. Firms cut back on investment spending, closed factories, and laid off workers. Output has fallen 20% since 2007, the unemployment rate is now above 25%, (for youth, 58%), household incomes have fallen by more than a third in the last three years, and government debt has surpassed 175% of GDP.

The eurozone trap. Greece's government could do little on its own to rescue its economy. With eurozone countries all using the same currency, individual countries could no longer use monetary policy to stimulate their economies (e.g., by devaluing the currency to boost exports or stimulating moderate inflation to reduce the real debt burden). Fiscal policy was also weakened by the Maastricht limits on deficits and debt, resulting in tight constraints on fiscal stimulus.

---

and haircuts (write-downs of the debt). While the country—really, the country's banks—got bailouts, the money flowed right back to repay lenders in Germany, France, and other countries. Very little actually went to Greek workers who fell into severe poverty. The bailouts invariably came with conditions in the form of austerity, privatization (e.g., water systems, ports, etc.), mass public-sector layoffs, labor-market "flexibilization" (making it easier to fire workers), cutbacks in unemployment insurance, and tax reforms (lowering corporate taxes and raising personal income and sales taxes). In sum, the neoliberal structural adjustment program for Greece shifted the pain onto ordinary people, rather than those most responsible for causing the crisis in the first place.

Austerity and internal devaluation

With steep cuts in government spending, neoliberal policy has been contracting the economy just when it needed to be expanded. Pro-austerity policy makers, however, professed their faith in "expansionary austerity." Harvard economists Alberto Alesina and Silvia Ardagna claimed that austerity (especially spending cuts) could lead to the expectation of increased profits and so stimulate investment. The neoliberals also hoped to boost exports through "internal devaluation" (wage cuts, resulting in lower costs and therefore cheaper exports). An economist

---

The Role of Goldman Sachs

Greece was able to "hide" its deficits thanks to Goldman Sachs, which had sold financial derivatives called credit-default swaps to Greece between 2002 and 2006. The credit-default swaps operated a bit like subprime loans, enabling Greece to lower its debts on its balance sheets, but at very high borrowing rates. Goldman Sachs had sales teams selling these complicated financial instruments not just to Greece, but to many gullible municipalities and institutions throughout Europe (and the United States), who were told that these deals could lower their borrowing costs. For Greece, the loans blew up in 2008-2009, when interest rates rose and stock markets collapsed. Among those involved in these deals included Mario Draghi (now President of the ECB), who was working at the Greece desk at Goldman Sachs at the time. While these sales generated huge profits for Goldman Sachs, the costs are now being borne by ordinary Greek people in the form of punishing austerity programs. (For more on Goldman Sachs's role, see part four of the PBS documentary "Money, Power, Wall Street.")

---

with Capital Economics in London claimed that Greece needed a 30–40% decline in real wages to restore competitiveness. A fall in real wages, along with the out-migration of workers, the neoliberals suggested, would allow labor markets to "clear" at a new equilibrium. Of course, they neglected to say how long this would take and how many workers would fall into poverty, get sick, or die in the process.

Meanwhile, international financial capitalists (hedge funds and private equity firms) have been using the crisis as an opportunity to buy up state assets. The European Commission initially expected to raise €50 billion by 2015 from the privatization of state assets (now being revised downward to just over €25 billion through 2020). The magnitude of the fire sale in Greece is still five to ten times larger than that expected for Spain, Portugal, and Ireland. Domestic private companies on the brink of bankruptcy are also vulnerable. As the crisis drags on, private-equity and hedge-fund "vulture capitalists" are swooping in for cheap deals. The other neoliberal reforms—labor and pension reforms, dismantling of the welfare state, and tax reforms—will also boost private profits at the expense of workers.

Default and exit from the euro

Another possible solution was for Greece to default on its debt, and some individuals and companies actively prepared for such a scenario. A default would lift the onerous burden of debt repayment, and would relieve Greece of complying with all the conditions placed on it by the Troika. However, it would likely make future borrowing by both the public and private sectors more difficult and expensive, and so force the government to engage in some sort of austerity of its own.

Some economists on the left have been supportive of a default, and the exit from the euro and return to the drachma that would likely follow. One such advocate is Mark Weisbrot, who has argued that "a threat by Greece to jettison the euro is long overdue, and it should be prepared to carry it out." He acknowledges there would be costs in the short term, but argues they would be less onerous "than many years of recession, stagnation, and high unemployment that the European authorities are offering." A return to the drachma could restore one of the tools to boost export competitiveness: allowing Greece to use currency depreciation to lower the prices of its exports. In this sense, this scenario remains a neoliberal one. (Many IMF "shock therapy" have included currency devaluations as part of the strategy for countries to export their way out of debt.)

The process of exit, however, could be quite painful, with capital flight, bank runs, black markets, significant inflation as the cost of imports rises, and the destruction of savings. There had already been some capital flight—an estimated €72 billion left Greek banks between 2009 and 2012. Furthermore, the threat of a Greek exit created fear of contagion, with the possibility of more countries leaving the euro and even the collapse of the eurozone altogether.

Keynesian Solutions

By late 2012, Keynesian proposals were finally being heard and having some impact on policymakers. Contrary to the neoliberal austerity doctrine, Keynesian solutions typically emphasize running countercyclical policies—especially expansionary fiscal policy (or fiscal "stimulus"), with deficit-spending to counter the collapse in private demand. However, the Greek government is already strapped with high deficits and the interest rates demanded by international creditors have spiked to extremely high levels. Additional deficit spending would require that the ECB (or the newly established European Stability Mechanism (ESM)) intervene by directly buying Greek government bonds to bring down rates. (The ECB has been lending to private banks at low rates, to enable the banks to buy public bonds.) In any case, a Keynesian approach ideally would waive the EU's deficit and debt limits to allow the Greek government more scope for rescuing the economy.

Alternatively, the EU could come forward with more grants and loans, in order to create employment, fund social-welfare spending, and boost demand. This kind of bailout would not go to the banks, but to the people who are suffering from unemployment, cuts in wages and pensions, and poverty. Nor would it come with all the other conditions the neoliberals have demanded (privatization, layoffs, labor-market reforms, etc). The European Investment Bank could also help stimulate new industries, such as alternative energy, and help revive old ones, such as tourism, shipping, and agriculture. In a European Union based on solidarity, the richer regions of Europe would help out poorer ones in a crisis (much as richer states in the United States make transfers to poorer ones, mostly without controversy).

Even some IMF officials finally recognized that austerity was not working. An October 2012 IMF report admitted that the organization had underestimated the fiscal policy multiplier—a measure of how much changes in government spending and taxes will affect economic growth—and therefore the negative impact of austerity policies. By April 2013, economists at UMass-Amherst found serious mistakes in research by Harvard economists Carmen Reinhart and Kenneth Rogoff, alleging that debt-to-GDP ratios of 90% or more seriously undermine future economic growth. Reinhart and Rogoff's claims had been widely cited by supporters of austerity for highly indebted countries. So yet another crack emerged in the pillar supporting austerity policies.

Keynesians have argued, contrary to the "internal devaluation" advocates, that the reduction in real wages just depressed aggregate demand, and made the recession deeper. Economists such as Nobel laureate Paul Krugman proposed that, instead, wages and prices be allowed to rise in the trade-surplus countries of northern Europe (Germany and the Netherlands). This would presumably make these countries' exports less competitive, at some expense to producers of internationally traded goods, though possibly boosting domestic demand thanks to increased wages. Meanwhile, it would help level the playing field for exporters in the southern countries in crisis, and would be done without the punishing reductions in real wages demanded by the Troika. The Keynesian solution thus emphasized stimulating domestic demand through fiscal expansion in both the northern and southern European countries, as well as allowing wages and prices to rise in the northern countries.

Signs pointing in this direction began to emerge in spring 2013, when some Dutch and German trade unions won significant wage increases. In addition, the Dutch government agreed to scrap its demands for wage restraint in some sectors (such as the public sector and education) and to hold off (at least until August) on its demands for more austerity. (Another €4.5 billion cuts had been scheduled for 2014, after the government spent €3.7 billion in January to rescue (through nationalization) one of the country's largest banks.)

Socialist Solutions

For most of the socialist parties in Greece and elsewhere in Europe, the neoliberal solution was clearly wrong-headed, as it worsened the recession to the detriment of workers while industrial and finance capitalists made out like bandits. Greece's Panhellenic Socialist Movement (PASOK) was an exception, going along with austerity, structural reforms, and privatization. (Its acceptance of austerity lost it significant support in the 2012 elections.) Other socialists supported anything that alleviated the recession, including Keynesian prescriptions for more deficit spending, higher wages, and other policies to boost aggregate demand and improve the position of workers. Greece's SYRIZA (a coalition of 16 left-wing parties and whose support surged in the 2012 elections) called for stopping austerity, renegotiating loan agreements, halting wage and pension cuts, restoring the minimum wage, and implementing a type of Marshall Plan-like investment drive. In many ways, these proposale resemble standard Keynesian policies—which have historically served to rescue the capitalist system, without challenging its inherent exploitative structure or vulnerability to recurrent crisis.

While Keynesian deficit-spending could alleviate the crisis in the short-term, who would ultimately bear the costs—ordinary taxpayers? Workers could end up paying for the corruption of the Greek capitalist class, who pushed through tax cuts, spent government funds in ways that mainly benefited themselves, and hid money abroad. Many socialists argued that the Greek capitalists should pay for the crisis, through increased taxes on wealth, corporate profits, and financial transactions, and the abolition of tax loopholes and havens. As SYRIZA leader Alexis Tsipras put it, "It is common knowledge among progressive politicians and activists, but also among the Troika and the Greek government, that the burden of the crisis has been carried exclusively by public and private sector workers and pensioners. This has to stop. It is time for the rich to contribute their share... ."

Slowly, the right-wing government began making gestures in this direction. In 2010, French finance minister Christine Lagarde had given a list of more than 2,000 Greeks with money in Swiss bank accounts to her Greek counterpart George Papaconstantinou, of the PASOK government, but Papaconstantiou sat on it and did nothing. But in the fall of 2012 the so-called "Lagarde list" was published by the magazine Hot Doc, leading to fury among ordinary Greeks against establishment political leaders (including the PASOK "socialists") who had failed to go after the tax dodgers. Another list of about 400 Greeks who had bought and sold property in London since 2009 was compiled by British financial authorities at the request of the current Greek government. In total, the economist Friedrich Schneider has estimated that about €120 billion of Greek assets (about 65% of GDP) were outside the country, mostly in Switzerland and Britain, but also in the United States, Singapore, and the Cayman Islands. The government also started a clamp down on corruption in past government expenditures. In the Spring of 2013, two politicians (a former defense minister and a former mayor of Thessaloniki, the country's second-largest city) were convicted on corruption charges.

Socialists have also opposed dismantling the public sector, selling off state assets, and selling Greek firms to international private equity firms. Instead of bailouts, many socialists have called for nationalization of the banking sector. "The banking system we envision," SYRIZA leader Alexis Tsipras announced, "will support environmentally viable public investment and cooperative initiatives.... . What we need is a banking system devoted to the public interest—not one bowing to capitalist profit. A banking system at the service of society, a banking system that serves as a pillar for growth." While SYRIZA called for renegotiating the Greece's public debt, it favored staying in the euro.

Other socialist parties have put forth their own programs that go beyond Keynesian fiscal expansion, a more equitable tax system, and even beyond nationalizing the banks. For instance, the Alliance of the Anti-Capitalist Left (ANTARSYA) called for nationalizing banks and corporations, worker takeovers of closed factories, and canceling the debt and exiting the euro. The Communist Party of Greece (KKE) proposed a fairly traditional Marxist-Leninist program, with socialization of all the means of production and central planning for the satisfaction of social needs, but also called for disengagement from the EU and abandoning the euro. The Trotskyist Xekinima party called for nationalizing not just the largest banks, but also the largest corporations, and putting them under democratic worker control.

Those within the Marxist and libertarian left, meanwhile, have focused on turning firms, especially those facing bankruptcy, into cooperatives or worker self-directed enterprises. Firms whose boards of directors are composed of worker-representatives and whose workers participate in democratic decision-making would be less likely to distribute surpluses to overpaid CEOs or corrupt politicians and lobbyists, or to pick up and relocate to other places with lower labor costs. While worker self-directed enterprises could decide to forego wage increases or to boost productivity, in order to promote exports, such decisions would be made democratically by the workers themselves, not by capitalist employers or their representatives in government. And it would be the workers themselves who would democratically decide what to do with any

---

Cooperatives Around the World

Efforts at transforming capitalist firms into cooperatives or worker-directed enterprises can draw upon successes in the Basque Country (Spain), Argentina, Venezuela, and elsewhere. The Mondragón Cooperative Corporation, centered in the Basque country, has grown since its founding, in the 1950s, to 85,000 members working in over 300 enterprises. In Venezuela, the Chávez government promoted the development of cooperatives. The total number surged more than 100-fold, to over 100,000, between 1998 and 2006, the last year for which data are available. In Argentina after 2001, failing enterprises were taken over (or "recovered") by workers and turned into cooperatives. The recovered enterprises boasted a survival rate of about 93%. By 2010, 205 of these cooperatives employed a total of almost 10,000 workers.

---

increased profits that might arise from those decisions.

One Greek company that is trying to survive as a transformed worker cooperative is Vio.Me, a building materials factory in Thessaloniki. In May 2011 when the owners could no longer pay their bills and walked away, the workers decided to occupy the factory. By February 2013, after raising enough funds and community support, the workers started democratically running the company on their own. (They do not intend to buy out the owners, since the company owed the workers a significant amount of money when it abandoned the factory.) They established a worker-board, controlled by workers' general assemblies and subject to recall, to manage the factory. They also changed the business model, shifting to different suppliers, improving environmental practices, and finding new markets. Greek law currently does not allow factory occupations, so the workers are seeking the creation of a legal framework for the recuperated factory, which may enable more such efforts in the future. Vio.Me has received support from SYRIZA and the Greek Green party, from workers at recuperated factories in Argentina (see sidebar), as well as from academics and political activists worldwide.

Whither Europe and the Euro?

As Europe faces this ongoing crisis, it is also grappling with its identity. On the right are the neoliberal attempts to dismantle the welfare state and create a Europe that works for corporations and the wealthy—a capitalist Europe more like the United States. In the center are Keynesian calls to keep the EU intact, with stronger Europe-wide governance and institutions. These involve greater fiscal integration, with a European Treasury, eurobonds (rather than separate bonds for each country), European-wide banking regulations, etc. Keynesians also call for softening the austerity policies on Greece and other countries.

Proposals for European consolidation have inspired criticism and apprehension on both the far right and far left. Some on the far right are calling for exiting the euro, trumpeting nationalism and a return to the nation state. The left, meanwhile, voices concern about the emerging power of the European parliament in Brussels, with its highly paid politicians, bureaucrats, lobbyists, etc. who are able to pass legislation favoring corporations at the expense of workers. Unlike the far right however, the left has proposed a vision for another possible united Europe—one based on social cohesion and inclusion, cooperation and solidarity, rather than on competition and corporate dominance. In particular, socialists call for replacing the capitalist structure of Europe with one that is democratic, participatory, and embodies a socialist economy, with worker protections and participation at all levels of economic and political decision-making. This may very well be the best hope for Europe to escape its current death spiral, which has it living in terror of what the next stage may bring. ❏

Sources: Amitabh Pal, "Austerity is Killing Europe," Common Dreams, April 27, 2012 (commondreams.org); Niki Kitsantonis, "Greece Resumes Talks With Creditors," *New York Times*, April 4, 2013 (nytimes.com); Mark Weisbrot, "Where I Part from Paul Krugman on Greece and the Euro," *The Guardian*, May 13, 2011 (guardian.co.uk); Alberto F. Alesina and Silvia Ardagna, "Large Changes in Fiscal Policy: Taxes Versus Spending," National Bureau of Economic Research (NBER), October 2009 (nber.org); Geert Reuten, "From a false to a 'genuine' EMU," Globalinfo, Oct. 22, 2012 (globalinfo.nl); David Jolly, "Greek Economy Shrank 6.2% in Second Quarter," *New York Times*, Aug. 13, 2012; Joseph Zacune, "Privatizing Europe: Using the Crisis to Entrench Neoliberalism," Transnational Institute, March 2013 (tni.org); Mark Weisbrot, "Why Greece Should Reject the Euro," *New York Times*, May 9, 2011; Ronald Jannsen, "Blame It on the Multiplier," *Social Europe Journal*, Oct. 16, 2012 (social-europe.eu); Landon Thomas, Jr., and David Jolly, "Despite Push for Austerity, European Debt Has Soared," *New York Times*, Oct. 22, 2012; "German Public sector workers win above-inflation pay rise," Reuters, March 9, 2013 (reuters.nl); Liz Alderman, "Greek Businesses Fear Possible Return to Drachma," *New York Times*, May 22, 2012; Landon Thomas, Jr., "In Greece, Taking Aim at Wealthy Tax Dodgers," *New York Times*, Nov. 11, 2012; Rachel Donadio and Liz Alderman, "List of Swiss Accounts Turns Up the Heat in Greece," *New York Times*, Oct. 27, 2012; Landon Thomas, Jr., "Greece Seeks Taxes From Wealthy With Cash Havens in London," *New York Times*, Sept. 27, 2012; Niki Kitsantonis, "Ex-Mayor in Greece Gets Life in Prison for Embezzlement," *New York Times*, Feb. 27, 2013; Sam Bollier, "A guide to Greece's political parties," Al Jazeera, May 1, 2012 (aljazeera.com); Alexis Tsipras, "Syriza London: Public talk," March 16, 2013 (left.gr); Amalia Loizidou, "What way out for Greece and the working class in Europe," Committee for a Workers' International (CWI), March 19, 2013 (socialistworld.net); Richard Wolff, "Yes, there is an alternative to capitalism: Mondragón shows the way," *The Guardian*, June 24, 2012 (guardian.co.uk); Peter Ranis, "Occupy Wall Street: An Opening to Worker-Occupation of Factories and Enterprises in the U.S.," MRzine, Sept. 11, 2011 (mrzine.monthlyreview.org); viome.org.

Article 10.5

EQUAL TREATMENT FOR IMMIGRANTS

BY ALEJANDRO REUSS
July 2013

In this age of mass migration, U.S. immigration policy has mixed relative open-ness to immigration (since 1965) with nativist hostility toward immigrants. On the state level, we have seen a wave of anti-immigrant legislation (like the Arizona "papers, please" law); on the federal level, the militarization of the U.S.-Mexico bor-der coupled with spasms of workplace immigration raids. Recent reform propos-als, including a bill passed by the Senate, have coupled "guest worker" provisions with still more military-police-prisons immigration enforcement. Nativist fantasies of walling off the United States, it is clear, are doomed to fail. Given the harm that such measures cause in both economic and human terms, moreover, it would be bad if they succeeded.

Immigration today is inextricably bound up with globalization. The interna-tional movement of people, no less than international trade or investment, connects different countries economically. Globalization in its current form, however, has been shaped by the wealthy and powerful to their own advantage. This is obvious when we compare the treatment of the international movement of capital to the international movement of people.

Under the guise of "equal treatment of investors in similar circumstances"—as put by the World Bank's "Guidelines on the Treatment of Foreign Direct Investment"—international trade-and-investment agreements have guaranteed corporations' ability to invest abroad without fear of unfavorable government intervention. A NAFTA tribunal, for example, notoriously decided against Mexico in a case where the govern-ment had blocked foreign investment in the form of a toxic-waste dump.

International agreements, in contrast, have varied dramatically in their treat-ment of international migration. The European Union, for all its shortcomings, allows nearly unencumbered migration between member countries. NAFTA, on the other hand, has created a three-country zone where goods and capital can move with little restriction, but people face harsh barriers to migration.

The U.S.-Mexico border is one of the most militarized in the world—lined with razor-wire, armed patrols, and even drone aircraft—and undocumented immigrants live in constant peril of arrest and deportation. A recent article in *The Economist* paraphrases University of California-San Diego economist Gordon Hanson on the results of U.S. immigration policy: "inflicting economic self-harm by spending so much to keep workers out." The self-harm hardly com-pares to that inflicted on undocumented migrants.

We can see the operation of unequal power here in three ways.

First, undocumented immigrants lack political power. In addition to being denied formal political rights, like the vote, their insecure status poses an addi-tional obstacle to legal social protest. On the other hand, the increasing significance of Latinos as an electoral constituency is a political counterweight. Many Latinos rightly see attacks on "illegal immigration" as thinly veiled attacks on them, so immigrant-bashing politicians risk an electoral backlash. That's why some Republicans are talking immigration reform now.

Second, labor wields far less political influence than capital. It is employers, not labor, who have gotten what they wanted from trade-and-investment agreements (mainly the ability to locate operations where labor costs are low and government regulation lax). While organized labor has not always (or typically) championed immigrants' rights, U.S. unions have turned more pro-immigrant in recent years, especially as they have come to see immigrant workers as crucial to their own futures.

Third, global corporations have powerful governments on their side. The U.S. government fights for agreements protecting the interests of U.S.-based companies. The governments of many lower-income countries advocate in favor of their nationals abroad, but they have less muscle on the international political scene. Unsurprisingly, these efforts have been less successful.

Today, discrimination on the basis of national origin is a central principle of immigration law. Even though U.S. labor laws, on their face, cover all workers regardless of immigration status, everyone knows this is a fiction because undocumented immigrants' precarious status keeps them from reporting violations to the authorities.

Imagine, instead, that the contours of political power were reversed. Instead of untrammeled freedom for globetrotting corporations, we would have guarantees for people of the right to move, live, and work where they wish. Instead of the "equal treatment" for global investors under trade-and-investment agreements, we would have equal treatment for workers, regardless of nationality, wherever they worked. That would be good not only for immigrants, but also for workers in general, by reducing labor-market competition and strengthening workers' overall bargaining power. As the late legal scholar Anna Christensen put it, in the context of Europe, "Equal treatment of foreign and domestic workers ... is no threat to the position of domestic labor. If anything, the reverse is true."

That is a far cry from the current situation. Indeed, it is a far cry from the Senate bill, which includes still more money for coercive enforcement measures, plus guest-worker provisions that would leave immigrant workers largely at the mercy of their employers.

Equal treatment, however, is the immigration reform we need. ❑

CONTRIBUTORS

Randy Albelda Is a professor of economics at the University of Massachusetts-Boston and a *Dollars & Sense* Associate.

Nicole Aschoff is a sociologist and writer living in the Boston area.

Dean Baker is co-director of the Center for Economic and Policy Research.

Robin Broad is a professor of international development at the School of International Service at American University.

John Cavanagh is the director of the Institute for Policy Studies in Washington, D.C.

James M. Cypher is a research professor in the doctoral program in development studies, Universidad Autónoma de Zacatecas (Mexico).

Elissa Dennis is a consultant to nonprofit affordable housing developers with Community Economics, Inc., in Oakland, Calif.

Nancy Folbre is an emeritus professor of economics at the University of Massachusetts-Amherst. She contributes regularly to the *New York Times* Economix blog (economix.blogs.nytimes.com).

Ellen Frank teaches economics at UMass-Boston and is a *Dollars & Sense* Associate.

Gerald Friedman is a professor of economics at the University of Massachusetts at Amherst.

Heidi Garrett-Peltier is an economist and research associate at the Political Economy Research Institute at the University of Massachusetts-Amherst.

Armagan Gezici is an assistant professor of economics at Keene State College, Keene, N.H.

Seth Grande is a graduate of Brandeis University and a *Dollars & Sense* intern.

Rob Larson is an instructor of economics at Tacoma (Wash.) Community College. His book *Bleakonomics* was published by Pluto Press in 2012.

Jonathan Latham is co-founder and executive director of the Bioscience Resource Project, which publishes Independent Science News (independentsciencenews.org).

Arthur MacEwan is professor emeritus of economics at the University of Massachusetts-Boston and is a *Dollars & Sense* Associate.

John Miller is a member of the *Dollars & Sense* collective and professor economics at Wheaton College.

William G. Moseley is a professor of geography at Macalaster College in Saint Paul, Minn.

Alejandro Reuss is co-editor of *Dollars & Sense* and author of *Labor and the Global Economy* (Dollars & Sense, 2013).

Katherine Sciacchitano is a former labor lawyer and organizer. She is also a professor at the National Labor College and a freelance labor educator.

Chris Sturr is co-editor of *Dollars & Sense.*

Marjolein van der Veen is an economist who has taught economics in Massachusetts, the Seattle area, and the Netherlands.

Brian Walsh is a social studies teacher at Essex High School, Essex Vt., and a graduate student at the Labor Relations and Research Center, UMass-Amherst.

Jeannette Wicks-Lim is an economist and research fellow at the Political Economy Research Institute at the University of Massachusetts-Amherst.

Marty Wolfson teaches economics at the University of Notre Dame and is a former economist with the Federal Reserve Board in Washington, D.C.